ATM and Multiprotocol Networking

McGraw-Hill Series on Computer Communications (Selected Titles)

ATM and Multiprotocol Networking

George C. Sackett

Christopher Y. Metz

McGraw-Hill

New York San Francisco Washington, D.C. Auckland Bogotá
Caracas Lisbon London Madrid Mexico City Milan
Montreal New Delhi San Juan Singapore
Sydney Tokyo Toronto

Library of Congress Cataloging-in-Publication Data
Sackett, George C.
    ATM and multiprotocol networking / George C. Sackett,
Christopher Metz.
        p.   cm.—(McGraw-Hill series on computer communications)
    Includes index.
    ISBN 0-07-057724-2
    1. Asynchronous transfer mode.   2. Internetworking
(Telecommunication)   I. Metz, Christopher.   II. Title.
III. Series.
TK5105.35.S23   1996
004.6'6—dc20   96-46027
                                                                        CIP

McGraw-Hill

*A Division of The **McGraw·Hill** Companies*

1 2 3 4 5 6 7 8 9 0   DOC/DOC   9 0 1 0 9 8 7 6

ISBN 0-07-057724-2

*The sponsoring editor for this book was Steven Elliot, the editing
supervisor was Virginia Landis, and the production supervisor was
Suzanne W. B. Rapcavage. This book was set in Century Schoolbook by
North Market Street Graphics.*

Printed and bound by R. R. Donnelley & Sons Company.

Illustrations by NetworX Corporation.

McGraw-Hill books are available at special quantity discounts to use as
premiums and sales promotions, or for use in corporate training programs. For more information, please write to the Director of Special
Sales, McGraw-Hill, 11 West 19th Street, New York, NY 10011. Or contact your local bookstore.

This book is printed on recycled, acid-free paper containing a minimum
of 50% recycled, de-inked fiber.

Only once in a lifetime does a dream come true. I dedicate this book to my dream, my wife, Nancy. Her love, encouragement, and thoughtfulness are matched by no one.
—GEORGE SACKETT

Dedicated to my late mother, Leila, whose smile, courage, and love is with me to this day and forever; my father, Frank, who was always there and taught us to do the right thing; and to my beautiful family: my wife, Leonor, my son Jonathan, and my daughter Leah—I could never be so lucky.
—CHRIS METZ

Contents

Part 2   Asynchronous Transfer Mode (ATM)

Preface

No, ATM is not the cash machine. It stands for Asynchronous Transfer Mode (ATM). Corporate networks provide the vital corporate data used to measure business processes. Networking professionals responsible for planning and designing data networks play a commanding role in the integration of ATM into these existing networks. Each type of network supported, i.e., TCP/IP, SNA, Novell, NetBIOS, APPN, needs special attention when being integrated with ATM. It is the intent of this text to provide the reader with detained understanding of integrating ATM in multiprotocol internetwork.

While the ATM architecture appears to be simple, its implementation and integration with existing network architectures and protocols can and will undoubtedly be complex. ATM was devised mainly to carry higher-bandwidth applications such as desktop video conferencing, imaging, and voice. The idea of carrying traditional application data was almost a second thought. ATM is being considered by corporations as a means of solving all their network application requirements now and into the future. However, to integrate the transport over ATM is critical to its acceptance as the preferred networking architecture. This book will lay out a detailed understanding of just how ATM is to carry the vital corporate data.

The text is in three sections. The first section of the book introduces the reader to the internetworking models along with shared media LANs, routing and routing protocols, and switched LANs. The second section details the concepts, definitions, and architecture of ATM. The final section will provide the reader with an understanding of the issues, concerns, and solutions for ATM to transport legacy protocols.

We hope this book provides you with the basics of understanding the current networking architectures and their implementations in preparation for migrating to ATM.

Acknowledgments

First and foremost I thank my wife, Nancy, for her constant encouragement, caring, and support during the writing of this book. She makes it all possible for me. Thank you, Nancy. Second, I give my thanks to Tony Colodonato whose straightforward way of viewing the world and concern for others is a refreshing trait. Many thanks go to Steven Elliot for his efforts and patience through this project. Finally, I thank my coauthor Chris Metz. Chris's constant enthusiasm, energy, expertise, and efforts have made this a great book. Thanks, Chris; the next six coffees are on me.

George Sackett

This book would not have been possible without my wife Leonor, whose spectrum of love and support ranged from pep talks to ultimatums. I needed all of it. I would also like to thank my manager, Bill Zuber, who has always provided me with encouragement and the latitude to explore so many interesting areas of networking. There are many colleagues at IBM who have unknowingly inspired me to explore, understand, and apply whatever expertise I have gained over the years. Laurant Nicolas and Francois Attia from IBM LaGaude, Jim Robinson from IBM Education, Roch Guerin from IBM Research, and Mark Morrison and Walter Barlow from IBM U.S. Herb Stubbmann and Ken Scerbo, also from IBM U.S., taught me about pride and the profession. I would also like to thank Dr. John McQuillan whose yearly conferences on ATM have provided a forum where I listen and learn. And then there are the many researchers and developers from the IETF, IEEE, ATM Forum, and elsewhere, whose hard work and efforts are reflected in the many professional contributions that are published. They make it so interesting. And finally, to my coauthor, George Sackett, whose knowledge and experience does not get in the way of his sense of humor.

Chris Metz

ATM and
Multiprotocol
Networking

Introduction

1

Network Models

Asynchronous Transfer Mode (ATM) is the near future networking architecture for all communications networks. In its first incarnation ATM was referred to as Cell Relay. This name aptly fit the architecture because the transmission unit is called a *cell*. ATM was devised mainly to carry high-bandwidth applications such as desktop videoconferencing, imaging, and voice. The idea of carrying traditional application data was almost a second thought. Corporate networks can reap the potential application opportunities with ATM as long as it is integrated with the transport of corporate data. The data transported over the corporate networks can be found in three types of network architectures: Systems Network Architecture (SNA), Open Systems Interconnection (OSI) and Internet Protocol (IP). All these models represent the networking infrastructures that must be planned for and designed when integrating ATM.

1.1 Systems Network Architecture (SNA)

SNA laid the groundwork for corporate wide area networking since its beginnings in 1974. The cornerstone for implementing an SNA network is the *virtual telecommunications access method* (VTAM). VTAM provides communication access for applications that execute on the SNA mainframe. The users of earlier applications resided in close proximity to the mainframe computer. As corporations grew, corporate personnel required access to corporate information from locations remote to the mainframe computer. This leads to the development of a *network control program* (NCP) that executes in a front-end processor such as the IBM 3745 Communications Controller. The NCP offloads the chores of polling, activation, and inactivation of networked resources from VTAM. The characteristics of SNA are:

1. SNA is a hierarchical master/slave architecture—no resource can participate until it is predefined and no resource can establish communication without authority from VTAM.

2. The SNA network topology for all intents and purposes is static. The traditional hierarchical network is interrupted when adding or removing resources, such as workstations, front ends, and lines. The latest versions of VTAM and NCP, however, allow for dynamic definitions.

3. The SNA routing mechanism can also be considered static and predefined. Again SNA's rigid structure for static definitions requires manual intervention for defining these routes.

4. SNA's strength is its ability to guarantee delivery of data between session partners. This includes inherent error/recovery of data transmission.

5. SNA is a proprietary seven-layer networking architecture developed by IBM.

1.1.1 SNA layers

Figure 1.1 diagrams the SNA layers. From top to bottom they are:

Transaction Service. This top layer of SNA is where applications reside. Applications are programs that execute on the mainframe computer providing services to the end user. These services entail the receipt and delivery of data to and from the data's origin.

Presentation Services. This layer presents the data delivered or received by the application layer. Its main concern is the representation of the data to another application or an end user. The services provided in this layer are 3270 data stream support, intelligent printer data-stream support, and program-to-program communications protocols. It also provides the controlling mechanism for conversational communications between transaction programs.

Data Flow Control. This layer assigns sequence numbers, correlates requests and responses, enforces session request-and-response mode protocols and coordinates session send-and-receive modes between SNA *logical units* (LU). SNA LUs are applications and logical representations for terminals and printers.

Transmission Control. The verification of sequence numbers and managing session level pacing set forth by the data flow control is provided by the transmission control layer.

Path Control. The path control layer provides the protocols needed for routing SNA *path information units* (PIU) through an SNA network.

Data Link Control. This layer controls the transfer of PIUs between two SNA nodes over a physical link. It also provides link-level flow control and error recovery. This layer supports System/370 and System/390 data channel, X.25, IEEE 802.2, and IEEE 802.5 protocols.

Physical Control.   This last layer defines the physical interfaces used over the transmission medium. These definitions include the physical signaling attributes to establish, maintain, and terminate physical connectivity.

Throughout SNA's evolution updates have been orchestrated with international standards. Implementation of the IEEE 802 LAN standards augmented SNA. The international standard that fostered the IEEE LAN standards is Open Systems Interconnection.

1.2   Open Systems Interconnection (OSI)

In 1977, the International Standards Organization (ISO) established a working group with the charter of developing the Open Systems Interconnection Reference Model. ISO identified a worldwide requirement for computer systems from all vendors to connect, exchange data, and communicate intelligently. The result is a set of international standards that are public domain and not specific to any vendor's hardware or software operating systems. In

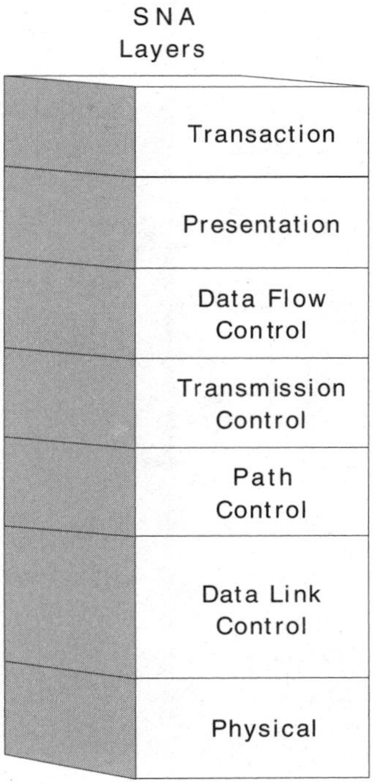

SNA
Layers

Transaction

Presentation

Data Flow
Control

Transmission
Control

Path
Control

Data Link
Control

Physical

Figure 1.1   IBM's Systems Network Architecture protocol stack.

short, nonproprietary. The reference model is defined to have seven layers, protocols, and basic commands. It is this set of standards that is known as *open systems interconnection* (OSI).

1.2.1 OSI layers

The layered concept deals with the constantly changing nature of standards and the products they employ. Systems that adhere to the OSI standards are said to be open to one another and thus are called *open systems*. Figure 1.2 identifies the seven layers of the OSI Reference Model and the services each layer provides and receives from adjacent layers. Each layer in an open system communicates with its equal in another open system by using protocols defined in OSI. It is OSI's modularity and flexibility to change based on nonproprietary standards that will thrust it into the mainstream in the mid-1990s.

The OSI Reference Model was accepted by ISO as an international standard in 1983. Again, as in SNA, the architecture is described from top to bottom. The seven layers provide the following functions and services:

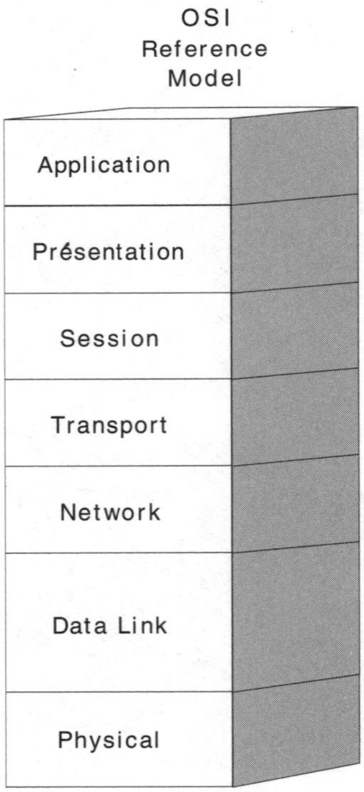

OSI
Reference
Model

| Application |
| Présentation |
| Session |
| Transport |
| Network |
| Data Link |
| Physical |

Figure 1.2 The ISO OSI seven-layer protocol stack.

Application layer.   This layer supports semantic exchanges between applications existing in open systems. It also provides access to the lower OSI functions and services.

Presentation layer.   Just as in SNA, this layer concerns itself with the representation of the data to the end user or application. This includes data conversions and code translations (e.g., ASCII to EBCDIC).

Session layer.   This layer provides the mechanism for organizing and structuring interaction between applications and/or devices.

Transport layer.   This layer is responsible for transparent and reliable transfer of data. The lower layers handle the attributes of the transfer medium.

Network layer.   This layer is the agent for establishing connections between networks. The standards also include operational control procedures for internetwork communications as well as routing information through multiple networks.

Data Link layer.   This layer provides the functions and protocols to transfer data between network resources and to detect errors that may occur in the physical layer.

Physical layer.   This layer defines the mechanical, electrical, functional, and procedural standards for the physical transmission of data over the communications medium.

The key to OSI is the adherence to the standard interfaces between the layers. As long as these standards are met, different implementations can satisfy the OSI Reference Model. But while ISO has been grappling with politics and vendor influence on the OSI standards, the U.S. government along with the scientific and educational communities established a working standard that has embraced the world of networking known as TCP/IP.

1.3   Transmission Control Protocol/Internet Protocol (TCP/IP)

The call for a simplified networking architecture that provided basic services was developed by the Advanced Research Projects Agency (ARPA) of the U.S. Department of Defense in the late 1960s. The goal of this network was to investigate any-to-any connectivity for computer network technologies by creating an internetwork between universities and research organizations. The resulting network, called ARPANET, was the first packet switching technology for data communications. ARPANET provides peer-to-peer communications between unlike computing devices. In its first incarnations ARPANET protocols were slow and networks were unreliable.

Transmission Control Protocol/Internet Protocol has its roots in a design specification proposed in 1974. This new protocol specification provided a robust, versatile protocol that is not dependent on the physical and data link control layers of such networking architectures as SNA and OSI. This architecture has accounted for its longevity and durability in data communications. Its protocol design is independent of hardware, operating systems, and telecommunications facilities, so TCP/IP has seen commercial success in recent years, since the advent of right-sizing MIS organizations and their applications. Therefore, it is appropriate to address the TCP/IP architecture and its role in information networks.

1.3.1   TCP/IP layers

The TCP/IP architecture is layered, providing a rational, simple, and easy-to-modify structure which has added to TCP/IP's success. The architecture is often referred to as a five-layer architecture but it actually defines only the three higher layers.

As seen in Fig. 1.3, the two lower layers, physical and data link control, can be defined by different networking architectures such as token-ring, Ethernet, frame-relay, ATM, SNA, and OSI. Recall that at these layers the physical attributes of the communications network are defined and adhered to. Data units at this level are called *frames*. Moving up to the third layer we find the one where Internet Protocol (IP) resides.

IP's single main function is to route data between hosts on the network. The data is routed in datagrams. IP uses connectionless network service for transmitting the datagram. Since it uses connectionless services, IP does not guarantee reliable delivery of the data or the sequencing of the datagram. Hence, the upper layers (e.g., TCP) must provide this function. What IP does provide is the ability to route traffic independent of available physical routes regardless of the application-to-application requirements. IP allows for datagrams to be rerouted through the network if the current physical route being used becomes inoperative. This is a valuable feature built into IP that SNA does not possess.

The transport layer, layer 4 of the OSI architecture, is where TCP resides. TCP connection-oriented services, as such, provide reliable delivery of data between the host computers by establishing a connection before the applications send data. TCP guarantees that the data is error free and in sequence. Data units at this layer are called *segments*. TCP passes its segments to IP which then routes the datagram through the network. IP will receive incoming datagrams and pass the TCP segment to TCP. TCP will analyze the TCP header to determine the application recipient and pass the data to the application in sequenced order. Standard applications provided with TCP/IP that use TCP are File Transfer Protocol (FTP), Simple Mail Transfer Protocol (SMTP), and Telnet terminal services.

At the transport layer another protocol is found in the TCP/IP architecture that provides connectionless-oriented services. This protocol is called User

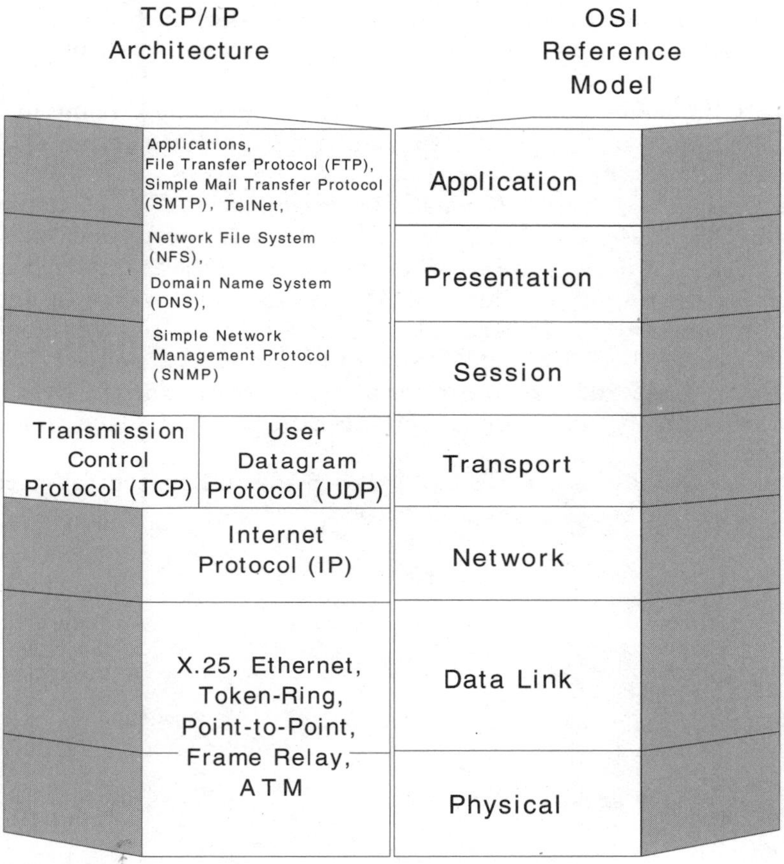

TCP/IP
Architecture

OSI
Reference
Model

Applications, File Transfer Protocol (FTP), Simple Mail Transfer Protocol (SMTP), TelNet,		Application
Network File System (NFS), Domain Name System (DNS),		Presentation
Simple Network Management Protocol (SNMP)		Session
Transmission Control Protocol (TCP)	User Datagram Protocol (UDP)	Transport
Internet Protocol (IP)		Network
X.25, Ethernet, Token-Ring, Point-to-Point, Frame Relay, ATM		Data Link
		Physical

Figure 1.3 The TCP/IP networking model as it relates to the OSI Reference Model.

Datagram Protocol (UDP). UDP is used by various applications to send messages to other applications where the integrity of the data is not as important. UDP passes user datagrams to IP for routing. UDP is used by the Simple Network Management Protocol (SNMP), Domain Name System (DNS), Network File System (NFS), and other applications. These user datagrams are usually small, single messages and hence it was thought that to resend such a message would not cause a network impact. This is in contrast to SNA, where every frame, no matter how small or large, is provided with guaranteed delivery.

1.4 IEEE 802 LAN Standards

The OSI and IP models provided a means for corporations to break away from the proprietary constraints that they have lived with for so long. The selection process for users is now wide open. Vendors must compete on equal ground for income. A standard networking platform that all vendors can develop to will inspire them to come up with software and hardware that will provide solutions to the business need rather than the business need being fit to the vendors solution. A case in point is the plethora of products adhering to the IEEE 802 LAN standards.

The *institute of electrical and electronic engineers* (IEEE) Computer Society established, in the winter of 1980, the data link and physical standards for local area networks. Figure 1.4 shows the IEEE 802 standard that implements local area networking into the two lower layers of SNA and OSI. The data link layer for the IEEE 802 LAN standard is subdivided into two sublayers. These are the IEEE 802.2 standard for *logical link control* (LLC) and the IEEE 802.3 and 802.5 standard for *medium access control* (MAC). The MAC standards will be discussed under the Ethernet and token-ring sections of Chap. 2.

The LLC sublayer is IEEE 802.2. It provides a flow control mechanism for LANs. The LLC has three types of services:

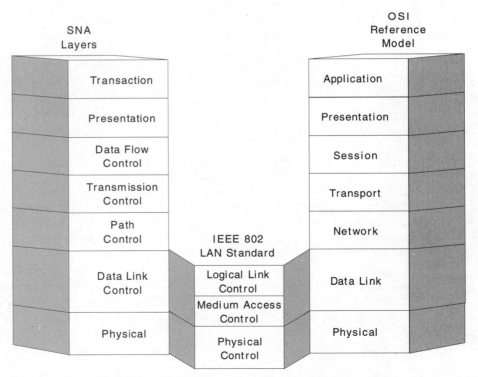

Figure 1.4   IEEE 802 LAN standard compared with the SNA and OSI models.

- Type 1—unacknowledged connectionless
- Type 2—connection-oriented
- Type 3—acknowledged connectionless

A connectionless mode of operation indicates that a logical data link connection is not established between the LAN stations before transmitting information frames. The LLC does not guarantee delivery of the information unit. This mode of operation provides no flow control, correlation between frames, error recovery, or acknowledgment of receipt of the information frame on the data link level (layer 2 of the OSI stack). These services must be provided by upper-layer network services. For example, IP does not provide guaranteed delivery. IP is a best-effort protocol. TCP, higher on the protocol stack, provides the functions of end-to-end data transfer. LLC type 1 services are typically used by protocols that deliver information in a datagram. With LLC type 1 services, data can typically be dropped, received out of sequence, or even duplicated, hence, the requirement for higher-layer protocols using connection-oriented services such as TCP.

Connection-oriented services require that a logical data link is established prior to transmitting an information unit. This is often referred to as a connection. This operation creates an LLC type 2 control block. The control block in association with delivery and error recovery services constitute a link station. The LLC type 2 service provides sequence numbering of information frames at the data link layer, error detection, and basic recovery and flow control including acknowledgment. The LLC type 2 acknowledgment allows for a window size of up to 127 outstanding frames sent before expecting an acknowledgment from the receiving station. This is also known as modulus 128. Once data has been sent between stations and the application function is complete, LLC type 2 services disconnect the stations.

LLC type 3 acknowledged connectionless is a stop-and-wait flow control mechanism. This mode of operation does not require a connection before transmitting information units. However, it does expect link-level acknowledgments for data delivered from the receiving station. In this way the receiving station can determine the rate at which it can accept data by acknowledging data when it is ready to receive more. This type of operation is particularly useful in LANs that may have high bursts of traffic like those used with file servers and backbone connectivity.

There are two classes of LLC services defined in the IEEE 802.2 standard:

- Class I—connectionless only
- Class II—connectionless and connection-oriented

All stations support connectionless operations. Only class II stations support type 1, type 2, and type 3 modes of operation.

The logical link control sublayer has three main functions:

1. A specification to interfacing with the network layer above.
2. Logical link control procedures.
3. A specification to interface with the medium access control sublayer below.

The interface specification to the network layer defines the calls for unacknowledged connectionless service. This type of service allows stations to exchange information units without establishing a connection or acknowledgments. This is also known as a *datagram*. The LLC sublayer also provides a connected service as an option to the network layer.

Service access points (SAP) provide the interface between the application and the logical link control. Each SAP is uniquely architected for an application existing on a specific device type. A main function of the SAP is to allow multiple applications executing on a device to access the token-ring network through a single connection or adapter. Service access points support connectionless and connection-oriented transmission.

Logical link control is concerned with the delivery of information. LLC, in conjunction with connection-oriented service, uses SAP to enable multiple applications to share a single connection to the LAN. Connection-oriented service utilizes link stations to manage the logical connections providing an extensive error recovery mechanism for maintaining data integrity. Connectionless service on the other hand provides no error recovery or guarantee of successful data transport.

1.5   Advanced Peer-to-Peer Networking (APPN)

The success of TCP/IP as the preferred internetworking protocol for corporate networks pushed IBM to enhance its SNA networking model to provide for an ease of connectivity and to allow for peer-to-peer networking between unlike processing platforms. IBM's answer to providing a peer-to-peer networking architecture is Advanced Peer-to-Peer Networking (APPN).

Although APPN is being represented as a peer networking architecture it does have its roots in SNA and hence it has the flavor of a hierarchical structure. IBM has taken the formality of SNA and successfully married it with the dynamics of a peer network to produce a sophisticated networking architecture. Figure 1.5 illustrates the APPN services and functions as they relate to the seven layers of the SNA model.

1.5.1   APPN and the SNA layers

APPN encompasses the SNA path control and transmission control functions. The physical and data link control layers of SNA are fully supported under

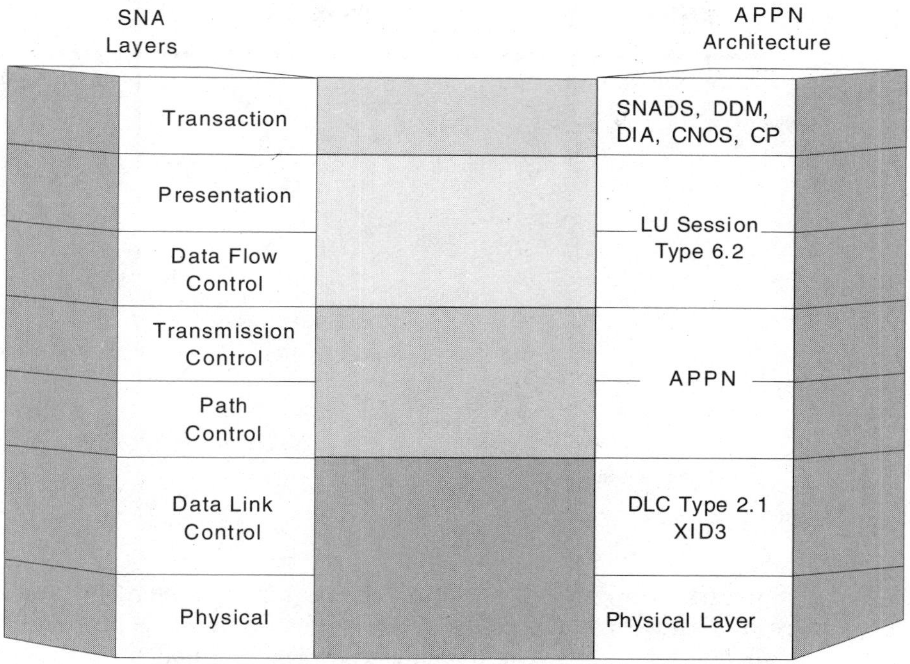

SNA
Layers

APPN
Architecture

SNA Layers	APPN Architecture
Transaction	SNADS, DDM, DIA, CNOS, CP
Presentation	LU Session Type 6.2
Data Flow Control	
Transmission Control	APPN
Path Control	
Data Link Control	DLC Type 2.1 XID3
Physical	Physical Layer

Figure 1.5 APPN comparison to SNA layers.

APPN. APPN will support any physical connection currently provided today. Session services in APPN are provided by logical unit (LU) 6.2 which takes on the SNA data flow control and presentation services layers. The LU 6.2 is IBM's peer-to-peer protocol as TCP is the peer-to-peer protocol for IP. Resources are located through the directory services functions of the control point. The *control point* (CP) in APPN resides at SNA layer 7 transaction services and is similar in functionality to IBM's VTAM on the mainframe computer and is considered an SNA node type 2.1, also known as an APPN network node (NN) or end node (EN). So, as you can see, even though the name implies a peer architecture, its functionality in certain areas reflects that of a hierarchy.

1.6 Asynchronous Transfer Mode (ATM)

Asynchronous Transfer Mode (ATM) is based on the concept of cell switching. Cells are set at a fixed length. Large blocks of user data are broken down to fit into the data area of the cell. The data area of a cell is called *payload*. In ATM, a cell is 53 bytes in length. The header takes up 5 bytes and the payload uses 48 bytes (Fig. 1.6). Even if the user data is only one byte in length the cell will be 53 bytes long.

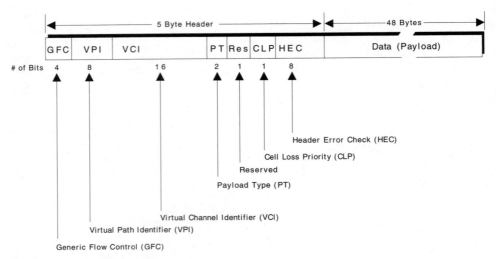

Figure 1.6   ATM cell format.

Short, fixed-length cells simplify the requirements on the switching hardware and therefore allows for higher speeds. Small cells result in shorter transit delay through a multinode network. The nodes on the network can handle cells more efficiently in its queues, reducing the variation in transit delays due to variable-sized-length frames. Finally, cell-based networks like ATM do not use link level error recovery. Only the header field of the cell is checked for errors in ATM and it is up to the higher-layer protocols to check for errors in the payload portion of the cell. All this adds up to the theoretical support of 2 gigabits per second (Gbps)! Cell switching is most suitable to concurrently carry voice, video, data, and image, over the same physical link.

1.6.1   ATM network architecture overview

An ATM network is composed of nodes, interfaces, links, and virtual resources, just as many of the other network schemes discussed. Figure 1.7 illustrates an ATM network. NNs perform the switching functions and data transport within the network. Note that the ATM NNs are not the same as the APPN NNs. At the endpoints of an ATM network are the *customer premise nodes* (CPN). This equipment is owned by the end user of the ATM network. Within each node there is an interface. On NNs, the interface is called the *network node interface* (NNI). CPNs have a user network interface (UNI). The NNI provides network signaling procedures for operation and control of the network besides the data transfer functions found in the UNI.

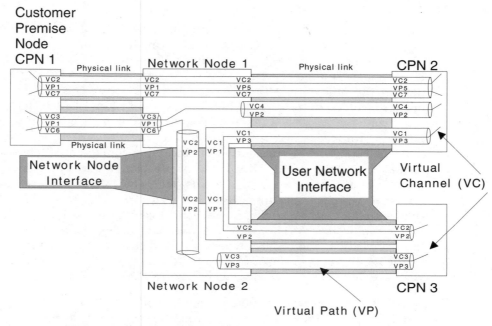

Figure 1.7 ATM network and connectivity illustration.

Physical links between nodes exist for the NNI and UNI to utilize. The physical links from NN–NN or UNI–NN are divided into *virtual paths* (VP) and *virtual channels* (VC). Multiple VPs can exist on a physical link and multiple VCs can be assigned to each VP on that physical link. Up to 256 VPs can be defined for each physical port and 4096 virtual channels for a single VP. A VP is a route over a physical link between two adjacent ATM nodes. A VC is a connection between the two ATM adjacent nodes that is mapped to the VP. Each VP and VC has an identifier assigned to it. The *virtual path identifier* (VPI) and the *virtual channel identifier* (VCI) are unique to specific physical links. These identifiers must be the same on each end of the physical link. They do not have to be network unique. Virtual channels are coupled through the ATM network to establish the connection between the CPNs. This connection is called the *virtual channel connection* (VCC). The VCC is analogous to an X.25 virtual circuit. However, under ATM, this connection establishes specific characteristics defined as the *quality of service* (QoS). Each VCC can have its own QoS defined, hence the VCC can be viewed as unidirectional. That is, each direction can have different QoS attributes. The VCCs themselves are bidirectional using the same VPI/VCI numbered pairs on each side of the physical link between the ATM nodes for sending and receiving cells. This pairing of VPI/VCI values is also called a *label*. Multiple VPI/VCI pairs make up the VCC.

1.6.2   ATM layer overview

At the physical layer of ATM the medium data rates and transmission technique are defined. ATM for the most part is media independent. The ATM specifications include unshielded and shielded twisted pairs, T45, SONET, IEEE 802.6, Fiber Channel, FDDI, and T1. The next layer in ATM, the ATM layer, defines the 53-byte cell that is transmitted through the network. A 5-byte header is added to the 48-byte information field received from the ATM *adaptation layer* (AAL) on transmission and the 5-byte header is removed and passed to the AAL on receiving the ATM cell.

The AAL, (Fig. 1.8), transforms the incoming signals into ATM cell-payload format. This layer is subdivided into two levels. The first level breaks up the incoming data into manageable pieces. The segmentation and assembly level breaks up the user data into a 48-byte field for transmission and reassembly at the receiving endpoint. ATM has specified several AALs to support different traffic requirements. These include voice, video, image, and data for leased-line, connection, and connectionless-oriented sessions. Support for the various traffic requirements over ATM results in data rates of up to 2 Gbps. These services are divided into four distinct categories. They are:

- *AAL-1.*   This service is used by applications that require a *constant bit rate* (CBR). These applications are uncompressed voice and video. This type of traffic is often referred to as *isochronous.* This type of application is extremely time sensitive and therefore end-to-end timing is paramount and must be supported. Isochronous traffic is assigned service class A.

- *AAL-2.*   Again this service is used for compressed audio and video (packetized isochronous traffic), however, it is primarily developed for multimedia applications. The compression allows for a *variable bit rate* (VBR) service without losing audio and video quality. The compression of audio and video,

Application	Isochronous voice/video	Compressed voice/video	Data	SMDS data
Connection mode	Connection-oriented	Connection-oriented	Connection-oriented	Connectionless
Bit rate	Constant	Variable	Variable	Variable
End-to-end timing	Required	Required	Not required	Not required
Service class	A	B	C	D
AAL type	1	2	5	3/4
	Adaptation layer			
	ATM layer			
	Physical layer			

Figure 1.8   The ATM layers and functions.

however, does not negate the need for end-to-end timing. However, timing is still important and is assigned a service class just below that of AAL-1.

- *AAL-3/4.* This adaptation layer supports both connection-oriented and connectionless data transport. Both AAL-3 and AAL-4 were specified for compatibility with IEEE 802.6 which is used by Switched Multimegabit Data Service (SMDS). Connection-oriented AAL-3 and AAL-4 payloads are provided with a service class D2 while connectionless-oriented AAL-3 and AAL-4 payloads are assigned the service class D. The support for IEEE 802.6 significantly increases cell overhead for data transfer when compared with AAL-5.

- *AAL-5.* For data transport, AAL-5 is the preferred AAL to be used by applications. Its connection-oriented mode guarantees delivery of data by the servicing applications and does not add any cell overhead.

ATM's small cell size, along with the various AALs and services compiled with the multiplexing of virtual paths and virtual channels on physical links, makes ATM ideal for mixing traffic of various types without each traffic type causing a delay or affect on the other. ATM is truly the multimedia, multiprotocol networking architecture.

1.7 Summary

The integration of transporting all information over a single network is the brass ring for corporate networks. This chapter has laid the groundwork for understanding the difficulty in supporting the integration of existing legacy SNA protocols, Internet protocols, and extensions to local area network standards to support these protocols and an overview of ATM itself. Now that we have a better understanding of the architectures and standards, a discussion of the shared media used on the physical layer along with data link control is in order to further understand the intricacies of integrating ATM.

2

Shared Media LANs

The cables and wires used to connect workstations to the LAN are called *shared media*. This shared media is defined in the physical layer of the OSI Reference Model. This physical connection is implemented with mechanical, electrical, functional, and procedural specifications that are understood by both endpoints of the connection, in other words, the type of connectors used, the voltage on the wire and the meaning of the voltage, and events initiated by the voltage.

The LAN uses shared media as a means of allowing any station on the LAN to communicate with any other station on the LAN without having a direct connection to the other station. This allows for a one-to-many configuration with only one cable connecting the station to the network.

Ethernet was one of the first shared media LANs and by far the most widely used shared media. Token-ring, made popular by IBM, is the second most popular type of LAN using shared media. Gaining some growth but not as popular for station access is the *fiber distributed data interchange* (FDDI) LAN. FDDI can usually be found as the backbone media when used for LANs.

Each of these popular LAN types utilizes standard cabling standards that must be adhered to in order for each of these LAN topologies to function properly.

2.1 LAN Cables

There are four major types of media used in LAN networking: coaxial cable, telephone twisted pair, shielded twisted pair, and fiber optic. The types and their characteristics are listed below:

Coaxial cable. This type of cable media has a low attenuation characteristic and drives signals at high-data rates over fairly long distances. *Attenuation* is the decrease in magnitude of an electrical or optical power between two points. The drive distance is the length a signal can be propagated over the cable before requiring a regeneration of the signal, using, for example, a repeater. Your cable television connection is made with coaxial cable.

Telephone twisted pair (TTP).   This is also referred to as *unshielded twisted pair* (UTP). *Unshielded* means that the wires do not have a metal shield around them. A metal shield reduces the interference of unwanted radio frequencies from having a negative effect on the cable. Therefore, UTP is very susceptible to unwanted radio frequencies and emit radio frequencies themselves when used for high-speed data transmission. Filters can be put in place to reduce or eliminate the unwanted radio frequencies but the filters reduce the signal strength. UTP also suffers from *crosstalk,* a signal generated from one pair affecting the signal on the other pair.

Data-grade media (DGM), shielded twisted pair.   As the name implies, this type of cable contains a shield. Within each shield there can be one or more twisted pairs. The pairs are twisted in such a way that they themselves help to alleviate radio frequency interference within the shielded cable. Shielded twisted pair cable is suited to handle data rates over 20 Mbps for most distances found in typical office buildings. Due to its low attenuation and high-data rates over long distances, DGM can be used for both low- and high-speed LANs.

Fiber optics.   The previous cables all use copper wiring. Fiber optics utilizes glass and light pulses. A fiber-optic cable can contain thousands of fibers. Each fiber is thinner than the thickness of human hair. Because fiber optics uses light as the transmission signal, it is basically impervious to radio-frequency interference. The rate of transmission in fiber-optic media is literally the speed of light. With minor signal attenuation, fiber optics has data rates that can approach terabits per second. In other words 1 trillion bits per second! Fiber optics provides enhanced security over copper wire. If tapped into, the fiber-optic signal will cause a loss of the transmission signal which will be immediately detected. Copper wire on the other hand can allow the tapping of the signal without great loss to the delivery of data.

Of the four cable types discussed, UTP, though suffering from high attenuation and radio frequency interference, is a well-understood inexpensive medium and yet undesirable for providing a stable network. However, newer NIC technologies and connectors have shown that UTP can sustain data rates as high as 100 Mbps with great stability. Fiber optics possesses the highest throughput but is relatively new technology and hence expensive to implement. DGM shielded twisted pair cable is the most cost-effective solution available today for providing both high-speed data rates and immunity to radio frequency interference. Figure 2.1 contains a table outlining the pros and cons of each cable type.

Medium Type	Pros	Cons
Unshielded Copper Wire Twisted pair	• Understood technology. • Knowledgeable technicians available. • Fast and simple installation. • Least expensive medium for LAN migration. • Can use existing telephone wiring found in building.	• Affected by electromagnetic interference. • Electrical and magnetic waves can be intercepted. • Cross talk between wires can cause transmission errors. • Exterior placement needs protection from lightning and corrosion. • Low data rate.
Shielded Copper Wire Twisted pair Coaxial Twinaxial Broadband (CATV)	• Understood technology. • Knowledgeable technicians available. • Fast and simple installation (except for CATV). • Minimal emanation of electromagnetic signals. • Shield provides some protection from interference, lightning, cross talk, corrosion.	• High-grade coaxial, twinaxial, and CATV cables are fairly expensive to use for migrating to LAN. • CATV cable is thick and ridgid requiring special tools to install around turns.
Fiber Optic Fiber Optic Cable	• Useful for high-speed applications. • No electromagnetic signal emanation. • Not affected by cross talk, electromagnetic interference, lightning, corrosion. • Less expensive medium than coaxial or CATV cable. • Signal transmitted over greater distances than copper wire without boosting the signal.	• Knowledgeable technicians are scarce. • Device connection more expensive than copper wire. • Bi-directrional communication requires two fiber optic lines. • High cost for installation. • Cannot be split, use for point-to-point topologies.

Figure 2.1 Table detailing the pros and cons of LAN cable types.

UTPs inexpensive solution for wiring a building and its ease of installation combined with improved NIC and connector technologies has made UTP the preferred cable in use today, governing over 50 percent of all LANs.

2.1.1 Cable classification

There are ten classes of cables and currently eight cable types available for use. Each type is used for specific installation requirements. These requirements are location and environment. The installation requirements of cables is dictated by the local or state electrical codes in your area. Be sure to follow these codes as they have been implemented for your safety. Figure 2.2 contains a table outlining the characteristics of each cable class. These cable classes are defined by the Electronics Industry Association in concert with the Telecommunications Industry Association (EIA/TIA). The EIA/TIA-568 cable standard and the enhanced standard 568B specify standards only for UTP. The five categories of EIA/TIA-568 are as follows:

Category 1.   Though this cable is categorized, its wide range of impedances and use of American Wire Gauge (AWG) 22 or 24 makes it an undesirable cable for use with data transmission.

Category 2.   This category of EIA/TIA-568 cable also uses 22 or 24 AWG solid wire. This cable is similar to category 1 but does not have a specific impedance. It is quite often used for Appletalk or IBM 3270 data transmission. These are low-bandwidth uses and as such the category 2 cable with its 1 MHz maximum is sufficient.

Category 3.   This cable uses 24 AWG UTP and is the most widely installed wiring. This wire is also known as *voice grade* (VG) wire. Category 3 wiring

Cable	Conductor	Twisted pairs	Shielding	Outdoor	Use
Category 1	Solid copper	2 or 4 pair AWG 22 or 24	No	No	Not recommended
Category 2	Solid copper	2 or 4 pair AWG 22 or 24	No	No	PBX Alarm Systems AppleTalk IBM 3270
Category 3	Solid copper	2 or 4 pair AWG 24	No	No	10BASE-T 100BASE-T 100VG-AnyLAN 4M Token-Ring
Category 4	Solid copper	2 or 4 pair AWG 24	No	No	10BASE-T 100BASE-T 4/16 Token-Ring
Category 5	Solid copper	2 or 4 pair AWG 22 or 24	No	No	10BASE-T 100BASE-T 100VG-AnyLAN 4/16/32 Token-Ring

Figure 2.2   Table of EIA/TIA-568 cable classifications.

has a typical impedance of 100 ohms and has a frequency range of 16 to 25 MHz. These characteristics make the cable suitable for 10 Mbps Ethernet and 4 Mbps token-ring. It has been shown to run 16 Mbps token-ring but the reliability of the transmission is not production safe.

Category 4.   This cable is identical to category 3 wiring with the exception that it has a bandwidth of 20 MHz. This extra four megahertz of bandwidth allows it to transmit 16 Mbps token-ring with added safety but is still not recommended.

Category 5.   This cable is the preferred UTP cable for use on LANs today. Category 5 cable is also referred to as *data grade* (DG) wire. It has a high-frequency bandwidth of 100 MHz and can transmit data up to 100 Mbps. This wire is also 22 or 24 AWG with an impedance of 100 ohms. Category 5 wiring has made the previous four categories obsolete.

IBM has always been a vendor to strive for higher standards where possible. In so doing, IBM has created its own cabling standards called *IBM Cable System.* These standards adhere to IBM's strict rules of protecting data integrity during transmission over a network as much as possible. Figure 2.3 contains a table of the IBM Cable System cable types. Though it highly recommends and prefers shielded cabling its cable system does support unshielded as does its own LAN equipment offerings. The following list details IBM's cabling standards:

Type 1: twisted pair.   This cable has a braided shield around two twisted pairs of #22 AWG solid wire for data communication. This cable type can support up to 16 Mbps data transfer rates and is used strictly for data. As with all cable types listed here, this cable can be installed in conduits. Type 1 can also come in two flavors: plenum and riser.

Plenum cable has an outer fire-resistant covering, such as Teflon, to reduce the fire hazard and emitted PVC fumes should a fire start. The resistance to fire and low-hazardous vapor emissions gives this cable adequate protection to allow installation in air ducts (plenums) and other spaces within a building used for air passages without the use of conduits.

Riser cable also has the characteristics of fire protection without the use of conduit. However, this cable is more suitable for use in a building riser. For example, *building risers* are elevator shafts and mail-drop chutes.

Type 1 cable can also be used outdoors. Used in this way the cable has a corrugated metallic cable shield around two twisted pair. Each wire of the twisted pair is made up of #22 AWG wire. This cable type can be used in an aerial installation or placed in conduit underground.

Type 1A: twisted pair.   This new standard has the same makeup as the type 1 cable; however, it has been enhanced to provide a frequency bandwidth of

300 MHz at 150 ohms. IBM highly recommends using type 1A cable for new construction.

Type 2: telephone twisted pair.   This is the same as type 1 cable but has an additional four twisted pairs of #22 AWG solid copper telephone wires. The cable contains six twisted pairs, two shielded, and four unshielded pairs. This cable type has the added advantage of supporting two token-ring connections and one voice connection concurrently. The shielded pairs can carry data at speeds up to 16 Mbps and data on the unshielded pairs (voice pairs) at 4 Mbps.

Cable	Conductor	Pairs	Shielding	Outdoor	Use
Type 1	Solid copper	2 twisted pair AWG 22 @ 20 MHz	Braided or corrugated	Yes	10BASE-T 4M Token-Ring
Type 1A	Solid copper	2 twisted pair AWG 22 @ 300 MHz	Braided or corrugated	Yes	10BASE-T 100BASE-T 4/16/32 Token-Ring
Type 2	Solid copper	2 pair AWG 22 and 4 pair VG AWG 22	Braided No	No	10BASE-T 4M Token-Ring
Type 2A	Solid copper	300 MHz 2 twisted pair AWG 22 and 4 twisted pair VG AWG 22	Braided No	No	10BASE-T 100BASE-T 4/16/32 Token-Ring
Type 3	Solid copper	4 twisted pair VG AWG 22/24	No	No	10BASE-T 100BASE-T 100VG-AnyLAN 4M Token-Ring
Type 5	Fiber optic	2 fiber strands 62.5/125 microns	No	Yes	10BASE-F 100BASE-F 16/32 Token-Ring
Type 5R	Fiber optic	2 fiber stands 50/125 microns	No	Yes	10BASE-F 100BASE-F 16/32 Token-Ring
Type 6	Stranded copper	2 twisted pair AWG 26	Braided	No	Patch or jumper cable
Type 8	Solid copper	2 parallel twisted pair AWG 26	Braided	No	10BASE-T 4/16 Token-Ring
Type 9	Solid/stranded copper	2 twisted pair AWG 26	Braided	No	10BASE-T 100BASE-T 4/16 Token-Ring

Figure 2.3   IBM Cable System cable types.

Type 2A: telephone twisted pair. Type 2A is an improved version of the type 2 cable. Like type 1A this cable provides for a bandwidth of up to 300 MHz at 150 ohms.

Type 3: telephone twisted pair. This is the recommended cable type for implementing token-ring networks over unshielded telephone twisted pair. This cable type has three or more twisted pairs at #22 or 24 AWG solid copper wire and support either voice or data. The solid copper wire must have a minimum of two twisted pairs per foot. The IBM Cabling System recommends that a maximum of 72 devices can be attached to a token ring using type 3 cable.

Type 5: optical fiber. Optical fiber itself is fairly inexpensive but costly to install. It is not provided for plenum specifications and therefore must be installed in some kind of protective conduit. The nonplenum optical fiber type 5 cable contains two optical fiber strands. One for transmit and one for receive. This nonplenum type 5 can be used indoors, aerial, or underground, as long as it is installed using a conduit.

These cables will contain multiple fiber strands which can be useful when making connections over long distances within a building. The cable may be laid horizontally and vertically. It does not require conduit but cannot be run through a plenum.

Outdoor fiber-optic cables also contain multiple fibers and are used primarily as backbone or campus connections between buildings. The use of this cable requires installation in a conduit.

Fiber optics can be used for both voice and data with speeds of 16 Mbps and greater. Fiber-optic cables are measured in microns instead of AWG. There are four thicknesses to a fiber as shown in Fig. 2.3. It is recommended that the fiber be 62.5 micron size for the fiber core and 125 microns for the cladding.

Type 6: twisted pair. This shielded twisted pair cable uses #26 AWG solid copper wire and is for data communications. The twisted pairs are surrounded by a braided shield. Type 6 cable is used only for patch or jumper cable.

Type 8: parallel pairs. This cable type consists of two parallel pairs of #26 AWG wires for data communications. This cable is used for under-carpet installation. The cable is used in situations where location of the endpoints do not allow for connection through plenums, conduits, or risers. Type 8 cables support data rates up to 16 Mbps. Each wire is a solid piece of copper.

Type 9: twisted pair. This cable type has two twisted pairs with a braided shield. Each wire of the pairs is #26 AWG. The wires can be made up of strands as well as a solid piece of copper. This cable is used mainly through plenum for main connections between token-ring segments or multistation access units. The cable can service data rates up to 16 Mbps. It can also be used in building risers. Type 9 cable is a lower-cost solution to implementing type 1 plenum cable.

With both the EIA/TIA-568 and IBM Cable System standards, it is very important to use the appropriate data connectors in order to sustain the specified data rates.

2.2 Ethernet

The Ethernet protocol was developed by Xerox Corporation and the final frame format was codeveloped by Digital Equipment Corporation (DEC), Intel Corporation, and Xerox. The popularity of Ethernet quickly grew and the IEEE architected a standard for all vendors to adhere to for Ethernet. This standard is known as IEEE 802.3. IEEE 802.3 and Ethernet frames are quite similar and for the most part the majority of vendors utilize the 802.3 standard. Unlike token-ring, Ethernet LANs use a contention-based bus architecture.

2.2.1 Ethernet bus topology and CSMA/CD

A bus topology can be considered a probabilistic architecture. In a bus architecture environment (Fig. 2.4) it is possible for two or more stations to simultaneously send data onto the LAN. This causes collisions on the LAN and hence a standard protocol to sense this type of error was developed. The standard is called Carrier Sense Multiple Access/Carrier Detect (CSMA/CD). Stations on an Ethernet LAN see all transmissions due to the bus architecture. This is the multiple access function of CSMA/CD. Each station analyzes the destination field for the destination address of the frame. If the address matches the station's address the frame is copied.

The transmission of an Ethernet frame onto the LAN is determined by a station "listening" to the wire. If the wire is busy then the station waits to send its

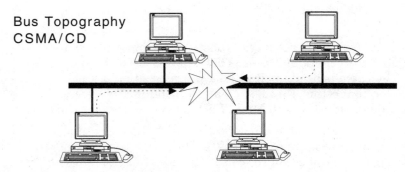

Figure 2.4   Bus topology of an Ethernet LAN.

data. If the wire is "silent" the station transmits its data. This is the carrier sense function of CSMA/CD. When two or more stations have a frame to send and they sense that the wire is silent they will send a frame out onto the wire. This will result in collisions. *Collision detection* (CD) causes a station to abort transmission and sends a jamming signal to the other stations on the LAN. This jamming signal is a random pattern usually 63 bytes in length. Stations on the Ethernet LAN will wait a random time after receiving a jamming signal before retrying transmission. This random wait time helps to avoid collisions. The number of collisions on an Ethernet LAN is a factor of the number of stations attached to the LAN.

2.2.2 Ethernet MAC frame format

The Ethernet frame format depicted in Fig. 2.5 shows the simplicity of Ethernet. This Ethernet frame format is the precursor to the IEEE 802.3 MAC frame format for Ethernet.

The first field is called the *preamble*. The preamble is 8 bytes in length and is a pattern of alternating bits. The preamble provides synchronization for Ethernet. The next field is a 6-byte field that contains the physical address of the Ethernet station adapter. This field is the destination address field. It contains the target address of the partner station. The following 6-byte field is the source address. This is the physical address of the originating station's Ethernet adapter. The next type is a 2-byte field that indicates the upper-layer protocol found in the data field. The more commonly found types are x'805D' for IBM SNA over Ethernet, x'8138' for Novell IPX, and x'0800' for TCP/IP. The data field in an Ethernet frame is variable in length and can range from 46 to 1500 bytes in length. The data found in this field is provided by the higher-layer protocols. The last field is the *frame check sequence* (FCS) field. This is a 32-bit field that is used for *cyclic redundancy checking* (CRC) using the destination and source address fields, type and data fields. Frames in Ethernet can range from 64 to 1518 bytes in length excluding the preamble. Frames outside of this range transmitted onto the LAN using Ethernet protocols are considered invalid. Frames shorter than 64 bytes are called *runts*. Frames longer than 1518 bytes are referred to as *jabbers*.

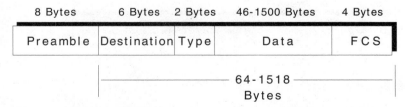

Figure 2.5 Ethernet MAC frame format prior to IEEE 802.3 standard.

2.2.3   IEEE 802.3/Ethernet
MAC frame format

Figure 2.6 illustrates the IEEE 802.3 frame format for Ethernet. Note that this is a MAC frame format which will allow IEEE 802.2 LLC data units to be encapsulated. Here again, the Ethernet frame begins with a preamble but in this format it is only 7 bytes in length.

The preamble is followed by the *start frame delimiter* (SD), a single-byte field. These two fields together create the identical pattern required for the preamble field of the Ethernet frame discussed previously. The SD is followed by the destination address field. Again the address found here is the address of the target station on the Ethernet LAN. However, instead of the address field being 6 bytes in length it can be 2 or 6 bytes in length. Six bytes is most common. In the IEEE 802.3 specification the fields of the address field will indicate whether the address is an individual station or a group address and whether it is universally assigned or locally administered. The source address follows the destination address and it too can be either 2 or 6 bytes in length. The requirement is that it must match the length used in the destination address field. Following the source address field is the length field. Note that in the IEEE 802.3 specification the length field replaces the Ethernet frame-type field. The length field provides the length of the data unit field in bytes. The data unit field is an IEEE 802.2 LLC protocol data unit. IEEE 802.3 requires that the data unit be a minimum of 46 bytes. If the data unit field is smaller than 46 bytes, the pad field is used to make up the difference. The data unit and the pad field combined cannot exceed 1500 bytes in length. Again the last field is the *frame check sequence* (FCS) field. This 32-bit CRC value is based on the contents of the two address fields, the length, data, and pad fields.

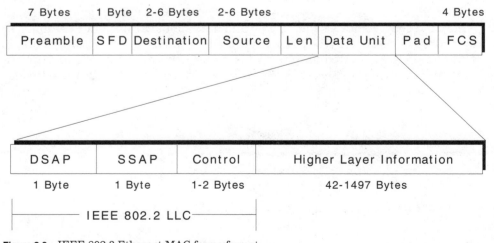

Figure 2.6   IEEE 802.3 Ethernet MAC frame format.

2.2.4 10 Mbps Ethernet

There are four ways that are used mainly for transmitting Ethernet at 10 Mbps. Each is defined using a standard naming convention. The convention is *10BASE-n*. The *10* identifies the speed of the medium. In this case it signifies 10 Mbps. The *BASE* means a baseband network. Baseband indicates that the full bandwidth is used for the specific purpose of transmitting data. This is opposed to a broadband network like Integrated Services Digital Network (ISDN) or Asynchronous Transfer Mode (ATM). Broadband networks have the ability to create narrower bands of frequency to transmit voice, video, and data simultaneously. The *n* in 10BASE-*n* identifies either the approximate length of a single Ethernet segment using the medium or the type of medium in use. The four most popular ways of transmitting 10 Mbps Ethernet are 10BASE5, 10BASE2, 10BASE-T, and 10BASE-F, compared in Fig. 2.7.

10BASE5 (Thicknet). As the name implies this Ethernet LAN has a data rate of 10 Mbps using baseband technology with a single Ethernet segment length of 500 meters supporting up to 100 connections. An *Ethernet segment* is the distance between two stations on the wire. 10BASE5 was developed in the 1970s and was dubbed Thicknet; short for thick Ethernet. Thicknet uses a 10-mm thick coaxial cable. Hence the name Thicknet. Ethernet segments can be extended with a device known as a *repeater*. A repeater simply boosts the signal on the wire and forwards the diagonal onto the next wire. Using Thicknet, a single Ethernet segment can be extended to a maximum of 2500 meters using four repeaters. This extended range is known as the *network diameter*. Station attachment to Thicknet requires the NIC, a DB-15 connector with a cable called an *attachment unit interface* (AUI), which in turn is connected to a *medium attachment unit* (MAU). The MAU contains the transceiver that connects to the coaxial cable.

	10BASE5	10BASE2	10BASE-T	10BASE-F
Max. segment length	500 meters	185 meters	100 meters	500, 1000, 2000 meters
Topology	Bus	Bus	Star	Star
Medium	50-ohm thick coaxial	50-ohm thin coaxial	100-ohm UTP	Multimode fiber
Connector	NIC—DB-15	RG-58	RJ-45	ST
Medium attachment	Medium attachment unit (MAU) bolted to coax	External or on NIC	External or on NIC	External or on NIC
Stations/segment	100	30	2 (NIC and repeater/hub) 12/hub	33 for 10BASE-FP, 2 repeaters for FB, FL or FOIRL
Max. segments	5	5	5	5

Figure 2.7 10 Mbps IEEE 802.3 Ethernet LAN comparison.

10BASE2 (Thinnet).   This cabling system for Ethernet was introduced in the early 1980s and is a thinner coaxial cable. Being thinner, it had a cost and installation factor that quickly caught on and replaced the majority of the 10BASE5 installations. Although 10BASE2 wiring is less expensive it reduced the number of connections per segment to 30 versus 100 for 10BASE5. Thinnets formal name implies a segment distance of 200 meters. However, this varies depending on the LAN configuration. If repeaters are in use, the four-repeater rule from 10BASE5 applies, creating a network diameter of 925 meters. A single nonextended Ethernet segment using Thinnet can be extended to 300 meters without the use of repeaters. The NIC used on a Thinnet LAN incorporates the MAU, transceiver, and AUI, making connection much simpler.

10BASE-T (twisted pair Ethernet).   This standard for Ethernet utilizes two pair UTP (4 wire) wiring. This wiring is a basic *voice grade* (VG) wiring and drastically reduced the cost for wiring buildings. One pair of the UTP is used for transmitting data and the other is for receiving data. The wire itself is connected to the NIC using RJ-45 connectors. 10BASE-T segments can be up to 100 meters in length and have a network diameter of 500 meters. 10BASE-T must use Category 3 cable or higher to handle the 20 MHz frequency requirement to transmit 10 Mbps over UTP.

This standard for Ethernet introduced a new feature called *link integrity.* This new feature is a keep-alive electrical pulse sent out by the hub port and the NIC interface every 16 ms. Receipt of this pulse by the NIC and the hub port indicates physical continuity. In a sense, it is a simple means of physical trouble management for 10BASE-T networks. Usually the NIC and the hub have LED indicators that display the state of the physical connection. A green LED for trouble free and a red LED for troubled connection.

A major effect on LAN topology occurs when using 10BASE-T. No longer is the Ethernet LAN a physical bus topology. The topology of a 10BASE-T network has changed to that of a star-wired topology. Each station connected to the LAN was on its own wire and centrally connected to a hub found in a wiring closet. Though the star topology greatly enhanced LAN physical management it reduced the number of stations per LAN segment to twelve.

10BASE-F (fiber Ethernet).   This cabling scheme uses fiber-optic cables of duplex fiber strands. Either two strands of multimode or single mode fiber may be used. One fiber is used for transmitting and the other is used for receiving data. Usually a 62.5/125-micrometer diameter is used to carry infrared light emitted by LEDs. This standard is broken down into three substandards:

10BASE-FP.   This standard uses a passive (the "P" in the name) star topology with a 1-segment length of 1000 meters (1 km) and 500-meter-per-segment length for an extended segment with a network diameter of 2500 meters. The medium access unit is built into the repeater or the *data terminal equipment* (DTE).

10BASE-FB. This standard is for backbone or repeater fiber networks. Again the medium access unit is integrated with the repeater, however, no DTE connections are specified. A single segment can be up to 2000 meters long and have a network diameter of 2500 meters.

10BASE-FL. This standard can be used only for connecting repeaters and utilizes an external medium access unit. A segment length between repeaters can be either 1000 or 2000 meters long and have a network diameter of 2500 meters.

Of these different 10BASE-*n* standards it was 10BASE-T that propelled Ethernet to dominate 90 percent of the LANs installed. Its cost-effectiveness using voice grade wire allowed companies to take advantage of low-cost cable along with preinstalled cable and the introduction of star-wired central hub devices to ease installation and allow flexibility in Ethernet LAN design.

2.3 Token-Ring

Though the name implies a circular ring, the Token-Ring network is actually a logical ring. The ring itself is defined as having ring stations with the transmission medium attaching them. The ring station is the combined functions of the token-ring adapter, logical link control, medium access control, service access point functions, and access protocols that allow a device attached to the ring to participate in token-ring communications.

In a ring there are two paths of unidirectional communications. Ring stations transmit on one physical path and receive data on the other. As the name indicates a ring is a continuous closed path. Figure 2.8 outlines a sample token ring and the flow of data on the ring. Traffic on the ring flows through each station adapter. A ring station transfers data to the ring. The data flows sequentially in one direction from one station to another. Each station receives the data. Upon receiving the data the station checks it for errors and inspects the destination address field against its own address. If there is a match, the station copies the data into its receive buffers and then regenerates the data back onto the ring to forward it back to the originating station. The originating station then removes the data from the ring. The determination of which station can send data on to the ring is determined by a token frame. It is the token that determines which station can send data and hence requires a complex logical algorithm implied in each interface card.

2.3.1 Star-wired ring topology

Local area networks that have each station attached to an adjacent station using point-to-point links form a physical ring. This type of configuration, depicted in Fig. 2.9, is known as a *ring topology*. Each station attached and active to the ring regenerates the information frame then retransmits it on

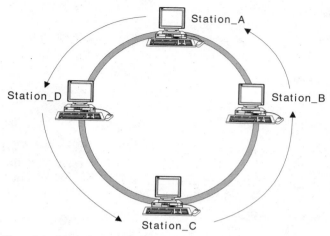

Figure 2.8   Logical token ring and logical flow of data on the ring.

the ring. The ring itself is physically circular and information travels in one direction.

Failure of a station in a ring topology disrupts the ring because the information frame is not regenerated. A break can also be caused by an outage in one of the point-to-point links. A loss of signal on the link will also cause a disruption. Though a fault in a ring can cause a complete outage, the exact location of the fault can be determined through timing or by determining the status of each station on the ring. Additions or deletions of stations to the ring can also be disruptive if the change is not managed properly.

These shortcomings of a ring topography are overcome by a star-wired ring topography, sometimes called *radial hierarchical wiring*. A star-wired ring

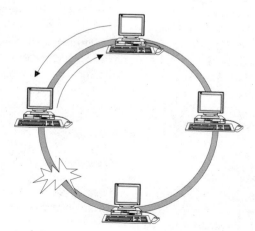

Figure 2.9 Ring topology for token-ring networks; its connectivity and weakness.

topology is a combination of a star and ring topography. This star-wired ring topography utilizes a relay center. Within the relay center the transmit path of one station is connected to the receive path of the next active station bypassing inactive stations. The connection between the relay center and the ring station is called a *lobe*.

The relay center is implemented as a wiring concentrator. The use of a wiring concentrator enables fault detection capabilities of a ring topography while providing the flexibility of installing, maintaining, and reconfiguring a star topography.

Typically, a token-ring network is implemented using the star-wired ring topography as diagrammed in Fig. 2.10. Stations are physically attached to the wiring concentrator with a point-to-point link. The wiring concentrator for a token-ring network can be passive or active. A passive wiring concentrator uses the electrical current on the lobe wire to power the relay mechanism. A passive wiring center is also called a *multistation access unit* (MAU). Active wiring concentrators provide their own power and thus can contain some intelligence to provide error recovery, error message processing, and management of the ring. Active wiring centers are also called *intelligent hubs*. Intelligent hubs can control physical access to the ring and provide a bypass methodology when faulty or inactive stations are detected. Star-wired ring topologies allow stations to be added or removed from the network, while it is in use, without affecting other stations on the network.

2.3.2 Token passing

Unlike the simplicity of Ethernet with its broadcast of data frames to each station, token-ring networks, use token passing, a more complex protocol on the network model stack.

Token-passing-ring LAN protocols define the length of a token to be 24 bits and the shortest possible MAC frame to be 200 bits in length. The transmission

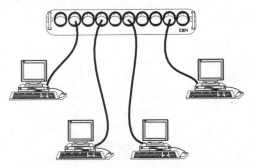

Figure 2.10 Token-ring star-wired configuration.

of data on a token-ring LAN is accomplished by a station capturing the token. The station sets the token bit in the access control field to indicate that the data is a frame and not a free token. The header of this frame is updated with destination and source MAC addresses, data, a new frame check sequence value, and the end delimiter and frame status field.

As the frame makes its way around the ring, each station will receive the frame, inspect it for its station address in the destination field, and perform CRC. If the stations address is not in the destination field the station retransmits the frame. Stations that receive frames, perform CRC checking, and then retransmit the frame are in normal repeat mode. Stations operating in normal repeat mode perform data checking on the tokens and frames they receive. Each station will set the error-detected bit in the end delimiter and the address-recognized and frame-copied bits in the frame status field accordingly. The destination station copies the information field from the frame, processes the end delimiter and frame status field to denote that the frames address was recognized and that the frame was copied, then sends the frame back out on the ring to the source station.

Once the source station receives the frame it removes the frame from the ring. The source station checks the frame with CRC checking and then interrogates the address-recognized and frame-copied bits of the frame status field for verification of successful delivery of the frame to the destination station. After receiving the frame header the source station releases a new free token onto the network for another station to capture for data transmission. This process of capturing and releasing a token is called *single token protocol* since only one token can exist on the ring at any given time.

2.3.3 Token claiming

A *token-claiming process* is the method used in determining the active monitor on the LAN. This process is also called the *monitor-contention process*. Token claiming begins under several different conditions. A loss of signal, expiration of the active monitor's Receive_Notification Timer or the expiration of the Ring Purge Timer, all detected by the current active monitor, will initiate the token-claiming process.

The expiration of the Receive_Notification Timer occurs when the active monitor does not receive the Active Monitor Present MAC frame it just transmitted in the Receive_Notification Timer time limit. The Ring Purge Timer expiration occurs when the active monitor does not completely receive Ring_Purge MAC frames it just transmitted in the time limit specified by the Ring Purge Timer.

Any ring station that is not acting as the active monitor is a *standby monitor*. The standby monitor will initiate the token-claiming process when its Good_Token Timer expires. This timer is started each time a token or frame is repeated by the station. If a token or frame is not received again over the course of the Good_Token Timer value, then the standby monitor will begin the token-claiming process. The expiration of the Receive_Notification Timer indicates that the standby monitor has not received an Active Monitor Present MAC frame during the length of this timer. Again, the standby monitor will begin the token-claiming process.

A third factor in determining the initiation of the token-claiming process occurs when a ring station attaches to the ring. The attaching ring station will start token claiming when it does not detect an active monitor. This occurs when the station enters the ring with one of the above conditions true and when the station is the first station on the ring.

Ring stations detecting one of the conditions above enters into claim-token-transmit mode by broadcasting a Claim_Token MAC frame and repeating it at a specific time interval. All ring stations can be optioned to participate in the token-claiming process. The default for each station is not to participate. However, a ring station must initiate the token-claiming process if it detects one of the conditions above. Each ring station participating in the token-claiming process analyzes the source address field of the Claim_Token MAC frame for its own address. If the source address is greater than the ring station's address it enters claim-token-repeat mode. If the source address is less than the ring station's address it transmits its own Claim_Token MAC frames. If the source address matches the ring station's address it broadcasts the Claim Token MAC frame until three of these frames have been received by the ring station. This indicates to the ring station that the ring is sound and that it has won the token-claiming process. The ring station then completes the process by adding the token delay to the ring, purges the ring, starts its activate monitors and issues a new token. At this point the ring station has become the new active monitor.

2.3.4 Active monitor

The *active monitor* is a station on the ring that performs detection and recovery functions for each LAN segment on a token-ring network. Only one station per LAN segment can perform the functions of the active monitor. All other stations function as standby monitors.

The active monitor sets the monitor bit of the access control field to a B'1' as it repeats the frame. If this bit was already set to a B'1' it is assumed the frame or token has circled the ring once. The active monitor removes the frame, purges the ring, and issues a new free token. This process also assists the active monitor in managing the ring speed. The active monitor delays the issue of the token by a 24-bit ring delay to ensure that a token can circle the ring before returning to the originating station.

The active monitor keeps a Good_Token Timer. This timer time-out value is greater than the time it takes for the longest frame to circle the ring. Expiration of this timer indicates that a token or frame has been lost. The timer is started every time the active monitor transmits a start delimiter.

At specified times the active monitor broadcasts the Active Monitor Present MAC frame. The receipt of this frame by ring stations forces them to initiate timers and obtain their *nearest active upstream neighbor* (NAUN) address.

2.3.5 Neighbor notification

The Active Monitor Present MAC frame is transmitted to the first ring station downstream from the active monitor. This first ring station begins the neighbor-notification process by recognizing the Active Monitor Present MAC frame and sets the address-recognized bit and the frame-copied bit of the frame status field to B'1'. The first ring station then saves the source address of the copied frame as its NAUN address. In this case the address is that of the active monitor. This station then starts the Notification_Response Timer and transmits the frame.

Ring stations active on the ring repeat the Active Monitor Present MAC frame but do not process it since the address-recognized bit and the frame-copied bit of the frame status field have already been set.

The Notification_Response Timer of the first active station downstream to the current active monitor expires during the passing of the Active Monitor Present MAC frame along the ring. This expiration initiates the transmission of the Standby_Monitor Present MAC frame to its next active downstream ring station. The ring station downstream from the standby monitor then copies the source address of the Standby Monitor Present MAC frame into its NAUN address, sets the address-recognized and frame-copied bits of the access control field to B'1' and starts its own Notification_Response Timer. At the expiration of this timer the ring station transmits a Standby_Present Monitor MAC frame to its next active downstream station.

The Standby_Monitor Present process is repeated around the ring until the active monitor copies the source address field from a Standby Monitor Present MAC frame as its NAUN address. The active monitor sets the Neighbor_Notification Complete flag to B'1' signifying that the neighbor-notification process is complete.

The neighbor notification, as demonstrated, enables ring stations on a token-ring network to learn its NAUN address and to give it to its active downstream neighbor.

2.3.6 Access priority

Access priority of a token or frame is determined by the values of the first three bits of the access control field. A station that requires a higher priority will set the last three reservation bits of the access control field. Ring stations select a priority and can transmit a token or frame at that priority if the available token priority is less than or equal to the priority assigned to the frame to be transmitted.

A ring station can reserve a priority to transmit frame by setting the reservation bits of the access control field in a passing frame or token. If the reservation bits have a value larger than what is requested, the bits remain unchanged and the station waits for the next token or frame. However, if the reservation bit values are lower than what is being requested, then the station sets the reservation bits to the required priority.

Interrogation of these bits by the originating ring station determines if the ring station will release a token with a higher priority than the frame it just transmitted. If the reservation bits are nonzero, the ring station must release a token of nonzero bits. Ring stations originating a token of higher priority are said to be in priority-hold state.

2.3.7 Ring-attachment process

Attachment of a station to the ring occurs in a five-phase insertion process. This process executes each time a station attaches to the token-ring network.

Phase 0: lobe testing. The station sends multiple Lobe_Media_Test MAC frames on the lobe wire to the multistation access unit (MAU). The MAU wraps the frames back to the sending station. The station's receive logic is tested. A successful test causes a phantom current of 5-volt DC to be sent to open the relay in the MAU creating a closed circuit between the stations adapter and the MAU.

Phase 1: monitor check. The now-attached station starts its insert timer, looking for Active_Monitor Present, Standby_Monitor Present or Ring Purge MAC frames before expiration of the insert timer. Expiration of the timer will initiate the token-claiming process. If this is the first active station on the ring it will become the active monitor.

Phase 2: duplicate address check. The station sends a Duplicate Address Test MAC frame where the destination address, source address, and the stations address are all equal. If a duplicate address is found the address-recognized bit will be set to B'1'. Upon receiving the Duplicate Address Test MAC frame the station inspects the address-recognized bit. If it is set to B'1' the station will then detach from the ring.

Phase 3: participation in neighbor notification. The station participates in learning its NAUN address and sends its own address to it next active downstream neighbor.

Phase 4: request initialization. This is the final phase of attachment to a ring. The bridge program on a ring may have a *ring parameter server* (RPS) function. During this phase the station issues a Request Initialization MAC frame to the RPS. If an RPS is not present, default values are used. The Request Initialization MAC frame may contain registration information for the LAN manager. This information may be the address of the ring station's

NAUN, the product identifier for this station and the ring station's microcode level. If an RPS is present, it responds with an Initialize Ring Station MAC frame response. The information in this frame is used by the ring station to set physical location, soft error report timer, ring number, and ring authorization level values. The last three values ensure that all stations on the ring will have the same values.

2.3.8   IEEE 802.5/Token-Ring MAC frame format

Communications between stations on a token ring require an addressing mechanism that will guarantee that each station address on a token ring is unique. This is needed to ensure receipt and delivery of information to and from the source and destination stations on a token ring. The medium access control (MAC) sublayer provides this addressing mechanism to control the transmission of data so that only one station is transmitting at any given time. The MAC determines whether a station on the token ring is in transmit, repeats to receive state, and controls the routing of data over the LAN. The main functions of the MAC are:

Addressing.   The MAC address is the physical address of the station's device adapter on a LAN. Recognition of the station's address found in the physical header of a MAC frame. Each station on a token ring must be able to recognize its own MAC address and an all-stations (broadcast) address or a null address for frames which are not to be received by the station. The MAC address identifies the physical destination and source of any frame transmitted over the token ring.

Frame copying.   After MAC has recognized its own address, meaning that the frame received has this device's MAC address as the destination address, it uses this function to copy the frame from the token ring into the device adapter buffers.

Frame recognition.   This function determines the type of frame received and its format—for instance, a system or user frame.

Frame deliminator.   The MAC must determine the beginning and ending of a frame. This is performed during transmission or receipt of a frame.

Frame status and verification.   This provides the checking and verification of frame check sequence bits and the frame status field in each frame to determine if transmission errors have occurred.

Priority management.   This function warrants fairness of access to the token-ring medium, based on priority, by issuing priority-level tokens for all participating stations on a token ring.

Routing.   This determines which function in a node should process the frame.

Timing. This keeps track of timers utilized by the MAC management protocols.

Token (LAN) management. This is used to monitor the LAN using management protocols to handle error conditions at the access control level.

A MAC frame is the *basic transmission unit* (BTU) for the IBM Token-Ring Network. These frames are composed of several fields, each 1 byte or more in length. Figure 2.11 details the MAC frame format. The high-order byte (byte 0) is transmitted first and the high-order bit within each byte is transmitted first. In other words, from left to right. The frame is composed of two sections with an optional section for information. The first section, the physical header, contains the *starting delimiter* (SD), the *access control* (AC), the *frame control* (FC) field, the destination and source address field, and an optional *routing information* (RIF) field. The second section of the MAC frame, the physical trailer, contains the frame check sequence, the *ending delimiter* (ED) and the *frame status* (FS) field.

The starting delimiter is a single byte field of the MAC frame. Token-ring frames and the tokens themselves are valid only when the right combination of bits are present that define the byte as the starting delimiter of a frame.

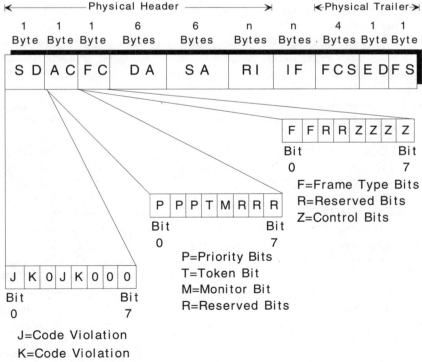

Figure 2.11 IEEE 802.5 Token-Ring MAC frame format.

The access control field is a 1-byte field to denote the access required by the frame on the LAN. The access defines the priority as well as the type of BTU (i.e., frame or token).

The next single byte field identifies the type of frame. This field is known as the frame control field. The frame control field identifies the type of frame, including specific MAC and information frame functions. There are currently two types of frames that can be identified with the FC field.

The 6-byte *destination address* (DA) field allows for a 48-bit representation of the MAC address for the receiving station. This address can be an individual or group address. The individual address can be assigned by a LAN administrator or by the adapter manufacturer. A value of hexadecimal FFFFFF means that this frame is an all-stations broadcast and that every station on the network will make a copy of the frame and interpret its information.

Like the destination addresses, the *source address* (SA) is 6 bytes in length (48 bits). The first byte of the SA field indicates whether the routing information field is present and whether the address is provided by a LAN administrator or by the manufacturer.

The routing information field is optional and is used only when the frame is going to leave the originating token or source ring. There are two fields that comprise the RI field. These are the route control field and the route designator. Each is 2 bytes in length. The route control field is followed by up to eight route designator fields. Routing performed in this fashion is also called *source routing*. The format of the RI field is detailed in Fig. 2.12.

When a station contacts another station on the token ring, it sends out a broadcast or test command. Token ring uses *source-route bridging* (SRB) to determine the physical path through the token-ring network between the station partners.

Since the total number of route designators in the route information field is eight, a frame cannot traverse more than seven LAN segments before reaching the destination address.

The route designator field is made up of 2 bytes which indicate the ring number and the bridge number. Each ring is assigned a networkwide unique number. Any bridge attached to a ring must define the same ring number. Bridges attached to different rings have different ring numbers. Each bridge is assigned a number. The bridge number can be the same for bridges attached to the same ring. However, bridges attached to the same two rings must have unique bridge numbers. Bridging in this manner is called *parallel bridging*. It is the ring number that guarantees a unique route designator. When a bridge receives a frame from the ring, it interprets the route designator fields. The bridge compares the route designator field values with its attached ring number and its own bridge number. The last route designator field in the routing information field will not contain a bridge number. This is because the end of a route is the target ring number.

The information field follows the route designator field. The information field for a MAC frame will contain MAC control information. If this frame had

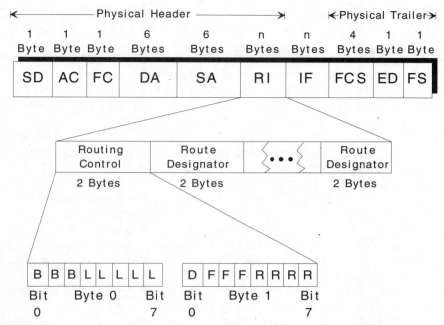

Figure 2.12 The format of the routing information field in the Token-Ring MAC frame.

been denoted as an LLC frame, then the information field would contain end-user data. The LLC information is also called a *logical link control protocol data unit* (LPDU).

The frame check sequence field is 4-byte value created using an algorithm that covers the frame control field, destination and source addresses, the optional routing information field and information field, and the frame check sequence itself. The algorithm results in the 4-byte cyclic redundancy check value placed in the frame check sequence field by the originating station. The frame type determines the position of the frame check sequence field and, therefore, the protection guaranteed by cyclic redundancy checking.

The ending delimiter will indicate either that there are code violations and errors, or that this frame is one of many associated frames being transmitted.

The frame status field indicates that the frame has been copied, the DA has been matched, or an error has occurred.

2.3.9 Token-Ring MAC addressing

Communications between any two stations on a token ring is established using an address mechanism. Each station, or a group of stations, is assigned a unique address in the MAC sublayer of the data link layer of OSI and the data link control of SNA. These unique addresses enable the attachment of any ring station to a token-ring network.

Individual and group addressing.   Ring stations are identified by a unique, individual ring station address. A group address identifies a group of ring stations that will acknowledge the group address found in the MAC destination address field.

Each 6-byte address field must be unique within the LAN segment. Ring station addresses can be duplicated on different LAN segments. As shown in Fig. 2.13, Station_A on segment_B has an address of x'000000000001' and Station_C has an address on x'000000000001' on segment_D. If Station_A becomes inoperative then stations on segment_B will access Station_C on segment_D. The reverse is true for stations on segment_D. To avoid inadvertent duplication of addresses the stations can be assigned universal or locally administered addresses.

Universal and locally administered addresses.   The universal address is assigned by IEEE. This address is found on all token-ring adapter cards. The address is unique for each token-ring adapter manufacturer. For example, IBM's assigned address is x'10005A'. This address is set in the token-ring adapter card's *read-only memory* (ROM) and is also commonly referred to as the burned-in address. Using the universal address eliminates the need for end-user involvement and thus less room for error on configuring the ring station for an individual address.

The universal address can be overridden by a *locally administered address* (LAA). Ethernet adapters use only universally administered addresses. A carefully orchestrated addressing scheme must be implemented to ensure unique addresses for each individual ring station using LAAs. The token-ring adapter sets the address at adapter-open time. LAA station addressing, however, requires someone to administer the LAA station addresses for each LAN segment.

Null address.   In a token-ring network address scheme a special, individual destination address can be sent with a value of x'000000000000'. This address is known as a *null address*. Frames carrying a null address are not addressed to any station on the LAN. Stations can send a null address but not receive a frame with a null address. When the sending station recognizes the null address frame the station strips the frame of its data and issues a new token.

All-stations broadcast addresses.   An all-stations broadcast address is received by all stations. The destination address values for all-stations broadcast address are x'FFFFFFFFFFFF' and x'C000FFFFFFFF'. All stations on the ring must be able to receive at least x'C000FFFFFFFF'.

Functional addresses.   The token-ring architecture calls for bit-specific functional addresses. There are currently 14 functional areas of the token-ring network architecture that have been assigned specific functional addresses. Ring stations use these functional addresses as a mask to identify these functions. These functions are defined at the access protocol level. There are a total of 31 possible functional addresses.

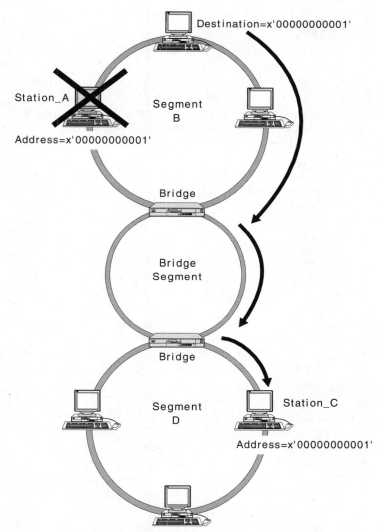

Figure 2.13 A diagram depicting the logical flow of using duplicate token-ring station addresses.

2.3.10 4 Mbps token ring

The release of a free token by the source station, after receiving a returned frame header, underutilizes the higher-speed mediums. On a typical 4 Mbps token ring the length of 1 bit has been determined to be approximately 50 meters, a 24-bit token is approximately 1200 meters and a 200-bit MAC frame is measured at 10,000 meters. Therefore, on a 4 Mbps token ring high-bandwidth utilization is maintained at high-traffic levels.

2.3.11   16 Mbps token ring

At 16 Mbps, 1 bit is measured at 12.5 meters, a token at 300 meters and the 200-bit MAC frame at 2500 meters. The concept of early token release was implemented to provide better utilization of the 16 Mbps token ring.

Early token release allows the source station to release a free token after transmitting the information frame but before the receipt of the transmitted header. After releasing the free token, an adapter indicator is set to stop the adapter from releasing a second free token after receiving the returned transmission header. The implementation of early token release allows multiple information frames to circulate on the network while still only using one token. Each station on a 16 Mbps token-ring network can be optioned to use early token release but it is not required on all stations. The early token release option is implemented by default on an IBM 16 Mbps Token-Ring Network.

2.3.12   32 Mbps (full duplex) token ring

As with all LAN media, pressure on standards to increase bandwidth never ceases. Token ring is no exception. Full-duplex token ring allows a 16 Mbps token-ring LAN to effectively have an aggregate bandwidth of 32 Mbps. This is accomplished by allowing the token-ring adapter at the MAC layer to send and receive at the same time. To do this, however, the token-ring adapter must contain a code that does not execute token protocols. In effect, a token ring executing in full-duplex mode is a tokenless network. As such, token access and recovery protocols along with frame repeating, frame stripping, and end-of-frame status update protocols and functions are no longer required. Permission to send by gaining control of a token is no longer needed. This is because in a 32-Mbps full-duplex configuration the adapter is directly attached to a compatible full-duplex port on a hub. The adapter will determine if it must operate in full duplex (32 Mbps) or half duplex (16 Mbps) mode. Since the token-ring protocols themselves provided the timing function for 16 Mbps, a new timing mechanism was created to allow 32 Mbps clocking. When no data is to be transmitted from the adapter transmit buffers, the adapter will send a steady stream of zeroes to the hub port and expect to receive them back. The time for the round trip is used as the clocking synchronization method. This type of method allows the full-duplex operation to detect physical errors on the cable. The requirement of a 32 Mbps token ring to connect to a hub that supports full-duplex transmission and eliminates the majority of the MAC layer token protocols results in a ringless token-ring network. Though the majority of MAC protocols and functions are not required, full-duplex token ring keeps the token-ring frame format intact.

2.4   Fiber Distributed Data Interface (FDDI)

Fiber Distributed Data Interface (FDDI) has been a proven shared LAN media since the late 1980s. FDDI is architected to operate at 100 Mbps. It is today primarily used to establish high-speed backbones. FDDI uses a dual counterrotating ring topology. Sharing many similarities with token-ring networks FDDI uses a token-passing protocol. Its main difference with token-ring networking is its extensive use of timers to determine ring stability.

2.4.1 FDDI dual ring topology

As shown in Fig. 2.14, FDDI utilizes two rings each in counterrotation to the other. The counterclockwise ring is considered the primary ring and the clockwise ring is considered the secondary ring. In this dual-ring configuration the primary ring carriers the data while the secondary ring is rarely utilized and is there specifically for ring reliability. Attachment by stations can be in two flavors. Class A stations attach to both the primary and secondary rings. These Dual Attachment Stations (DAS) will internally wrap the ring to bypass a break in the primary ring. This selfhealing architecture makes FDDI the highest-availability network around. To maximize the cost-effectiveness of FDDI, dual-ring architecture Class B stations attach only to the primary ring. These stations are known as Single Attachment Stations (SAS). It is possible to use an SAS on only the secondary ring as shown in Fig. 2.15 to further maximize the cost-effectiveness of FDDI even further. However, in this configuration Class B stations do not gain the redundancy characteristics of DAS.

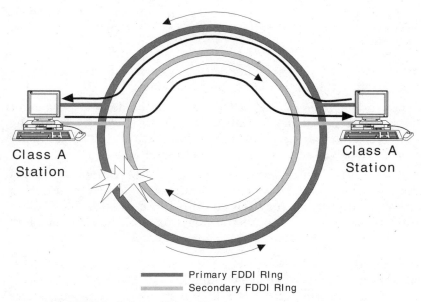

Class A
Station

Class A
Station

▬▬▬ Primary FDDI Ring
▬▬▬ Secondary FDDI Ring

Figure 2.14 FDDI dual-ring configuration.

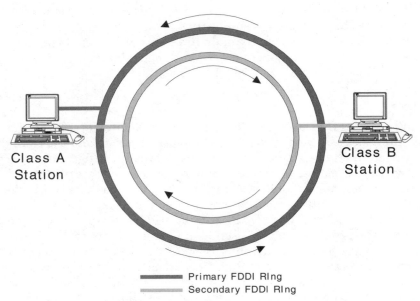

Figure 2.15   FDDI dual ring with class B station attached to secondary ring.

2.4.2   FDDI access protocol

Remember that FDDI uses a token just as in token ring. However, FDDI uses timers rather than events to determine token availability and ring stability. There are three timers that each station attached to the FDDI network use. The timers are:

Token rotation timer (TRT).   This timer is used by each station to determine the time elapsed since the station last received a token.

Target token rotation timer (TTRT).   This is a station-defined parameter whose value is negotiated at ring initialization. All stations agree to use the smallest value offered by any station. The value indicates the target maximum time between opportunities for a station to send tokens.

Token hold timer (THT).   This value determines the maximum amount of data a station can transmit during a token rotation. If time is leftover during the token rotation, the station may send multiple frames until the TTRT is reached. After transmission, the station sends a new token. FDDI employs early token release.

The drawback to FDDI as a LAN topology for corporations is its cost. FDDI fiber-optic cable is much more expensive to purchase and install than category 3 or 5 cable. The station adapter cards required for FDDI connectivity are almost ten times that of category 3 and 5 wiring. Some companies have tried to answer this cost problem by taking the FDDI protocols and 100 Mbps data rate and implement it on category 3 and 5 wiring. The resulting technology defend is Copper Data Distributed Interface (CDDI). However, though an exciting new technology, its limited distance of 100 meters and added intelligence on adapters did not do much for reducing the cost of implementing 100 Mbps LANs using existing wiring infrastructures. The result of this search is what has come to be known as Fast Ethernet.

2.5   Fast Ethernet

Fast Ethernet has its roots with Grand Junction Networks, a company formed by the original developer of Ethernet. Fast Ethernet came about as a means to leverage the wiring infrastructure in place at over 90 percent of all LAN installations for 100 Mbps support. Fast Ethernet is 100 Mbps data rate over twisted wire (100BASE-T). The specification of 100BASE-T is defined in the IEEE 802.3u standards. The IEEE 802.3u 100BASE-T standard requires a star-wired topology. The IEEE 802.3u specification supports UTP and fiber.

2.5.1   Fast Ethernet CSMA/CD

A main objective in the development of the 100BASE-T standard was to keep the IEEE 802.3 MAC frame format and parameters intact as much as possible. This was accomplished with only the InterFrameGap (IFG) time changed from 9.6 to 0.96 microseconds as a minimum due to the increased data rate of Fast Ethernet (10 times faster than 10 Mbps Ethernet). Though stations on 100 Mbps Ethernet are not on a bus topology they still implement the listen-before-sending CSMA/CD protocol prior to sending. The CSMA/CD protocol is implemented on 100BASE-T over four different types of physical layer specifications. These are 100BASE-TX, 100BASE-T4, 100BASE-T2 and 100BASE-FX and are compared in Fig. 2.16

2.5.2   100BASE-TX

100BASE-TX uses two pairs of data grade category 5 UTP cable. Each station cannot be further than 100 meters from the hub. One pair of the wiring is used for transmitting and the other is used for receiving data. 100BASE-TX uses the same RJ-45 connector and conductors used for 10BASE-T Ethernets. This allows corporations to leave the current Ethernet and wiring infrastructure in place when migrating from 10BASE-T to 100BASE-TX. The actual transmission of the data is based on FDDI over wire, meaning CDDI technology.

2.5.3   100BASE-T4

This physical layer implementation of IEEE 802.3u utilizes category 3 voice grade UTP wire as well as category 4 and 5. The physical specification requires 25 MHz bandwidth, which is available on category 3 wire.

	100BASE-TX	100BASE-FX	100BASE-T4	100BASE-T2*
Max. segment length	100 meters	Multimode: Repeater 150 meters DTE-DTE 412 meters Full-duplex DTE-DTE 2000 meters Singlemode: As high as 10 kilometers	100 meters	500, 1000, 2000 meters
Topology	Star	Star	Star	Star
Medium	100-ohm UTP category 5 2-pair or 150-ohm category 1 2 pair or IBM type 1/1A	Mulitmode or singlemode fiber	4 pair of UTP Category 3/4/5	2 pair of UTP Category 3
Connector	RJ-45	SC or ST	RJ-45	RJ-45
Medium attachment	External or NIC	External or on NIC	External or on NIC	External or on NIC
Stations/segment	1024	1024	1024	1024

* IEEE 802.3u is currently working on standardizing 100BASE-T2. It is not currently a working standards.

Figure 2.16   Table comparing Fast Ethernet 100 Mbps standards.

To implement 100 Mbps, four pairs of voice or date grade shielded or unshielded wire is used. Three of the pairs are used for transmission and the fourth pair is used to receive data. No separate receive-transmit pairs are present. 100BASE-T4 also uses the standards 8-pin RJ-45 connector. Each station can be a maximum of 100 meters from the hub.

2.5.4   100BASE-T2

Though this is not a formal standard it is currently being worked on and is close to completion. This standard allows 100 Mbps transmission over two pairs of category 3 UTP wire. Completing this standard makes 100BASE-T2 backward compatible, leveraging the networks infrastructure in place. To implement this requires that each pair is used for sending and receiving. The idea behind using only two pair for the transmission on category 3 wiring is to allow the other pair to be used for voice or some other type of transmission requirement at the desktop.

2.5.5   100BASE-FX

This standard for 100 Mbps Ethernet utilizes FDDI technology and fiber-optic networks. As in FDDI, 100BASE-FX Ethernet uses two strands of multimode or single-mode fiber. 100BASE-FX is used typically for Ethernet high-speed backbone networks and not to the desktop. Distance between stations can be 412 meters but can be extended with repeaters to 2000 meters using full-duplex communications. Some repeater manufacturers using full-duplex technology and single-mode fibers can allow for connection lengths of 10 kilometers.

2.6 Summary

In this chapter we reviewed and discussed the various medium technologies, standards, and formats required to implement shared media LANs. A review of the three different types of cables (coaxial, twisted pair and fiber) revealed that from a cost-efficiency perspective over 90 percent of today's LANs are implemented using twisted pair wiring. This wiring infrastructure became the focal point for improving LAN technology bandwidth demands from 10 Mbps to 100 Mbps. Of the two dominating LAN architecture, Ethernet and Token-Ring, Ethernet is the preferred LAN shared media for departmental and desktop infrastructures. Fiber-optic LANs have become the infrastructure in place for high-speed LAN backbone networking.

3

Internetworking Models

The rapid growth of local area networks has lead to a requirement for devices to allow the interconnection of the various physical media and logical architectures. This interconnection is performed by bridges, routers, and switches. Bridges perform their primary functions on OSI layer 2. Routers perform their primary functions on OSI layer 3 and switches perform their functions on OSI layers 2 and 3. These devices provide the internetworking of a myriad of network protocols and mediums. The terms interconnection and internetworking are not one in the same. *Interconnection* refers to the physical connectivity of the LANs concentrating on the physical and data link layers of the OSI Reference Model. *Internetworking* encompasses not only the physical and data link layers but the entire seven layers of the OSI Reference Model for networking.

3.1 Bridged Networks

The *personal computer* (PC) took the business world by storm in the mid- to late-1980s. Since then practically every company, small and large, in one way or another has a network of personal computers. Local area networks (LANs) are the networking infrastructure for connecting personal computers. Figure 3.1 illustrates a typical LAN connecting personal computers. Though the networking of personal computers is what brought LANs to the forefront, UNIX workstations have been networked over LANs since the late 1970s.

The most widely used LAN communication transport protocols are Ethernet, token-ring and Fiber Distributed Data Interface (FDDI). As shown in Fig. 3.2, Ethernet uses a bus topology; token-ring and FDDI use a ring topology. In a bus topology the information is sent in a message unit called a *packet*. A ring topology transports the message unit in a *frame*. The difference in the two topologies is that with a bus topology each station on the LAN receives the same information packet whether it is destined for the station or not; in a ring

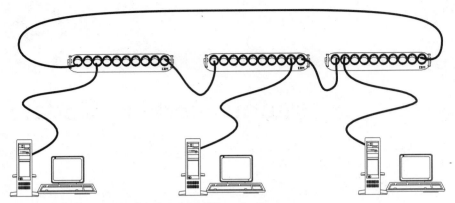

Figure 3.1   Diagram depicting typical LAN topologies.

topology, some but not all stations on the ring will receive the same information frame depending on where the destination station resides on the ring. These transport protocols fall within the *data link* (DL) layer 2 of the seven-layer communications protocol stack.

The data link layer of the seven-layer protocol stack derives the hardware-addressing schema for the *network interface card* (NIC) used in attaching to the LAN. For ease of explanation, a LAN segment is a stand-alone LAN whether it is Ethernet, token-ring, or FDDI. Traditionally, interconnected multiple LAN segments use a device known as a *bridge*. Bridges use the data link addressing schema to interconnect multiple LANs. Since bridges are focused on data link control, they perform their functions on a store-and-forward mechanism using the destination address found in the MAC frame after receiving the full frame. Using only data link control makes bridges protocol insensitive. Figure 3.3 diagrams single and multisegment LAN configurations using bridges for the interconnection. As you may notice in Fig. 3.3, the LAN segments interconnected can be of different types. The various LAN topologies, however, dictate the type of bridging in use. There are four types of bridging methodologies in use for interconnecting LAN segments. These are transparent bridging, *source route bridging* (SRB), translational bridging, and *source route transparent* (SRT) bridging.

3.1.1 Transparent bridging

The concept of transparent bridging is based on the fact that stations view all LAN stations as being on the same segment. Transparent bridges do not use routing information fields like that found in source routing. Instead, transparent bridges inspect the source address of each frame on a segment. The transparent bridge builds a routing table called the *filtering data base*. This routing table contains the source address of stations that communicate with the bridge

Bus Topography

Ring Topography

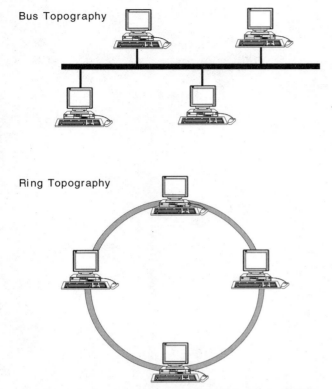

Figure 3.2 Comparison of bus and ring topologies for LANs.

over a specific interface. In this way, the transparent bridge can determine if a frame is destined for a station on the source ring or off the source ring. A timer value is also placed with the entry. The entry will be removed from the routing table if the station has not sent a frame in a specified amount of time.

As diagrammed in Fig. 3.4, Bridge_1 receives a frame from Ring_A. Bridge_1 inspects the source address field against the routing table for Ring_A. If the source address matches an entry in the Ring_A routing table then the bridge knows that the source station is on Ring_A. The destination address field is inspected but the address is analyzed for both Ring_A and Ring_B. If the destination address is found on Ring_A then the bridge ignores the frame. If, however, the destination address is found to be on Ring_B then the bridge forwards the frame. An intermediate transparent bridge places the source address of a frame whose source and destination address are not in the routing table into the on-ring routing table and the destination address into the off-ring routing table.

Transparent bridging requires a single route between stations. There can be only one active route through a LAN when using transparent bridging. This is

Single Segment

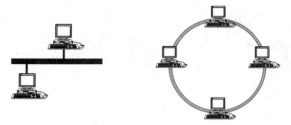

Multiple Segment

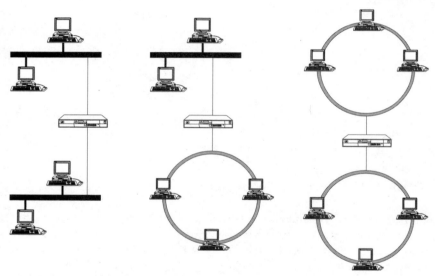

Figure 3.3 Single and multisegment LAN configurations.

due to the fact that parallel bridges will always assume that all source and destination stations are on the originating ring, therefore looping a frame endlessly. To minimize the impact of this, an automatic single-route selection process is required for transparent bridging. This single-route selection process is known as the *spanning tree algorithm*.

3.1.2 Spanning tree algorithm

Multisegment LANs configured with transparent bridges use a spanning tree algorithm to always ensure a single active route. Bridges have incorporated this algorithm for use with source route bridges ensuring a single route for single-

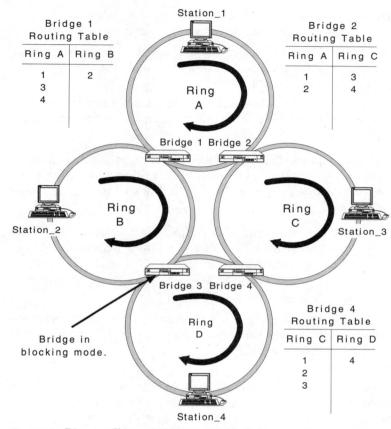

Figure 3.4 Diagram illustrating transparent bridging.

route broadcast frames. The difference between the two implementations is that the functional addresses used by transparent and source route bridges are not the same. The result of this is that a single-route broadcast configuration will be performed by all transparent bridges and separately by each source route bridge in a network that utilizes both. The algorithm is called a spanning tree because there is no closed loop between LAN segments; the tree connects the subnetworks.

In a spanning tree algorithm there are five possible states that may be considered by the bridge:

1. *Disabled.* In this state the bridge is not participating in any way with the spanning tree algorithm.

2. *Blocking.* This state prohibits the forwarding of frames and address learning and does not participate in the spanning tree algorithm except to ensure that another bridge is forwarding frames onto the segment.

3. *Listening.* This state provides no frame forwarding or address learning but does allow the bridge to participate in the spanning tree algorithm.

4. *Learning.* This state allows the bridge to build address tables from passing frames and participates in the spanning tree algorithm. It does not, however, provide for frame forwarding.

5. *Forwarding.* As you might assume, this enables all three functions of the bridge: frame forwarding, address table building, and spanning tree algorithm participation.

To fully understand spanning tree algorithm there are eight terms that must be defined. These are: unique bridge identifier, port identifier, root bridge, path cost, root port, root path cost, designated bridge, and designated port. These terms are described below:

1. *Unique bridge identifier.* The bridge identifier is made up of the MAC address on the bridges lowest-port number and a 2-byte priority level that is defined during bridge customization.

2. *Port identifier.* Each port on a bridge has a unique 2-byte port identifier. This value is unique only within the bridge itself.

3. *Root bridge.* The bridge assigned the lowest-bridge identifier becomes the root bridge. This bridge may carry the bulk of the traffic, since it connects the two halves of the network.

4. *Path cost.* Preferred routes in an interconnected LAN have the least amount of impact on LAN performance. Fast bridges are preferred over slow bridges. LAN segments with minimal traffic are preferred over heavy-traffic segments. These preferences lead to the cost of a bridge port. The higher the cost the less-preferred route. Each bridge adds the cost of transmission through each port of the bridge to come up with the total cost of transmission for a path to any LAN segment through the root bridge.

5. *Root port.* This is the bridge port with the least cost for a path to the root bridge.

6. *Root path cost.* This is the path with the minimum cost to the root bridge from each bridge.

7. *Designated bridge.* The only bridge on a LAN segment that forwards frames is the designated bridge. All other bridges on the LAN segment are in the blocking state.

8. *Designated port.* The minimum-cost path for all traffic from this bridge and subordinate LANs will travel through this port. This is the port that connects the LAN to the designated bridge.

Bridges broadcast frames called *bridge protocol data units* (BPDU) to determine a single loop-free topology. Figure 3.5 details a BPDU. The BPDU frame

Bytes

2	1	1	1	8	4	8	2	2	2	2	2
Prot. ID	Prot. Ver ID	BPDU Type	Flags	Root ID	Root Path Cost	Bridge ID	Port ID	Msg. Age	Max Age	Hello Time	Fwd. Delay

Figure 3.5   Format of the bridge protocol data unit (BPDU).

is exchanged quickly, reducing the time in which LAN service is unavailable between stations.

In a LAN using spanning tree algorithms, the tree itself is learned after the passing of BPDUs. Each bridge in the network assumes one of three roles. The bridge with the lowest bridge identifier becomes the root bridge. The root bridge forwards frames and periodically issues a 'HELLO' BPDU to all LAN segments connected to the root bridge. Each bridge, based on information from the exchange of BPDUs, will then select its root port. The bridge that provides the lowest path cost to the root bridge becomes the designated bridge for that LAN segment. The designated bridge is responsible for recognizing and receiving the 'HELLO' BPDU over the root port and updating the path cost and timing information and the forwarding of the BPDU across the bridge. The port on the designated bridge that connects it to the LAN becomes the designated port. The designated port transmits BPDUs. Bridges that are parallel to the root or a designated bridge will not have a designated port assigned. These bridges are called *standby bridges* and will not forward frames. Standby bridges monitor the 'HELLO' BPDU but do not update the fields or forward them. During network reconfiguration the standby bridge may be needed to assume the role of the root or designated bridge. This is determined by the BPDUs which are monitored by the standby bridge. It is through the use of BPDUs that the topography of the LAN is maintained when using the spanning tree algorithm.

While the spanning tree algorithm provides the automation necessary for transparent bridging, it has its drawbacks. For one, the single path between two stations is only as fast as the slowest link. Second, all intersegment traffic is directed to a single root bridge whose processor speed and capacity may degrade network performance. Source route bridges overcome these drawbacks by supporting parallel routes.

3.1.3   Source route bridging

Source routing is an IBM bridge architecture defined for the IBM Token-Ring Network architecture. The source routing architecture has since been accepted into the IEEE 802.5 standard.

There are two distinct numbers required in source routing a ring number and a bridge number. Ring and bridge numbers are defined during the configuration of a bridge. Ring numbers are assigned to each segment that a bridge connects. The bridge itself is characterized by the set of ring numbers. Each bridge in a network must have a bridge number. The pair of numbers together require a network uniqueness. It is up to the communications staff of a company to determine which of these two numbers will be network unique to give the bridge/ring pair its unique identity. Together, these two numbers form the route designator field of the routing segment of the routing information field in the MAC frame format.

The originating station (i.e., the source station) issues a TEST or XID LPDU command on its ring with the destination address set to the null service access point address. If the destination station responds with a TEST or XID LPDU response, then the source station does not set the route information indicator bit to a B'1' since the destination station is on the same ring or LAN segment. However, if the source station does not receive the TEST or XID LPDU response, it determines that the destination station is off the ring. Off-ring determination is found in the IBM Token-Ring Network using all-routes and single-route broadcast route determination.

In all-routes broadcast route determination the source station issues a TEST or XID LPDU command to all rings as seen in Fig. 3.6. Copies of the TEST or XID LPDU command are forwarded by the bridges except in the following circumstances:

- The frame has been on the next segment.
- The hop-count limit would be exceeded in that direction. The hop count is set at bridge configuration time.
- The bridge is set to filter this frame from being forwarded.

As the frame is sent to the bridge the source sets the all-routes indicator. The first bridge then adds a route designator field identifying the source station ring number and bridge number and then a route designator field identifying the ring number and bridge number of the next ring followed by a null bridge entry. Any bridges that may be crossed after the initial bridge will then add its bridge number and another 2-byte designator field. In Fig. 3.6, there are two possible routes between station 1 and station 2. Station 2 will respond to as many frames as there are available routes. In this example there will be two frames. Station 2 responds with a nonbroadcast frame, flipping the direction bit and containing a completed-route information field. The frames are returned over the route received in the reverse order of the route information field. The route chosen is usually the first nonbroadcast reply frame to arrive at the source station. However, variables such as the number of hops or the supported-frame size can be used to determine the most efficient route.

Single-source routing reduces the overhead of the destination station during the routing discovery process. Using this mechanism the source station again issues a TEST or XID LPDU command but sets the single-route broadcast indi-

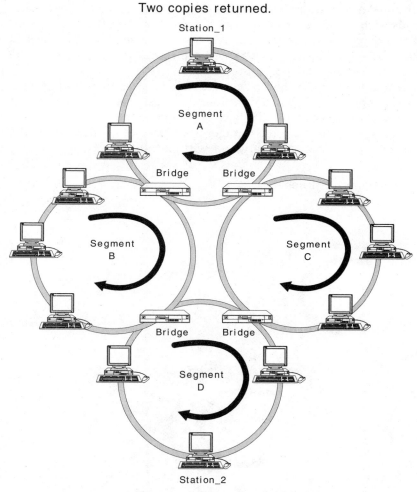

Figure 3.6   TEST or XID LPDU broadcast on the LAN.

cator in the route control field of the routing information field. The single-route broadcast allows only one copy of the frame on each segment. The single-route broadcast frame is propagated according to the following:

1. The bridge configuration allows the bridge to forward a single-route broadcast frame.

2. The route designator field indicates that this frame has already been on the next segment.

3. The bridge filters this frame.

The destination station, after receiving the single-route broadcast route command, responds with an all-routes broadcast frame, as shown in Fig. 3.7, with the destination being the source station. The source station then receives as many all-routes broadcast responses as there are routes in the network. The source station chooses the preferred route.

Single-route broadcast is the chosen favorite of the two source-routing techniques. The bridge options program determines if a single-route broadcast is to be forwarded. This can be set manually (local or remote) or automatically when using parallel bridges. The main advantage of single-route broadcast is the elimination of redundant frames in networks with parallel paths.

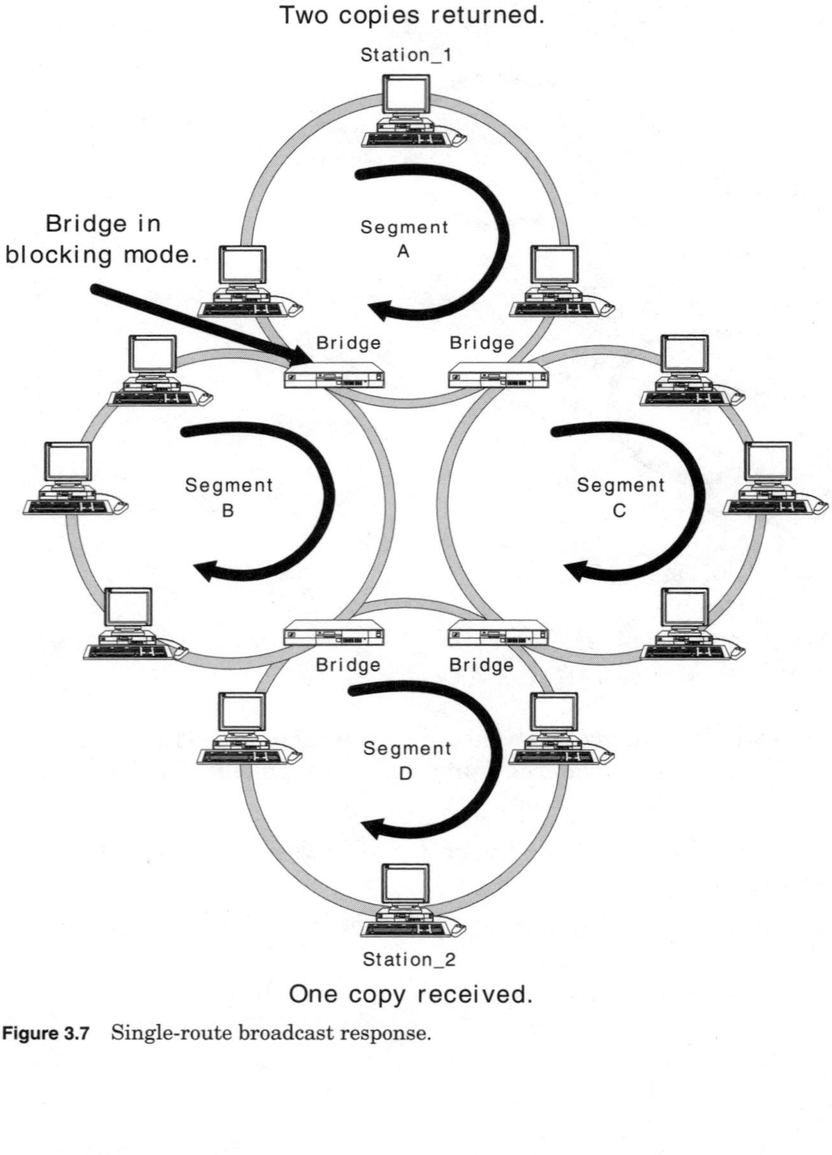

Figure 3.7 Single-route broadcast response.

3.1.4 Translational bridging

Translational bridging allows for unlike LANs to communicate. That is, Ethernet LANs can send and receive information from and to stations residing on token-ring LANs. Figure 3.8 illustrates this configuration. Translational bridges incorporate bridging methods specific to both Ethernet and token ring. The key to Ethernet-to-token-ring translation is the reverse order of significant bits for the MAC addresses in the destination and source address fields. Ethernet uses most-significant bit first of each byte and token ring uses least-significant bit order first of each byte.

3.1.5 Source route transparent bridging

In March 1990, IBM proposed to the IEEE 802.1 (internetworking) committee a bridging concept called *source route transparent*. SRT was proposed by IBM to answer the committees requirement that source-route bridges and stations must have the capability to interoperate with transparent bridges and stations on the same network.

A problem with interoperability is the instance where two stations, one understanding source-route route information fields and the other (depending on transparent bridging) not understanding route information fields, attempt to establish communications with each other. The goal of SRT is to provide for this interoperability by having source-routing stations interpret and understand the functions of the transparent bridge station.

The SRT bridge concept is based on the transparent bridge but will also include a tower on top of the base function to support source routing. The transparent function of the SRT bridge will be to forward frames based on the transparent routing table. The tower comes into play when a frame contains a routing information field. The SRT bridge will interpret the routing information frame and then base its decision on forwarding the frame from the information found in the routing information field.

SRT bridges form a single spanning tree with other SRT and transparent bridges in the same method as that used under a pure transparent bridging network. SRT stations will use the source-routing path, if one exists, or fall back to the spanning tree path. SRT stations use a single on-segment route explorer frame. This route explorer mechanism results in one single-route broadcast frame at the destination station.

The destination frame responds with one single-route broadcast message containing no routing information. The originating SRT station will choose the route or use the spanning tree path. Transparent bridging stations do not respond to frames that contain routing information.

3.2 Routed Networks

Routers perform store-and-forward just as bridges do; however, they can also interrogate the entire frame and perform protocol analysis on the frame by

IEEE802.3/Ethernet

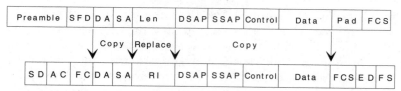

Token-Ring

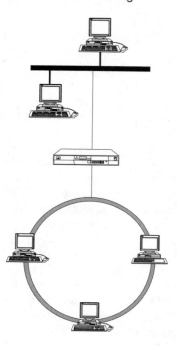

IEEE802.3/Ethernet

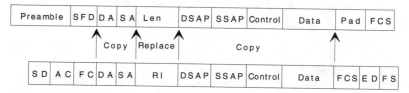

Token-Ring

Figure 3.8 Diagram depicting the functionality of translational bridging.

interpreting the protocol header and making a decision on the type of frame and its characteristics. This type of forwarding is called *modified cut through*.

Routers were once concerned with only the network layer (layer 3) of the OSI Reference Model. Routers were the means for supporting TCP/IP networks, a network layer 3 protocol. IP networks assign an address to a wire or LAN segment. A router's sole existence was to route information frames from one wire to another using IP as the protocol. However, as routers became incorporated into mainstream Fortune 500 companies they have taken on all the functions of a bridge and merged these functions with those of a router. The first incarnations of this new offering was dubbed a *brouter* for bridge router. Today these devices are termed more aptly multiprotocol routers.

3.2.1 LAN networking with routers

A router's ability to perform the functions of a bridge and to examine the protocol header of a data frame on the LAN gives the router the added benefit of segmenting a LAN into subnetworks based on protocols and destination addresses.

LAN segmentation provides for a means of protecting other LAN segments that do not necessarily require the same protocol services as the other LAN segments. Figure 3.9 illustrates this example. LAN_A and LAN_D use Novell IPX

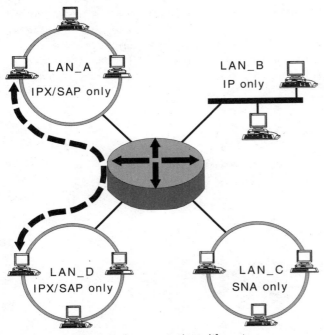

Figure 3.9 LAN protocol segmentation with routers.

services while LAN_B uses only TCP/IP and LAN_C requires SNA. Through the use of a multiprotocol router, Novell SAP broadcasts for printers and servers are passed only between LAN_A and LAN_D. Novell SAP broadcasts are prohibited from LAN_B and LAN_C. Likewise, LAN_A and LAN_D do not see TCP/IP or SNA traffic from the other LAN segments. In this fashion, routers become traffic managers for segments, but between different network types.

As with translational bridging, routers have the ability to transport information between dissimilar LAN types. Figure 3.10 depicts a routed internetwork that utilizes Ethernet, Token-Ring and FDDI. As shown in the figure, a frame is destined for a station on Ethernet LAN_B from Token-Ring LAN_A. The router accepts the incoming frame from the token-ring LAN_A and interrogates the destination address and protocol header. The router understands that the destination is the Ethernet LAN_B and translates the token-ring frame format (IEEE 802.5) to the Ethernet frame format (IEEE 802.3) and then sends the translated frame out to the FDDI backbone network by encapsulating the Ethernet frame in an FDDI frame. The Ethernet LAN_B router receives the frame, de-encapsulates it, and sends the translated Ethernet frame to the destination address. This translation can happen in either direction as long as the appropriate definitions are specified on the routers.

As distributed LANs grew, IP gained acceptance as the transport protocol. Routers became the cornerstone for LAN design. Many networks have incorporated routers as the keystone for the *wide area network* (WAN). Interoffice connectivity became paramount as client/server applications were rolled out into remote offices that primarily used IP as the transport mechanism. Figure 3.11 illustrates some of the more common WAN connections found on routers today. The routers have tried to become the answer to all corporate data networking needs. As shown in the figure, the router can transport data over the

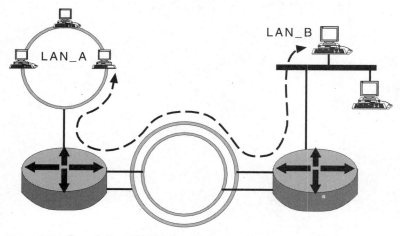

Figure 3.10   Translational bridging on routers.

WAN that originated as SNA, SDLC, IP, IPX, NetBIOS, AppleTalk, and DEC-Net. Routers encapsulate bridged protocols such as SNA and NetBIOS in TCP or IP prior to transporting the data frame over the WAN. IBM SDLC traffic can be encapsulated in TCP or it can be converted to LLC-2 format and then encapsulated into TCP or IP for transport over the WAN. IP, IPX, AppleTalk, and DECNet are all routeable (network layer 3) protocols and hence do not need special handling. However, routers can still be used as traffic managers on the WAN protecting the lower-speed links of WANs from being inundated with broadcasts.

3.2.2 Routing techniques

There are three various routing techniques most widely used. The techniques differ in the manner in which routes are defined and selected and how route information is shared between the networking nodes. The three routing techniques are source routing, label swapping, and destination routing.

Source routing. This is the familiar source routing technique discussed in the bridging section. Source routing pertains to the concept that each information frame contains the complete route needed for the source station to transport data to the destination stations. The source station in some manner, either through broadcast searches or static definitions, provides the road map (directions) to the destination station. Replies from a destination station would use the same directions but only in reverse. While this technique may be the most efficient for routing information frames it comes with an an overhead cost because each frame contains the complete description of the route. The size of the descriptor field varies depending on the protocol being used.

Label-based routing. This routing technique is often referred to as address swapping and is the dominant technique used in switching network models. Switching networks exercise label swapping at layer 2 and router networks use

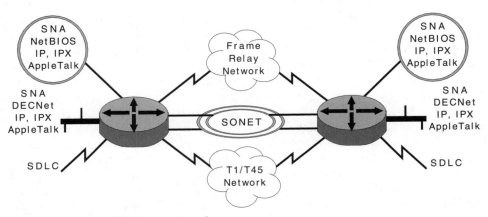

Figure 3.11 Common WAN connections for routers.

label swapping at layer 3. The label or address is in actuality an index into a switching table at each intermediate routing node in the network. The intermediate node uses the label as an index into the switching table to determine which port or link the information frame should be sent out on and provides a new label for the next node on the route to use as an index into its table.

Destination routing.   This routing technique is based on layer 3 information. The information provides the destination and source addresses but does not include a specific route. The concept for this technique in routing can be summed up in a question: "How can I get there from here and which is the best way?" Each node and intermediate node, after interpreting the layer 3 information, will assess the current topology and congestion of the network and make its decision based on predefined information on routing to the destination. The three most widely used protocols, IP, IPX, and SNA utilize destination routing.

Each of these routing techniques requires a routing algorithm to determine the optimal route. These algorithms are distance vector and link state.

3.2.3   Routing algorithms

The physical route taken by an information frame or packet is computed for optimization. That is to mean the best possible route based on network topology. Congestion at the time will determine the optimal path for the transmission of data between two endpoints over the network. The routing algorithms are based on tables in each routing node found on the network. There are two fundamental routing algorithms in use: distance vector and link state.

Distance vector.   As the name implies, this routing mechanism is based on the distance (hops) between the routing node and the destination routing node and the vector (direction) in which to send the data. Distance-vector routing is based on the Bellman-Ford algorithm. The routing tables contain entries on each known destination network. As each router determines its own table of network topology, it exchanges the entire table with its adjacent routers. These routers, in turn, update their tables and then pass the new one on to the next adjacent router. The tables are updated whenever the router has received changes from a neighboring router or when they themselves have a new link added or deleted. The actual exchange of routing tables occurs on a time and not a change basis. This means that the tables can be exchanged even if no network change occurred. This passing of routing information and the resulting update is known as *convergence*. The convergence time is increased in a distance-vector routing algorithm based on network size. The larger the network the longer the convergence time. The advantage to using a distance-vector routing algorithm is its simplicity. The cost of the simplicity is the long convergence time needed in large routed networks. Examples of a routing protocol that utilize distance-vector algorithms are: Routing Information Protocol (RIP) and Cisco Systems Interior Gateway Routing Protocol (IGRP). Both are used as IP routing protocols.

Link state.   An approach to reduce the convergence time on a network and to allow each router to have a topology map of the network is accomplished using link-state routing algorithms. Link state is based on the Djikstra algorithm. This algorithm determines the optimal path based on the shortest distance to the destination network at that time. It is also called *shortest-path-first* (SPF). In link-state routing, only each router is responsible for contacting its adjacent or neighbor router. Each router "advertises" the links and networks available from each link to its neighbor. Note that it is only link information that is exchanged and not the entire network topology database as in distance-vector routing. Convergence of changed network topology is drastically reduced and more dynamic in link state because only when a router discovers a new router, link, or link-status changes are updates exchanged. The exchange occurs as soon as the topology change is recognized and not on a timed exchange. Examples of routing protocol using link-state algorithm are: IBM's APPN, OSI Intermediate System–Intermediate System (IS-IS), Cisco Systems Enhanced–Interior Gateway Routing Protocol (E-IGRP), and IP Open Shortest Path First (OSPF).

3.3 Switched Networks

Switched network configurations have come about as a means of preserving network infrastructure investment while increasing bandwidth and throughput. The term switching refers to information coming in on a specific port and being sent out on another specific port. No more, as in Ethernet or token-ring networks, does each station on the LAN necessarily need to receive every frame for analysis. The switch has basically moved this process away from the station. Switch network environments, such as token-ring, 10BASE-T, and 100BASE-T, employ a star-wired configuration.

3.3.1 Switching functions

Switches can be employed to act as bridges, routers, and topology managers. When acting as a bridge, the switch must adhere to the underlying protocol standards for bridging traffic. In the role of a router, the switch must deliver the frames based on layer 3 protocols. As a topology manager, a switch can ease the physical reconfiguration of a LAN through port switching and create *virtual LANs* (VLANs) based on IP subnetwork numbers. The function of the switch is determined by the traffic it services, the protocol in use, and the switches position as a component of the network.

A switch is comprised of ports, buffers, address tables, and a backplane as shown in Fig. 3.12. The port is the physical interface used to connect the wiring. The buffers are used to store frames for analysis and latency. The address tables are used to determine on which port the destination station can be found. The backplane is the switching matrix that delivers the frame from one port to another. The aggregate bandwidth available on the backplane is the sum of the bandwidth/port and the number of ports. A 16-port 100 Mbps port switch has an aggregate bandwidth of 1.6 Gbps. Each port on a switch has a buffer and address table. Each LAN segment or station attached directly to the switch port receives only frames destined for the station(s) on that specific LAN segment. If the destination segment is busy, data would be temporarily held in the destination-port buffer. In a switched environment, the only reason why an outgoing frame would be buffered is if the transmit pair is already busy sending frames to the station(s).

Switches implement the three basic types of forwarding mechanisms. These are store-and-forward, cut-through, and modified cut-through. Figure 3.13 depicts the choice of fields used for each type of forwarding mechanism. Store-and-forward switching provides an excellent means of error checking. Since the entire frame must be analyzed prior to sending it out, the latency of the transmission is determined by the size of the frame. This makes the use of store-and-forward a good choice for critical locations in the network but not necessarily for workgroups. Cut-through forwarding has the lowest latency because it will begin sending the frame out to the destination station as soon as the destination address field is read and verified. This, however, means that all frames, valid or invalid, will be forwarded to the destination station. It is thought that end stations already possess the intelligence to verify frame errors, thus, this level of checking is not needed in the switch. Cut-through forwarding is a good choice for workgroups over backbone configurations if they tend to encounter low error rates. Modified cut-through in switches, as in routers, tends to merge the best of both of the other mechanisms. Since modified cut-through reads the first 64 bytes of the frame, it acts more like cut-through for large frames and store-and-forward for small frames. This is a weakness of modified cut-through

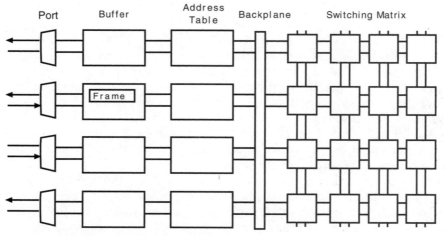

Figure 3.12 Components of a switch.

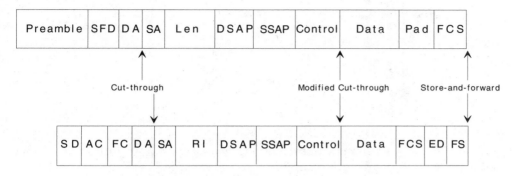

Figure 3.13   Fields used for switches to forward frames.

because small frames are generally control and management frames which require a quick turnaround and large data frames which require thorough error checking. Selecting the appropriate forwarding mechanism for your switch is dependent on your specific networking criteria and the position of the switch in your network.

Switches must still support the IEEE 802.3 or 802.5 MAC sublayer protocols of the OSI data link layer 2. Recall that the MAC protocol regulates access to the LAN cable. For token-rings, this access is determined by the station controlling the token frame, and on Ethernet this is accomplished using CSMA/CD. The MAC protocol role in a switched configuration, where each port has a single station on the LAN segment, is greatly diminished. Since the LAN segment and the full bandwidth is dedicated to the single station there is no contention to transmit data. For that matter there is also no contention for receiving data. Switching, therefore, allows for full-duplex communication to the dedicated station on the LAN as shown in Fig. 3.14. The ability to have full-duplex operations for a LAN station can be utilized in workgroup and backbone configurations.

3.3.2 Switched workgroups

Large LAN topologies can benefit from implementing switches. Through microsegmentation, using switching stations on a LAN can gain extra bandwidth and still be considered a part of the same workgroup. Figure 3.15 illustrates this point. Typically, LAN segments have 20–50 stations attached to it. Using switching microsegmentation would provide 5–6 stations on a shared media LAN segment, thus increasing bandwidth fourfold. While the end-user stations still operate in half-duplex mode following all the MAC protocols spe-

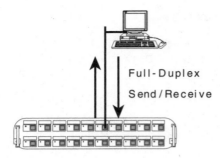

Figure 3.14   Full-duplex dedicated-shared media.

cific to the LAN architecture, the servers would operate in full-duplex mode allowing for full bandwidth availability to each server.

3.3.3   Switched backbone

Backbone configurations allow traffic segmentation as well as full-duplex versus half-duplex microsegmentation to occur. As shown in Fig. 3.16, a typical backbone configuration provides access for each workgroup to the print, file, database, mail, and gateway servers. The workgroup switches are connected to

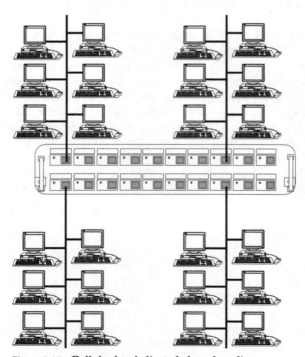

Figure 3.15   Full-duplex dedicated-shared media.

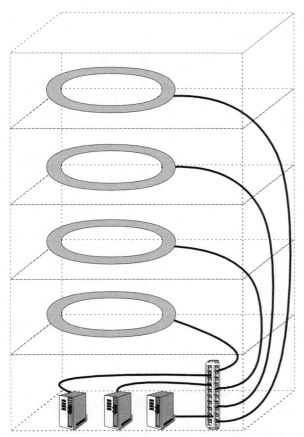

Figure 3.16   Full-duplex segmentation for common workgroup servers.

the backbone switch to service all the users of the building and provide the high-speed full-duplex transmission to the common servers of the corporation.

Another use of a backbone switch is to implement a virtual LAN (VLAN) backbone where the switch is the backbone for the building and, through advanced management of the switch, virtual LANs can be designed. As shown in Fig. 3.17, stations on the third floor can be logically associated as a single workgroup with stations on the second and first floor. This again allows the switch to better manage the traffic patterns through the LAN and to dynamically change the logical configuration of the workgroups when required.

3.4   Summary

Internetworking models are based on the abilities of three devices: bridges, routers, and switches. Each device must provide functions specific to either layer 2 or layer 3 or both of the OSI Reference Model.

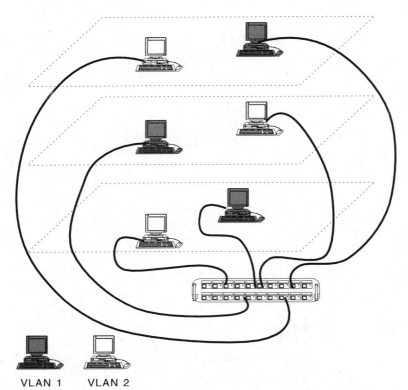

VLAN 1   VLAN 2

Figure 3.17   A VLAN configuration using advanced switch management.

Bridges interconnect LAN segments using four types of bridging methodologies: transparent, source route, translational, and source route transparent bridging. Bridges primarily use the data link layer 2 of the OSI Reference Model.

Routers, as internetworking devices, at first concentrated on the network layer or layer 3 of the OSI Reference Model. Initially, routers dealt specifically with the Internet Protocol (IP) network address. But since their introduction, they have become multiprotocol devices with the ability to bridge and route information frames. Routers use one of two routing algorithms. Distance vector is used as a simple means for exchanging the entire network routing table between routers on a time interval. Link-state routing algorithms exchange only the addition or deletion of new connections in the network on a dynamic basis.

Switching devices provide both bridging and routinglike routers, however, they increase the available bandwidth per segment through the use of full-duplex transmission and microsegmenting. The ability of a switching device to create virtual LANs and to dynamically switch a dedicated-shared media (single station segment) to a new logical ring greatly increases LAN management.

These three devices provide the interconnecting seam for today's internetworking environments.

4

Routing

The term routing used in context with networks immediately conjures up the image of a meshed network consisting of routers. However, routers are not the only devices that use a routing algorithm to move information from a source to a destination. In fact, that's all routing is: a means of determining a suitable path between a source and destination. The various algorithms used for routing result in connection versus connectionless networking. These two networking techniques will determine if the routing algorithm can be trusted or just uses a best-effort for delivery of information.

4.1 Connection-Oriented Networks

In a connection-oriented network, the path used for the transmission of information between the source and destination is predetermined prior to the sending of the data. Once the path is selected the information utilizes the established path for the duration of the transmission. The most well-known and used connection-oriented network is the telephone system.

Conceptually, a data connection-oriented network is very much like a telephone call. Figure 4.1 depicts the two connection-oriented calls side by side for a clear illustration. The caller establishes network connectivity by picking up the telephone handset. This connectivity is recognized and the network responds with a dial tone. The caller is considered the source station at this point. The caller identifies the receiver of the call by entering the telephone number of the destination station. At this point the telephone network will determine the best path between the source and destination phone numbers. Once the path is selected, the destination phone begins to ring and the selected path is the only one used during the rest of the call. When the handset on the destination phone is picked up a conversation may begin. The conversation protocol now takes over and confirmations of connectivity are processed. As the conversation goes on, information is exchanged. At some point, one of the endpoints (the people) will begin ending the conversation and the call will be disconnected.

In the data-network world the call is often referred to as the *virtual circuit*. The transfer of information is referred to as the *conversation*. The hang-up in a voice network is called a *disconnect* in the data network. People in the voice world of networking are considered to be the *applications* in the data world. It is the applications (i.e., people) that have conversations, not the equipment. Finally, the telephone set in the voice world is equivalent to the *computing workstation* in the data world. Understanding this concept by relating it to the telephone system will make it easier to comprehend connection-oriented networks.

True connection-oriented networks have four primary characteristics. These are:

1. The guaranteed delivery of information in an assigned, orderly fashion without loss or duplication.

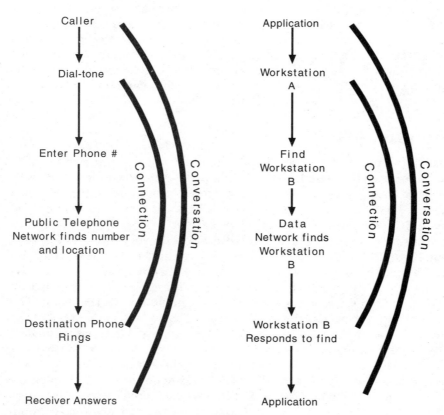

Figure 4.1 Illustration of connection-oriented system.

2. A single path used during the call. Information will flow only on this designated path (route) for the call duration.

3. Minimal bandwidth guarantees are established at the connection time and reserved for the length of the call. Underutilization of the minimal will waste valuable bandwidth.

4. Call establishment is refused if network parameters that govern the previous characteristics are not possible. The caller is notified of the request with some kind of message. For example, in a voice network this is the fast-busy signal. In data networks, connection establishment will not be successful and the application will notify the user with a message of some type indicating the possible reason (e.g., unavailable network resources).

Failure of the network to guarantee the orderly delivery of information, path reliability, and bandwidth availability will result in a call disconnect. Examples of connection-oriented protocols are SNA and source route bridging.

4.2   Connectionless Networks

A main difference between connection-oriented and connectionless networks is in the responsibility for error correction and message unit sequencing. Connection-oriented networks place error detection, recovery, and sequencing clearly in the network. The end nodes (i.e., users, applications) are not to be concerned with these networking functions when using connection-oriented conversations. Connectionless networks, however, view these functions in the end nodes themselves. They are responsible for delivering the data in any way possible. This is known as a *best-effort delivery system.*

A best-effort delivery system is akin to the postal system. Figure 4.2 diagrams the two systems side by side for conceptual clarity. A message unit in a connectionless network is referred to as a datagram. When an end node in the network begins transmitting information to another end node in the network, it includes the address of the end node in each datagram. In a postal system, each letter can be considered a datagram. On each envelope is a completed address of the recipient. The mailbox in the postal system can be analogous to the network interface in a data network. Once the envelope is placed in the mailbox it is routed to the recipient. If two envelopes with the same address were sent at the same time from the same mailbox, one envelope may arrive at the destination prior to the other. In a data network, each envelope is a datagram and each datagram contains the destination end node address. Though the datagrams, in reality, cannot be entered into the network at the exact same time, for all intents and purposes, they can be considered to be simultaneously transmitted from the same source end node when one immediately follows the other. In a connectionless-oriented network there is a presumption that datagrams will get lost, duplicated, or altered due to the routing of the datagram through the network to the destination end node. Since each datagram is independently routed, there is no guarantee of sequenced order. As in the receipt of letters out of order from the postal system, the end user (i.e., end node, application) must resequence the order and determine if there is missing data. Connectionless networks have the following characteristics:

1. Best-effort delivery is used. The network will make judgments on delivery of the datagram based on network resources as they occur, allowing for rerouting, duplication, and altered datagrams to be delivered.

2. Information units (datagrams) are routed independently of each other. On-the-fly rerouting of data, due to network congestion, resource outages, and

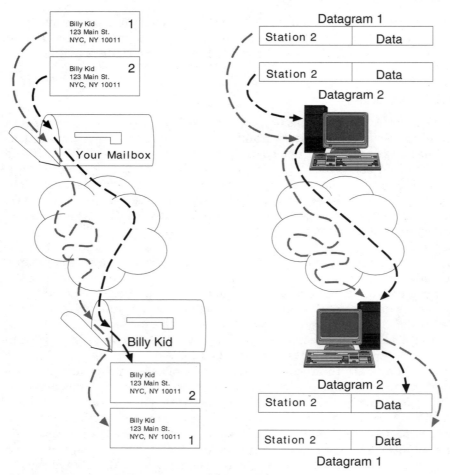

Figure 4.2   Illustration of connectionless delivery systems.

timing thresholds exceeded, allows a connectionless-oriented network to meet its obligation of delivering each individual datagram to its destination.

3. Error recovery and sequencing are a function of the end node. The delivery of the datagram is provided by the network. Datagram content, integrity, and sequence become the responsibility of the end node applications.

4. A better mechanism for sharing network resources by not guaranteeing a uniform service is provided. The absence of guaranteed bandwidth, sequencing, and delivery allows a connectionless-oriented network to share bandwidth more efficiently and reduces network processing time.

Examples of connectionless-oriented network protocols are IP and IPX.

4.3   Network-Layer Addressing

The OSI network layer is the one concerned with addressing, routing, and relaying information. It is in this layer that connection-oriented and connectionless networks operate, network addresses are assigned, network topology is known, and route-decision processes are performed.

A single network can be represented by a single identifier. In some cases the identifier is a number, in others it may be alpha characters, and in still others a combination of both. Regardless of the identifier's format, the network addressing schema used must provide a means for a quick-decision process. This is facilitated by the network address being subdivided into subnetworks (analogous to the postal system concept previously discussed under connectionless networking).

The postal address is actually read in reverse by the postal system to facilitate quick sorting and routing of the mail. For example as shown in Figure 4.3, in the United States the network identifier is the state. A subnet of that state would be the city. Within the city is an identifier of the home, which would be the identifying equivalent to the last portion of a network address, and finally, the destination is the recipient's name. This hierarchical addressing is common in all the most widely used networking protocols. Without a hierarchical routing of information on a network each individual routing node would need a complete map of the entire network. Network routing nodes know how to get to the destination end node, based on the end node's address. This information is stored in routing tables on each routing node.

Postal Address   Network Address

123 Main St. ⟺ Host
      NYC ⟺ Subnetwork   **Figure 4.3** Network address as
       NY ⟺ Network   compared to a postal address.

4.4 Routing Tables

The network layer is concerned with a logical mapping of the network entities. Routing tables provide the data necessary for that route-decision process. Each routing node must contain a table that uses various parameters to determine the best route for the message unit. There are two basic types of routing tables: static and dynamic.

Static routing tables are predefined routes through the network. This type of routing table is very reminiscent of the hierarchical routing used in SNA networks. Each routing node is defined with an entry that details how a message unit can be routed to the destination network. Figure 4.4 details such an entry. Station A begins transmitting data to station B. Station A sends its data to its router. In this case router A. Router A knows it can get to station B one of two ways. The first way is the direct route to router B and the second way is the alternate route through routers C and D. Router B must have the reverse static route defined in its static table for station B to send information back to station A. Routers C and D must also have forward and reverse routes defined for the alternate route used between routers A and B. Static routing provides the network engineer with the ability to have full control of traffic through the network. It is apparent from the example, static routing has its limitations. One is that the routing node searches the table sequentially from first to last entry, thus overloading the first route with traffic, while the alternate route is never used. Another limitation is that static routing does not weigh in the factor of bandwidth. In a static environment, should a link become inoperable, the router will continue to try to send data over the static route until the static router from A or B is deleted. As shown in Fig. 4.4, the alternate route actually has higher

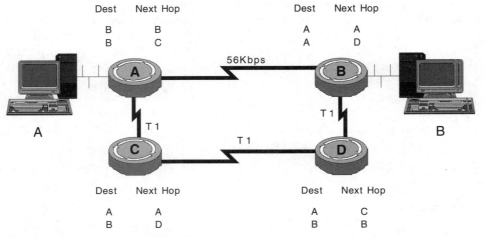

Figure 4.4 Static routing table example.

bandwidth capacity than the direct route. So, as can be surmised, static routing in large networks can become quite complex and time consuming.

Dynamic route tables are established by the routing node during initialization time. As each routing node initializes it advertises to the network the networks that it knows are directly attached to it. Figure 4.5 illustrates this type of dynamic routing table. The network takes care of itself. In fact, link failure and recovery between routing nodes is now taken into consideration. So dynamic routing tables not only supply enough data for all the routing nodes to discover the routes between each other, they also constantly update each other allowing for dynamic network topology changes to take place, be recognized, and used. The downfall to dynamic routing tables is the network overhead created. Depending on the routing protocol in use, the network can be inundated with routing table updates even though the network topology could remain static.

4.5   Routing Table Updates

As routing nodes learn of the network topology they store it in a table. Depending on the routing protocol used (e.g., RIP, OSPF, IGRP, E-IGRP), the table entries will be of different formats and the updates themselves will be governed differently. For the most part, all routing tables have the following fields in their entries: destination network address, metric, interface, and mask. The first field explains itself and identifies the network associated with this entry. A calculated metric is included in the entry making it a best-choice route to send message units to the destination. The interface field indicates which network interface on the routing node is associated with this entry. The interface could be a serial line, an FDDI ring, Ethernet or token-ring LAN, or even a switched interface connection. The last field is a mask, applied to the network address for subnetting. Without this field the routing node would not know how to interpret the addresses associated with the destination networks accessible through the identified interface. There may be multiple entries in a routing table for some networks because of the network topology. However, the metric value will provide a least-cost ascending sequence of the available

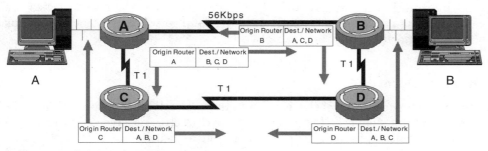

Figure 4.5   Dynamic routing table example.

entries, where the lowest metric value is tried first. The metric value provides a preferred-route search key for the routing node during the route-decision process.

4.6   Route-Decision Process

Each message unit that enters a routing node must be interrogated by the node to determine the destination of the message unit. In most routing nodes the following process occurs in delivering information message units:

1. If the message unit destination network/subnetwork address is indeed a network attached directly to the routing node, the node will deliver the message unit to the corresponding network interface associated with the direct, attached network.

2. If the message unit destination network/subnetwork address is accessible through another routing node, this node will send the message unit to the designated routing node over the associated interface having the lowest least-cost metric value for the destination network.

3. If the message unit destination network/subnetwork address is not found in the routing table entries, the routing node then determines if a default route or "gateway of last resort" has been defined. If there is a default route for message units that do not have a network match in the routing table, the routing node sends the message unit on to the default gateway of last resort. However, if there is no default gateway, the router will return a network response to the source of the message unit indicating that the destination network is unreachable through this routing node. The routing node at this point will discard the message unit.

This decision-making process is performed for every message unit entering a routing node on its way to the destination network.

The expression *routing node* has been used to mean any type of node that must contain network topology information and make decisions of where to send information in the network. The most notable of these node types are called *routers* and have historically used the Internetwork Protocol as a means of routing information through a network.

4.7   Internetwork Protocol (IP)

The Internetwork Protocol (IP) resides in the network layer of the five-layer IP architecture as shown in Fig. 4.6. The IP architecture is layered, providing a rational, simple, and easy way to modify structure, which has added to IP's success. The architecture is often referred to as a five-layer architecture, but it actually defines only the three higher layers.

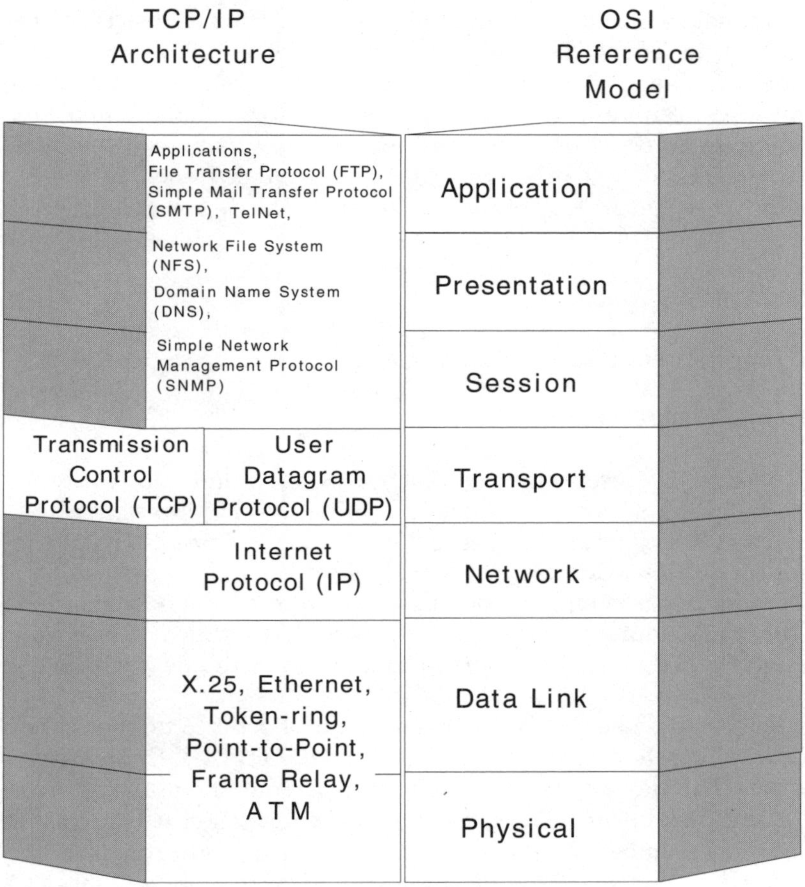

TCP/IP
Architecture

OSI
Reference
Model

TCP/IP Architecture		OSI Reference Model
Applications, File Transfer Protocol (FTP), Simple Mail Transfer Protocol (SMTP), TelNet,		Application
Network File System (NFS), Domain Name System (DNS),		Presentation
Simple Network Management Protocol (SNMP)		Session
Transmission Control Protocol (TCP)	User Datagram Protocol (UDP)	Transport
Internet Protocol (IP)		Network
X.25, Ethernet, Token-ring, Point-to-Point, Frame Relay, ATM		Data Link
		Physical

Figure 4.6   Diagram of the Internet Protocol IP architecture.

As seen in Fig. 4.6, the two lower layers, physical and data link control, can be defined by different networking architectures, such as token-ring, Ethernet, frame-relay, ATM, and OSI. Recall that at these layers the physical attributes of the communications network are defined and adhered to. Data units at this level are called *frames*. Moving up to the third layer we find the network layer where Internet Protocol (IP) resides.

4.7.1   IP addressing

Internet Protocol has an addressing scheme that is based on the network layer. Hence, it is a logical address versus the address found in the data link control layer which denotes a physical interface address. Every host in an IP network is assigned an IP address. An IP host can be a mainframe computer, UNIX workstation, personal computer, or midrange processor. The address is 32 bits (4 bytes or 4 octets) in length. This allows for a total of 2^{32} addresses. That's over 4 billion hosts on an IP network! The addresses are used in binary form but represented in a decimal form. This representation is called *dot notation*. Since 8 bits make up an octet, or byte, and there are 32 bits to an IP address then there are 4 octets or bytes that must be represented. Hence, in the dot notation, 4 values represent the IP address of an IP host. For example the address:

130.11.31.132

is the decimal representation of the binary value:

10000010 00001011 00011111 10000100

Obviously the decimal representation is easier to comprehend and is the reason why the dotted decimal notation is used to define the IP address. If all the binary values are 1s, then the IP address is 255.255.255.255 and is considered a broadcast address which every IP host will receive.

The IP address format is comprised of a network address and a local or host address. The network address identifies the network to which this host is attached. The local address is the unique local address of the host within the network.

The IP address formats use the first 4 bits of the first octet to further subdivide the IP addressing scheme into classes. As shown in Fig. 4.7, there are five IP address classes. The classes are denoted by the starting bits of the address. For example, if the first bit of the address has a 0 value, then it is a class A address with address numbers starting from 0 and continuing through to 127. A class A networking scheme is used for large IP networks, providing over 2^{24} or 16,777,216 addresses within its networking scheme. Class B is used for medium-sized networks with as address space of 2^{16} or 65,536 addresses, and class C is used for small networks using 2^8 or 256 addresses. In IP, a network consists of all the addresses within a given network. For instance, a class A address of 56 is a different network than a class A address of 15.

Class A, B, and C addresses are employed by the user community to build networks. Class D addresses are used by IP for a mechanism called *multicasting*. Multicasting allows for the distribution of a single message to selective hosts on a network. The class E addresses are used for experimental purposes and are therefore reserved.

4.7.2 IP subnet addressing

The IP address schemes, class A, B, and C, can be further subdivided using a partitioning of the IP address to include a subnet address. Subnetting provides

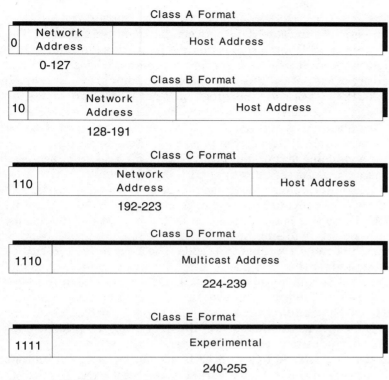

Figure 4.7 IP address class formats.

a sliding mechanism to extend the network address into the host address field. For instance, in Fig. 4.8 we have extended the network address by creating a subnet. In the figure, class A network of 34 (which is denoted as 34.0.0.0) has been subnetted by applying a mask to the bits in octets 2 and 3. This mask is denoted in decimal form as 255.255.255.0. The value of the mask sets the bits used in the subnet and network addresses to 1 and the host address bits to a 0. So in the example, the network is 34, the subnet is 128.80, and the host field is the last octet. This type of subnetting will provide 253 host addresses for the network 34.128.80.0. It is only 253 because the 0 host address is reserved to represent the network in the host and the value of 255 is reserved for broadcasting. By applying a mask of 255.255.252.0 the number of hosts can be increased to over 4000 for the subnet.

Class A network address	34.0.0.0	00100010.00000000.00000000.00000000	34.0.0.0
16-bit subnet mask	255.255.255.0	11111111.11111111.11111111.00000000	0.128.80.0
Class A subnet address	34.128.8.0	00100010.10000000.00001000.00000000	34.128.80.0

Figure 4.8 Example illustrating the use of IP addresses and subnets.

4.7.3 IP routing

IP's single main function is to route data between hosts on the network. The data is routed in datagrams. IP uses connectionless network service for transmitting the datagram. Since it uses connectionless services, IP does not guarantee reliable delivery of the data or the sequencing of the datagram. Hence, the upper layers (e.g., TCP) must provide this function. What IP does provide is the ability to route traffic, independent of available physical routes, regardless of the application-to-application requirements. IP allows for datagrams to be rerouted through the network if the current physical route being used becomes inoperative. This is a valuable feature built into IP that SNA does not possess.

The IP uses connectionless services to send data between TCP/IP hosts. Hence, it does not guarantee delivery or the sequence of the datagrams. IP was architected in this way to provide internetworking for any device. As can be seen in Fig. 4.9, the IP header is quite large. In fact, the length of the header can reach as high as 60 octets in length.

The first octet in the header contains two fields. The *Version* field identifies the IP version being used for this datagram. This value is always 4. Datagrams received with a previous version number are discarded by the receiving device. The *Header Length* field of the first octet contains the length of the IP header in 32-byte boundaries. The *Padding* field is used here just as in TCP to ensure this requirement. If no options are included in the datagram, then this header length field will always indicate a length of 20 octets or five words.[1]

The *Type of Service* field is used to give precedence and priority to different types of IP traffic flowing through the network. For the most part, this field is ignored by most implementors of IP and is a serious drawback to the current IP implementation. However, some vendors, like the router-provider Cisco Systems, are implementing a Type of Service field in their routing software that is analogous to providing a class of service to the various protocols and applications.

The length of the datagram is calculated by adding together the length of the IP header and the data fields. This 2-octet field architecturally provides for a datagram to be up to 65,535 bytes in length. However, networking restraints and host computer buffer constraints do not make this a reality.

Though IP does not support sequencing it does support *fragmentation*. Fragmentation occurs when the data field makes the overall length of the datagram larger than the size that any node can accept on the way to the destination host. The *Identification* field is used to assist in determining which datagram fragments belong together for reassembly at the receiving host. The *Flags* field indicates whether a frame can be fragmented and whether it is one of many or the last fragment. The *Fragment Offset* field contains the number of 8-byte

---

[1] A word is 4 octets in length. An IP header has a minimum length of five words and a maximum length of fifteen words.

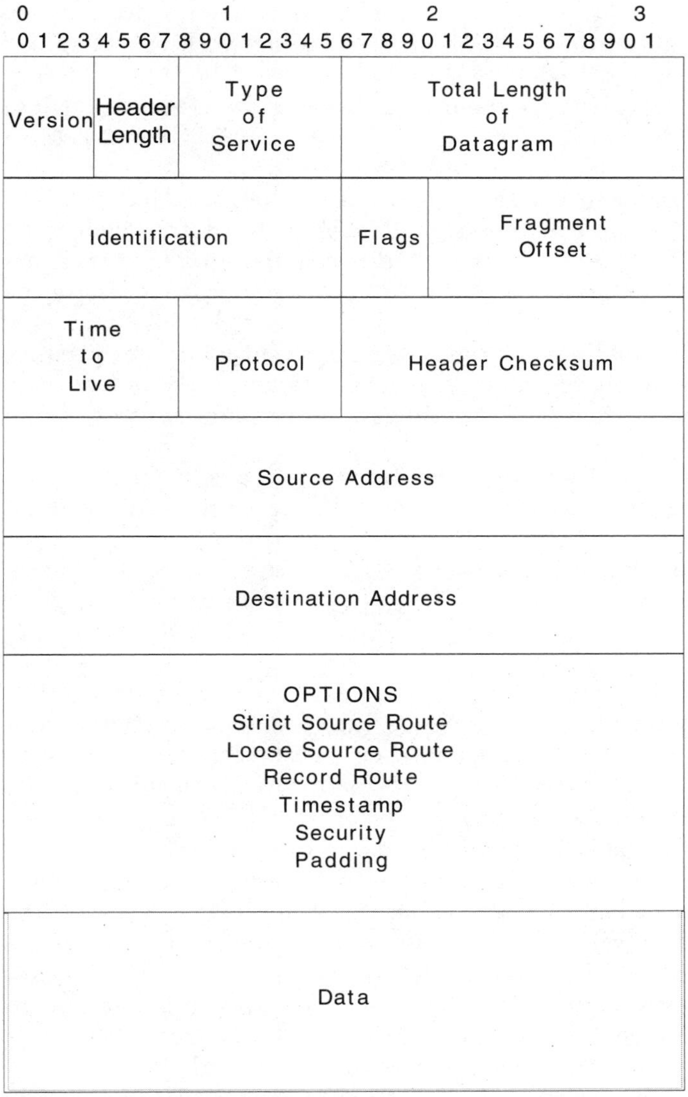

```
 0                   1                   2                   3
 0 1 2 3 4 5 6 7 8 9 0 1 2 3 4 5 6 7 8 9 0 1 2 3 4 5 6 7 8 9 0 1
```

Version	Header Length	Type of Service	Total Length of Datagram

Identification	Flags	Fragment Offset

Time to Live	Protocol	Header Checksum

Source Address

Destination Address

OPTIONS Strict Source Route Loose Source Route Record Route Timestamp Security Padding

Data

Figure 4.9 Format of the IP header.

units of this datagram's data from the start of the first datagram. This 8-byte unit is called a *fragment block*.

The *Time-to-Live* field is a measurement in seconds. This field is decremental by 1 on each router along the path to a destination station. The value for the field is set by the sending host and can be set as high as 255. If the TTL value reaches 0 before reaching the destination host then the datagram is discarded.

In reality, it is not a timer at all but a hop-count mechanism. Once the hop count is exceeded, the datagram is removed from the network by the router that decrements the TTL field to 0.

The *Protocol* field indicates which upper-layer protocol is to receive the data field of the datagram. For instance, a value of 6 indicates that TCP is to receive the data.

The *Header Checksum* field of the IP datagram is a value based on the 16-bit 1's complement of the 1's complement sum of all 16-bit words in the header. The checksum value itself is set to all 0s prior to this calculation. This checksum calculation is performed by the sending host and every router traversed in the network.

The *source* and *destination address* fields are the 32-bit addresses used for the IP address. Recall that these are not the hardware addresses but the network layer addresses of the devices. The hardware (MAC) addresses are found in the data link layer.

The *options* field contains several different options that can be implemented by the sending host. For the most part these are self explanatory and will not be discussed here.

The last field in the datagram is the *data* field. The data field of an IP datagram is the TCP or UDP segment.

4.8   Address Resolution Protocol (ARP)

IP has gained great popularity as the preferred protocol for client/server systems. In a client/server environment the end-user workstation (i.e., client) contacts the server over a LAN. Recall that LAN protocols use medium access control (MAC) addresses on the data link layer of the OSI Reference Model. The conversation between the client and the server, however, takes place at a higher level in the network layer. In an IP networking environment, a logical network (IP) address is used for connectivity between the client and server. The requesting station, in this case the client, is aware of the IP address of the server but does not know the MAC address of the server network interface card (NIC). The MAC address is required in order to use the LAN protocol (e.g., Ethernet or token-ring). IP resolves the issue of mapping its address to the MAC address through the use of the Address Resolution Protocol (ARP).

Figure 4.10 illustrates the use of the ARP. Station A sends an ARP request on to the LAN using the all-stations broadcast MAC address for the LAN protocol. In both Ethernet and token-ring, this broadcast results in a destination MAC address of FFFFFFFFFFFF (all bits set to 1). This MAC frame containing the ARP request is received by every station on the LAN. Each station inspects the request to determine if (1) it is using the specified protocol, in this case ARP and (2) the IP address defined in the target protocol address field is equal to its own IP address. If the IP address is matched, then the station sends back an ARP reply to the originating station with the target hardware-address field completed. Now that the client station is aware of the hardware address of the server, it can set up the TCP conversation needed for the client/server application.

This type of ARP is considered a *local* ARP. Local ARPs are ARP requests and responses that occur on the same subnet and LAN segment. ARP is used for any type of communication between IP stations on a network.

As each station learns of the hardware-to-network address mappings from ARP requests and replies, it builds an *ARP cache*. The ARP cache is a table that keeps track of the hardware-to-network address mappings. Without such a cache, each time a new connection is made between previously connected stations the ARP must be used, wasting bandwidth and connection time. Figure 4.11 depicts the use of an ARP cache. Most ARP caches are kept for a period of time before the station clears out each entry. The ARP cache is added to by stations even if they are not the destination recipient of the ARP request. In this way, each station can maintain its own table. As the table is built and the station now needs to connect with another station on the LAN, it first checks its own ARP table to resolve the address mapping prior to sending out an ARP request.

4.8.1   Proxy ARP

Suppose the destination station is on a different LAN segment and a different subnet. The IP-to-hardware mapping is resolved using a function of ARP called *Proxy* ARP.

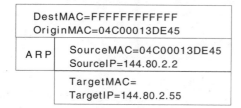

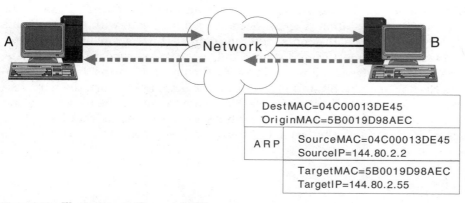

Figure 4.10   Illustration on the use of ARP.

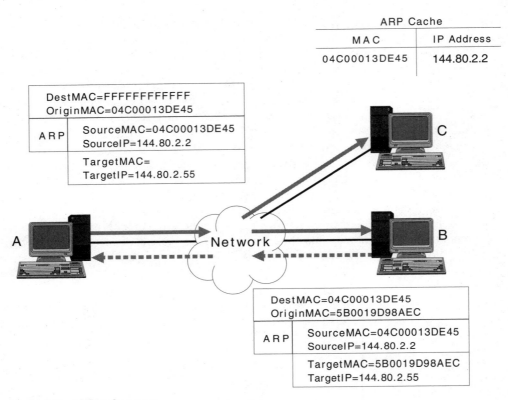

ARP Cache

MAC	IP Address
04C00013DE45	144.80.2.2

DestMAC=FFFFFFFFFFFF
OriginMAC=04C00013DE45

ARP | SourceMAC=04C00013DE45
SourceIP=144.80.2.2

TargetMAC=
TargetIP=144.80.2.55

DestMAC=04C00013DE45
OriginMAC=5B0019D98AEC

ARP | SourceMAC=04C00013DE45
SourceIP=144.80.2.2

TargetMAC=5B0019D98AEC
TargetIP=144.80.2.55

Figure 4.11   ARP cache usage.

Proxy ARP is actually a function of an ARP server that resides somewhere on the network. In today's networking environments, this ARP server is usually the stations default router. Since it is the function of a router to provide connectivity to other subnets, it makes sense that it should build its own ARP cache. As shown in Fig. 4.12, station A again needs to communicate with station B this time. However, station B is on a different subnet (LAN segment). The router receives the ARP request from station A and, using its knowledge of the subnets, inserts its own hardware address into the ARP reply and returns the ARP to station A. Each frame sent by station A to station B actually contains the hardware address of the router and not station B. The router, receiving the frame from station A, places station B's hardware address in the frame as the destination address before sending the frame out to the LAN segment, where station B is actually found.

4.8.2 Reverse ARP (RARP)

There are some instances when the workstation knows its hardware address but not its IP address. This occurs on diskless workstations and in LAN proto-

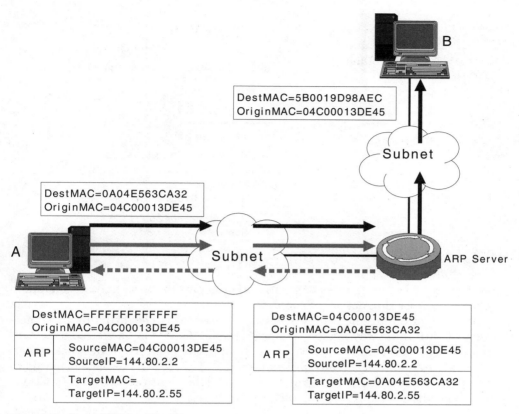

Figure 4.12   Proxy ARP functionality.

cols such as Banyan VINES. The format of the RARP is the same as the ARP except that the operation code field indicates an RARP reply or request function and the protocol type field will be set to RARP instead of ARP. In an RARP request, the frame is again broadcast to all stations as shown in Fig. 4.13. Only stations that are configured as RARP servers will respond to the request. If more than one RARP server exists on the network, the requesting station will accept only the first reply and discard the rest. The RARP server uses a table that keeps a map of the hardware-to-IP address associations. As the RARP server scans the table and finds the matching hardware address, it places the IP address in the protocol address field of the RARP packet and sends back the reply. The station can then proceed to use IP services as it normally would.

4.9   Internet Control Message Protocol (ICMP)

The Internet Control Message Protocol (ICMP) is as close as IP gets to providing a network management function. ICMP is used by the router or destination

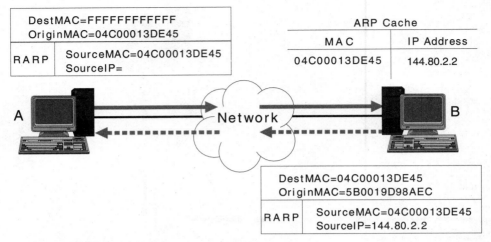

Figure 4.13   RARP function and usage.

station in two ways: to report operational problems to the source station and to obtain network diagnostic information.

ICMP is a requirement of any station or device participating in an IP network. ICMP in no way makes IP more reliable. ICMP can be viewed as a feedback mechanism for intelligence at the IP stations to interpret network issues. Figure 4.14 details the ICMP message format. This ICMP message is placed in the data area of the IP datagram. The type field identifies thirteen functions possible with an ICMP message. These types are:

0	Echo reply
3	Destination unreachable
4	Source quench
5	Redirect
8	Echo
9	Router advertisement
10	Router solicitation
11	Time exceeded
12	Parameter problem

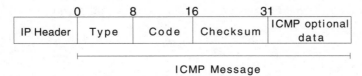

Figure 4.14   ICMP message format.

13   Timestamp

14   Timestamp reply

15   Information request

16   Information reply

The two most widely used and known ICMP messages are destination unreachable and echo/echo reply. As shown in the example depicted in Fig. 4.15, station A sends an IP datagram to station B. Station A's router receives the message and attempts to determine the appropriate route for delivering the data to station B. However, the router is not aware of the IP network address for station B and replies back to station A with a destination unreachable ICMP message. For this type of ICMP message the ICMP code field further delineates the reason. The values possible in the code field for destination unreachable are:

0   Network unreachable

1   Host unreachable

2   Protocol unreachable

3   Port unreachable

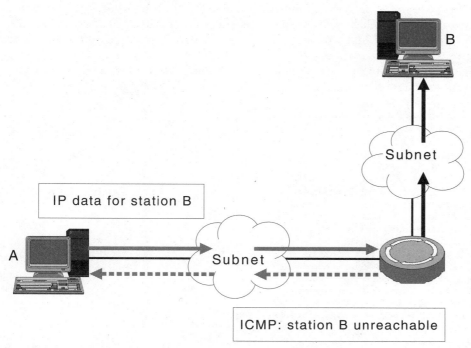

Figure 4.15   ICMP destination unreachable example.

4   Fragmentation needed and DF set

5   Source route failed

One of the most commonly used IP functions for determining connectivity between stations and networks is the ICMP echo function. The echo function of ICMP is basically a test message that is returned to the sending station. A most popular debugging tool for IP called Packet Internet Groper (PING) is, in fact, a program that utilizes the ICMP echo function. The PING function allows the network administrator to set a message size, destination IP station, and number of echo requests for debugging network connectivity. The PING program provides identifiers, sequence numbers to match the requests and replies, as well as simple statistics after the program has completed. The statistics provide the number of packets transmitted, total packets received back from the destination station, a percentage of packet loss, and the minimum, average, and maximum round-trip time in milliseconds. These statistics can provide an inroad to the health and stability of the network. Figure 4.16 provides a sample output from the PING program.

4.10   Transmission Control Protocol (TCP)

TCP provides a valuable piece of networking that is not provided by IP: a guaranteed sequential delivery of message units. The TCP message unit format is called a *segment*. Each TCP segment is made up of a TCP header and a data field. Figure 4.17 illustrates a TCP segment which begins with the source and destination port identifiers.

Ports in TCP can be viewed as identifiers for applications. Each TCP application is assigned or selects a port number. In TCP/IP the standard or well-

```
ping hq.company.com
hq.company.com is alive
ping hq.company.com: 100 data bytes
100 bytes from 34.82.0.1:icmp-seq=0 time=20ms
100 bytes from 34.82.0.1:icmp-seq=1 time=20ms
100 bytes from 34.82.0.1:icmp-seq=2 time=60ms
100 bytes from 34.82.0.1:icmp-seq=3 time=10ms
100 bytes from 34.82.0.1:icmp-seq=4 time=40ms
100 bytes from 34.82.0.1:icmp-seq=5 time=60ms
100 bytes from 34.82.0.1:icmp-seq=6 time=20ms
100 bytes from 34.82.0.1:icmp-seq=7 time=20ms
100 bytes from 34.82.0.1:icmp-seq=8 time=80ms
100 bytes from 34.82.0.1:icmp-seq=9 time=100ms
100 bytes from 34.82.0.1:icmp-seq=10 time=20ms
—hq.company.com ping statistics—
10 packets transmitted, 10 packets received, 0% packet loss
round-trip (ms) min/avg/max = 10/45/100
```

Figure 4.16   Example of PING program output.

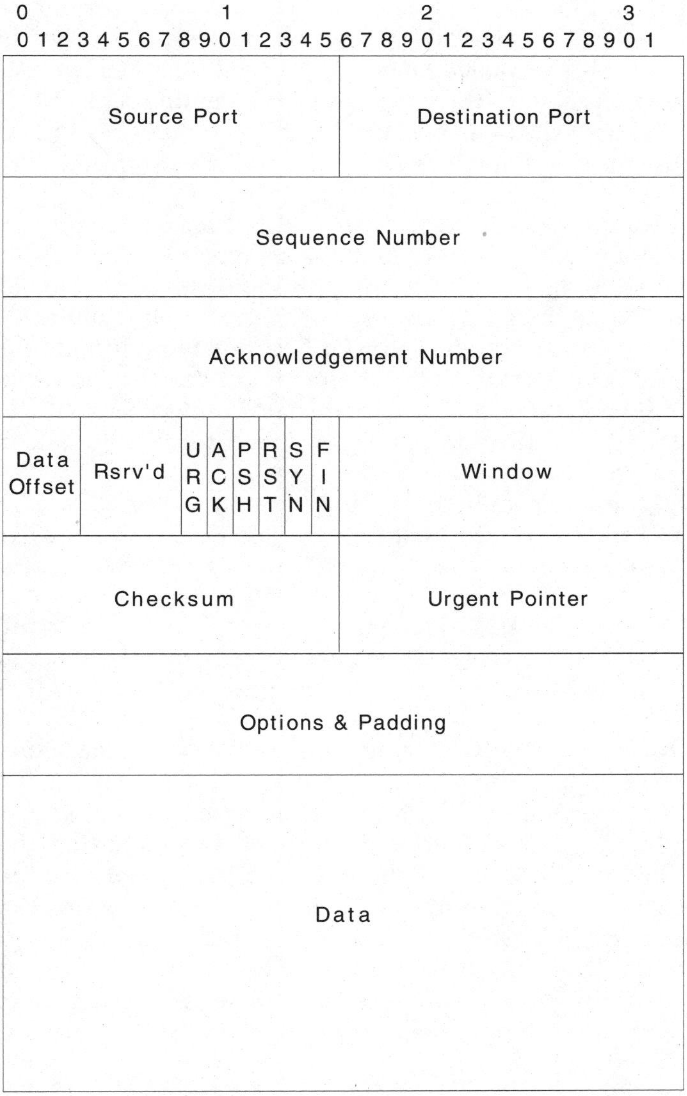

```
0                   1                   2                   3
0 1 2 3 4 5 6 7 8 9 0 1 2 3 4 5 6 7 8 9 0 1 2 3 4 5 6 7 8 9 0 1
```

Source Port		Destination Port	
Sequence Number			
Acknowledgement Number			
Data Offset	Rsrv'd	U R G / A C K / P S H / R S T / S Y N / F I N	Window
Checksum		Urgent Pointer	
Options & Padding			
Data			

Figure 4.17 Format of the TCP segment.

known applications, like File Transfer Protocol (FTP), are given standard port numbers that no other application can use. For example, FTP is always port number 21. Each Port Number field in the TCP header is 2 octets in length. As can be seen from the Fig. 4.17, the source and destination port values take up the first 4 octets of the TCP header following the port number identifiers is the Sequence Number field. Just as in SNA, the sequence number identifies the position of this TCP segment in relation to the other outgoing segments found in the data stream. This sequence number field is 4 octets in length. The next field is the *Acknowledgment* (ACK) field. The ACK identifier indicates the sequence number of the expected next incoming segment. If the ACK number field is entered, then the ACK indicator field is set to a 1. The Sequence and ACK number fields are equivalent to the N(s) and N(r) fields in SNA/SDLC.

The *Data Offset* field contains the length of the TCP header. This field is 4 bits in length and measures the TCP header in 32-bit increments. The header must end on a 32-bit boundary and, hence, the options and padding field found at the end of the header is used to pad the header out to the 32-bit boundary.

The *Urgent* (URG) field is set to a 1 when the data contains urgent data for the TCP application. The TCP applications locate the urgent data by the value placed in the *Urgent Pointer* field. This value points to the last octet of the urgent data. Any data found after this location is ignored. A terminal break or interrupt is often sent as urgent data.

The *Window* field is the number of bytes, beginning with the Acknowledgment Number field, that can be received by this host. This field is continually updated as the host determines the number of bytes that it can receive into its buffers.

The PUSH flag that follows the ACK flag, when set to a 1 indicates to the receiving TCP host that once TCP receives the segment it is to deliver the data to the destined application identified by the destination port number field in a timely manner.

Connections are aborted when the REST flag is set to a 1. It is also sometimes used in response to a segment error.

Connections are closed by setting the FIN bit to a 1 in disconnect messages.

The Checksum field in the TCP header is determined by computing the length of the TCP header and the length of the data. Incoming segments are validated by using this computation and then verifying the results against the value found in the Checksum field. If the values do not match, then the segment is discarded. Note that the Checksum field itself is also included in the calculation, since it resides in the header. Also realize that this checksum value is at the Transport layer. IP also performs a checksum at the Network or the Data Link layer as well.

4.10.1 Sliding windows

Flow control between two connecting stations using TCP is accomplished using a *window* mechanism. A window is an expression used for communications protocols to determine the number of units that can be transmitted to the receiver from the sender before the sender can expect an acknowledgment that the receiver has indeed received the units, unabated. For most protocols the unit in question is either a frame or a packet.

TCP uses a byte-stream connection with sequence numbers assigned to each byte. This byte stream is broken up into segments for transmission. The window size in TCP is not based on segments but on bytes. The value of the window size is found in the Window field of the TCP header. This window-size value is determined at connection establishment. The ACK sent back to the sender identifies the sequence number of the byte received. Each ACK message will include the size of the window the receiver is ready to handle on the next transfer. The sending station must receive an acknowledgment for each sequence number prior to sliding the window to allow the data to be transmitted.

As the sends and receives occur, the window slides on the outbound buffer till all the data has been sent and acknowledged. In Fig. 4.18, station A has already sent three segments to station B. At connection time, station B set the window size to a value of 8. As station B begins acknowledging sequence number 1 through 3, sequence numbers 4 through 8 are received and acknowledgment of these continues. As an ACK for sequence number 1 is received, the sender slides the window to include sequence number 9. The window does not slide until each outstanding sequence number has been acknowledged.

Using this technique, TCP can ensure a reliable transmission. Retransmission of a sequence number due to a lost segment or damaged segment will not allow the window to slide. Although the receiving station may accept sequence numbers out of sequence it will not allow the window to slide until all the sequence numbers have been received. For example, in Fig. 4.19 station B received sequence numbers 1, 2, 4, 5, and 6. Sequence number 3 has not been delivered to station B. Station B, however, will send an ACK for 4, 5, and 6 but indicate that the last received sequence number was 2. Sending station A will eventually time-out the acknowledgment for sequence number 3 and then send it again. This time, station B receives it and sends an ACK with the sequence number of 6, indicating that all six have been received and the window can now slide forward.

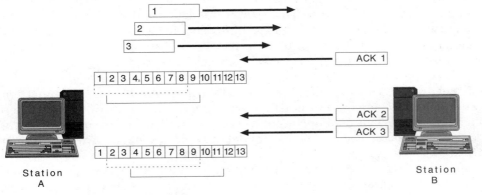

Figure 4.18 Depiction of sliding window.

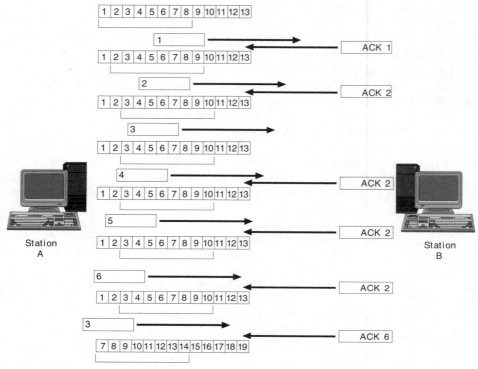

Figure 4.19 TCP technique for ordered sequence transmission.

4.10.2 Slow-start congestion avoidance

The sliding-window algorithm works but has been known to have some issues with timing and congestion. For one, the sender can immediately flood the network with messages for a specific station, overrunning the station and poorly using its own output buffers. This type of problem has been corrected using a slow-start congestion-avoidance algorithm. This algorithm was developed by Van Jacobson in 1988. It is in place in today's TCP standards. This new algorithm places the onus of sizing the window on the sender and not the receiver. When the connection between the stations is established, the sending station will set a small window size of 1, allowing for a low data rate. As the connection progresses, the window size is increased by twice the number of acknowledgments received. This doubling is governed by either transmission errors or statistical processing of acknowledgment delay. The delay is measured by keeping track of the *round-trip time* (RTT) for the sender to receive the acknowledgment. The average and standard deviation of the acknowledgments is measured at the beginning of the transmission. As the RTT begins to increase past the average and standard deviation and the window or a network error is observed, the window will be decreased to 1 immediately. The optimal window size is determined by the sender noting the window size in use at the time of the congestion or error and halving it. This enables efficient retransmission due to many different types of network conditions.

4.11   IP Next Generation (IPng)

The Internet, E-mail, and one of the most popular applications residing on it, World Wide Web (www), have been publicized in papers, journals, magazines, and on news programs to the point where these technologies have become celebrities. The result of this is a sudden flood of requests for Internet access resulting in a strain on the Internet in both addressing and bandwidth utilization.

Corporations are beginning to use the Internet to conduct business not only with customers but with its own locations. A main reason for this is the cost effectiveness of using a public utility like the Internet is less expensive than private networks. So, as these corporations begin to push the envelope and try to capture virtual markets through the Internet, they require a quality of service for their applications.

These new networking requirements prompted the Internet Engineering Task Force (IETF) to provide solutions. The outcome is IPv6. The celebrity name for this new IP standard is IP Next Generation (IPng).

4.11.1   IPng addressing

The current IP is version 4. This version uses the standard IP addressing scheme published in 1978. IPv4 uses a fixed 32-bit addressing scheme. At the time it was thought that a 32-bit address would be more than enough for supporting the Internet and the hosts attached to it. However, since 1978 and the corporate embrace, the popularity of the Internet has grown to worldwide proportions and address space is in danger of being depleted.

Recall that IPv4 addresses are assigned based on classes and that each network address is registered to avoid duplication. IETF members began pondering this problem four years ago and began work on providing relief to this addressing constraint. If the current addressing space were not modified to allow for more growth, it is estimated that the Internet would exhaust its available addresses by the year 2004. Other estimates are less optimistic, sighting 1999, and still others give a greater leniency by estimating the year 2008. In any case, the IETF members have come up with a new version of IP addressing to solve the address-depletion problem.

What the IETF has decided on is expanding the IPv4 address from 32-bits to 128-bits. Alignment for the address remains on a 32-bit memory boundary, which is important for programming. This addressing space provides for approximately 18 billion IP addresses. Depletion will no longer be an issue with IPv6. For IPv6 to accommodate this new addressing scheme the IETF had to redefine the IP header.

4.11.2   IPng header

The IPv6 header is defined not only to accommodate the new features of IP but also to coexist with IPv4. Figure 4.20 compares the IPv4 and IPv6 header formats. The IETF provides space in the IPv6 header for 128-bit addresses by removing some of the IPv4 fields that were either reserved, never used, or considered optional. For example, the options field in the IPv4 header can span 40 bytes on its own. Removing this field provides ample space for two 128-bit addresses. A new field that is found in the IPv6 header is the Flow Label. This field provides IPv6 with the other requirement: providing QoS.

The Flow Label is a 28-bit field divided into two areas: a 4-bit traffic class (TCLASS) subfield and a 24-bit Flow Identifier (FLOWID) field. The FLOWID subfield provides a unique ID to the flow of sequenced packets from the source to the destination for this particular QoS. The 4 bits of the TCLASS subfield provide the first means of IP supporting a true QoS function. Figure 4.21 illustrates the format of the Flow Label and the breakdown of the TCLASS subfield. The values in the TCLASS are listed and defined in an ascending order which correlates with low to high QoS. As with most, if not all network protocols, message units carrying network operational and diagnostic information is provided with the best possible QoS. IPv6 enables the QoS to be determined on a hop-by-hop basis using the TCLASS bits. For a more guaranteed QoS, IPv6 can set up the QoS during connection establishment between the source and destination stations prior to transmission by reserving network resources. This resource reservation is accomplished using the Resource Reservation Protocol (RSVP).

4.12   RSVP and Integrated Services

TCP/IP networks to date have relied on the best-effort model. There are no implicit or explicit guarantees that the data packets will be delivered in a timely fashion or even delivered at all. If something happens in the network and the packets are lost or delayed, then it is up to the end station and its underlying mechanisms to resolve the situation. A TCP/IP workstation that has detected congestion or the loss of packets will retransmit the data. Data is transported through the network on a best-effort basis.

This is satisfactory for the current breed of applications such as E-mail and FTP. These applications do not depend on the data reaching the destination within a specified amount of time. These applications do not require a minimum amount of bandwidth. In fact, whatever bandwidth is available will suffice.

The introduction of multimedia applications has placed new demands on the network. These applications providing video on demand, audio, desktop conferencing, and audio/video multicasting require a network that can deliver

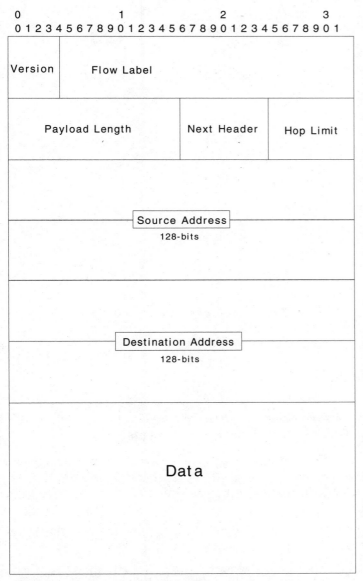

Figure 4.20 Comparison of IPv4 and IPv6 header formats.

data from the source to the destination(s) within a certain period of time. The network, in fact, must ensure that there are sufficient resources in terms of bandwidth, buffers, and so on to service the needs of these applications. At the same time this should not be done at the expense of the traditional best-effort data traffic.

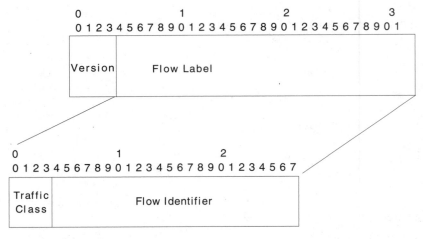

0 - Uncharacterized traffic
1 - "Filler" traffic
2 - Unattended data transfer
3 - Reserved
4 - Attended bulk data transfer
5 - Reserved
6 - Interactive traffic
7 - Internet controller traffic (e.g., SNMP, IGPs)
15 - Highest QoS

Figure 4.21   Format of the IPv6 Flow Label format.

Solving the problem of supporting both real-time and best-effort data traffic in TCP/IP networks introduces several basic requirements:

- *Resource reservation.*   Applications must have a way of telling the network how much bandwidth and delay they need to operate. The network, in turn, should be able to check its available resources and either accept or deny the application's request.

- *Traffic control.*   The network should identify the application data flows and then deliver the requested levels of network resources.

To address these requirements the IETF is developing the Integrated Services Architecture (ISA). ISA is an enhancement to the current best-effort model that will enable TCP/IP networks to deliver QoS guarantees to those applications that request them. There are two separate but very related efforts under way to develop and define the mechanisms that comprise ISA:

- Integrated Services
- RSVP

ISA introduces the concept of a flow. A *flow* is a series of packets with a common source, destination, and QoS. To deliver a requested level of service to an application, it is necessary to install flow-specific state in the network. This enables an ISA network to distinguish between flows that request resources and those that do not.

4.12.1 Integrated Services

Integrated Services defines several functional elements that are incorporated in hosts and routers that support ISA:

- *Reservation setup protocol.* This is used by hosts and routers to reserve resources along a path between the two endpoints.
- *Admission control.* This is used by hosts and routers to determine if they can accept or deny the reservation request.
- *Classifier.* This is used by hosts and routers to identify and map packets to a specific service class. A *service class* is a broad classification of network services that a specific flow can fall under. Two examples might be real time and best-effort.
- *Scheduler.* This is used by hosts and routers to schedule packets on the outgoing link, based on their service class and associated priority.

The traffic characteristics of a flow are defined in the traffic specification or Tspec. A Tspec takes the form of a token bucket consisting of a token rate equal to r and a bucket size equal to b. Essentially the r parameter specifies a sustainable data rate and the b parameter specifies the extent to which the data rate can exceed the sustainable rate for a period of time.

The QoS level for a flow is defined in the service-request specification or Rspec. The Rspec might contain a service class, a maximum delay, or other associated service parameters.

4.12.2 RSVP

RSVP stands for Resource Reservation Protocol (or some variant). RSVP is the reservation-setup protocol defined in ISA. RSVP is a signaling, not a routing protocol. It is used by a host, on behalf of an application data stream, to request a specific level of service from the network. RSVP is also used by routers to deliver service requests to all routers along the route from the source to the destination and to maintain these resource reservations once they have been accepted.

The RSVP protocol defines two basic messages: PATH and RESV. A sending application that is RSVP-capable will first send a PATH message into the network and address it to the destination. (It is the receiver of the data flow and not the sender who is responsible for issuing reservation requests.) The destination can be a unicast or multicast address. The RSVP PATH message is forwarded to the destination using normal IP unicast or multicast routing protocols (e.g., RIP, OSPF, MOSPF).

The PATH message is used by the sender to establish a path from the sender to the receiver. As the PATH message traverses the network, each router along the way will record the upstream IP address from where it originated. The router may also update the PATH message with information about its own resources. In addition, the PATH message contains a description of the sender's Tspec. Once the PATH arrives at the destination, the receiver has a specific path to follow back to the sender and a pretty good idea about the available network resources.

At this point the receiver may issue an RSVP RESV message. This message contains a *flow specification* (flowspec). A flowspec carries a reservation request (receiver's Tspec and Rspec) that is generated by the receiver. In addition, the RESV message will carry a filterspec which is used by the routers along the path to identify which packets will receive the requested QoS.

The RESV flows upstream toward the sender and follows the reverse path of that taken by the PATH message. Along the way, each router will invoke admission control and determine if it can support the requested level of service. If so, then it will update the classifier with the filterspec and the scheduler with the flowspec. Once the sender receives the RESV message, it will begin transmitting data. The data flows over the same path that the PATH and RESV messages took.

The features of RSVP can be summarized in the following:

- Supports both unicast and multicast IP flows.
- Makes reservations for unidirectional data flows.
- Receiver of data flow issues reservation requests.
- Receiver heterogeneity. Different receives can request and receive different QoS levels from the network for the same IP multicast flow.
- Maintains soft state in routers. If reservations time out or a route changes packets will continue to flow over best-effort path to destination.
- Supports several reservation styles that enable in some cases multiple reservations to be merged into a single reservation, thus better utilizing network resources.
- Supports both IPv4 and IPv6.

4.13 Summary

There are two basic types of networking protocols: trusted and best-effort. Connection-oriented networks are trusted for use with applications requiring sequencing-of-information message units. Connectionless networks use a best-effort approach and are employed by applications not concerned with sequential delivery of data. The connections made by these networks are predicated on a network addressing scheme and the ability to route the information between the source and destination. Internet Protocol (IP) has become the defacto standard for the routing between source and destination. Its popularity has grown such that its current incarnation will not provide the expected address requirements for the near future, fostering the need for a new IP standard. The IP IPv6 provides for an address space almost 4.5 times that of the current IP, thus enhancing the service given to various applications by applying a QoS. The QoS is enhanced even more with the use of RSVP. Using RSVP connections between IP stations can guarantee minimal service requirements that best fit the applications needs.

Routing Protocols

The movement of data between source and destination is accomplished by means of routing. In the multiprotocol world of networking the routing is performed by means of a routing protocol. There are four types of *routing algorithms* in use today. *Static* routing is a nondynamic and requires operational intervention for the network administrators and operators to circumvent a network outage or event. *Distance vector* routing algorithms offer a dynamic but simplistic way of computing the best path between the source and destination based on hop counts (distance). *Link-state* routing algorithms employ the concept of a distributed map: each routing node in the network has a complete copy of the network database allowing the selection of the shortest path first. *Interdomain* routing allows for the division of a large singular network into smaller autonomous systems. Each of these routing protocols has grown, developed, and borrowed useful concepts from each other.

5.1 Static Routing

Static routing may be the preferred routing mechanism for very small networks. Figure 5.1 illustrates a small static routing network. As you can see from the figure, each router is told how to get to the other subnets in the network through specific definitions. For example, router A knows it can get to subnet 212.21.22.0 via interface 1. Also note that a default gateway has been defined in each routing node. The default gateway is often referred to as the gateway of last resort. This means that if for some reason the destination subnet is either not found in the static routing table or if the static defined route is for some reason not usable, the router will forward the packet through the default gateway definition.

Since each routing node on the network may have a direct connection to the other node, static routing seems suitable for both defining the specific routes

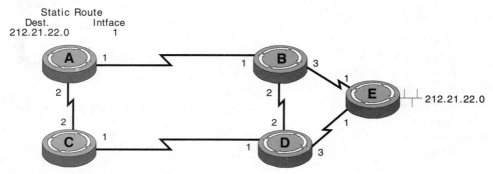

Figure 5.1 Small static routing network.

and for reduced traffic overhead. But as the number of routing nodes grows with the size of the network, static routing may become an administrative nightmare due to its operational intervention constraints and lack of dynamic change. Though the disadvantage to static routing is the manual reconfiguration of routing tables with the addition or deletion of network resources, it can play an important role in providing a backup route for switched connections or to networks defined with passive interfaces. Figure 5.2 diagrams this configuration. A *passive interface* is one that will receive routing table updates in a dynamic routing network but will not broadcast its own routing table through the interface. These situations are usually those where the router is referred to as a *stub*. A stub router is one that connects only to one other router. It is usually defined at remote locations with a single communications link and attaches an office LAN to the backbone WAN.

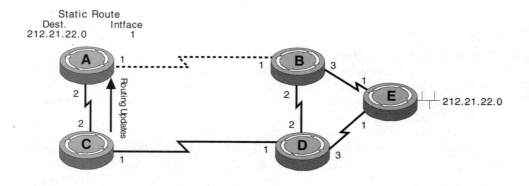

Figure 5.2 Diagram depicting the use of a static route for a switched connection.

5.2 Distance Vector Routing

Distance vector routing protocols have their roots in the Bellman-Ford algorithm. This elegant algorithm provides for a simple means of routing nodes to determine the distance from itself to every other routing node in the network. This distance value is determined using the routing information at the routing node and combining it with the information received from neighboring nodes. The vector identifies which interface on the routing node is the direction of the destination network.

In a distance vector algorithm there is the destination network, the interface, and the cost associated with sending the packet to the destination through an interface. This cost is measured by the number of links or hops that must be traversed between the source and destination. Each hop or link is assigned a cost. The cost is some arbitrary number that identifies the distance between a routing node and its neighbors. The value used is usually 1. Using Fig. 5.3 we can gain an appreciation of the simplicity of the algorithm. Each router in the network will go through the following steps to calculate its routing table:

1. Each routing node is identified with its own unique identifier. This could be a name or an address.

2. A cost for each link attached to the routing node is assigned. This can be a fixed cost like the value of 1 or a calculated cost based on various parameters such as hops, bandwidth, delay, or interface.

3. The first entry in the routing table is a route to itself with a cost of 0.

4. As each link is activated, the routing node sends a distance vector message to each of its directly attached neighbors. Distance vector messages will also be sent whenever there is a change in the links or connections or on a periodic basis.

5. The distance vector messages are saved by each routing node as they are received from the neighboring ones.

6. The routing node calculates its own distance to the destinations identified in the distance vector message by determining the minimal cost. The minimal cost is calculated by adding, in turn, the link cost of the hop associated with the neighboring routing node and the cost received from the neighboring routing node for the destination. The lowest-cost route is the preferred route for the destination.

7. The routing node will recalculate the distance vector when either a neighboring routing node sends a distance vector message that contains different information than before or when a link has been subtracted or added between the routing node and its neighbor.

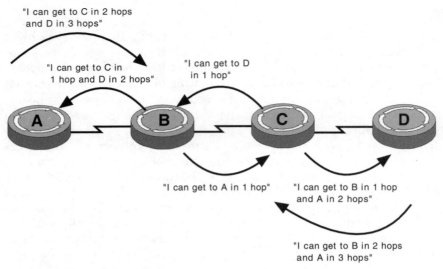

"I can get to C in 2 hops
and D in 3 hops"

"I can get to C in
1 hop and D in 2 hops"

"I can get to D
in 1 hop"

"I can get to A in 1 hop"

"I can get to B in 1 hop
and A in 2 hops"

"I can get to B in 2 hops
and A in 3 hops"

Figure 5.3   Diagram of a distance vector routing topology.

Distance vector routing can be viewed as a *hear-say* algorithm. No routing node in the network will know about other routers until it has heard how to get to the other routers from its neighbors. For instance, if the direct route to A from D is through C, D hears of it from C. In turn, C hears from B which is directly attached to A. The reverse is true for A learning that the direct route to D is via B-C-D. The simplicity of distance vector has made it a favorite for coding, however, its need to determine preferred routes based on the neighbors information causes a slow convergence of the routing tables.

Convergence is the process of settling down the stable routing information that is used for the network. A distance vector routing protocol may take a long time to converge. Figure 5.4 diagrams a simple topology to help explain slow convergence on distance vector protocols. In this topology R1 is connected to R2 which in turn is connected to R3. To establish a baseline, let's view the distance vector from the point of R3. R3, as described above, will establish its own distance as 0. Assuming the cost value is based on hops, each link in the topology has a cost of 1. Therefore, R2 calculates its distance to R3 as a cost of 1. R1 calculates its distance to R3 as a cost of 2.

Typically, outages will occur in any network. If connectivity between R2 and R3 should fail for any reason, R2 must recalculate its distance vector to R3. R2

Figure 5.4   Topology used for illustrating convergence with distance vector protocols.

will delete the current distance vector entry in the routing table for R3. However, R2 does not completely disregard the existence of R3. This is because R2 has knowledge that R1 is the distance of 2 from R3. Knowing this, R2 recalculates the distance to R3 by adding the distance of 1, which is the distance between R1 and R2, with the distance for R1 to get to R3, which is 2. R2 adds to its routing table a distance vector entry of 3 for R3 through R1. R2 will not send its updated routing table to R1. R1 receives the routing table update and determines that the route to R3 from R2 has been modified. R1 will then recalculate the distance to R3 through R2 with a cost of 4 (R2's cost of 3 plus the cost of the link (1) between R1 and R2). R1 then sends its updated table to R2 and the process continues. This iterative process is what is known in a distance vector algorithm as counting to infinity.

Counting to infinity is a term used in distance vector algorithms but may not actually be the outcome. In reality you will never reach infinity, therefore, the table updates will never end. Most distance vector routing protocols will define infinity with a parameter value. The value is usually set to a low number, for instance 16 or 20, if the protocol is based solely on hop counts. Still others may multiply the largest link cost by a factor of 20 if the cost is based on more than just the hop count. Either way the routing software for distance vector algorithms will actually reach infinity. Once reaching infinity, the routing node will mark the destination network as unreachable.

During the counting to infinity process, network source stations connected to the subnets of R1 and R2 may still send packets destined for a network on R3. The result is what is called the *bouncing effect*. This bouncing effect is, in fact, a routing loop, for R1 packets destined for R3 are sent to R2. Once the packet reaches R2, it will send it back to R1 because it is the best path to R3 from R2. Again, we are seeing an iterative process where the packet will go back and forth between the R1 and R2, using up bandwidth with no real destination available. Eventually, because the packets are bouncing back and forth, the time-to-live (TTL) timer will expire and the routing node will discard the packet.

The effects of counting to infinity and bouncing can create havoc on a large, distance vector routing network. The iterative process of recalculating distance vectors causes delay in the routing node because each node can only go through the recalculation process upon receiving information from its neighbor nodes. This delay allows more packets to enter the network that may end up in the bouncing effect, utilizing routing node processing and network bandwidth. One popular technique for alleviating the slow convergence, counting to infinity, and bouncing is called *split horizon*.

The main contribution of the split horizon technique is to not tell R2 that R1 can get to R3 through R2. The rule being that: if R1 is routing packets to Rx through R2, then do not tell R2 that Rx can be reached through R1. Remember, in distance vector routing table updates the whole table is sent. Thus, R1, as shown above, without using split horizon would tell R2 that it can get to Rx through R1. This results in the routing nodes broadcasting what can be considered uncompleted routing tables because of the use of split horizon.

There are actually two versions of split horizon as shown in Fig. 5.5. The simple form omits any information about destinations routed over the neighbors link. The second form is known as split horizon with poisonous reverse. This poisonous reverse form of split horizon has the routing nodes sending the entire routing table to its neighbors but sets the cost of destination networks to infinity for those networks that are reachable through the neighbor routing node. Using split horizon with poisonous reverse fixes the two-hop routing loop but does not correct all routing loops.

One final mechanism that is used by many of the distance vector protocols is *triggered updates*. Recall that the distance vector algorithms use a timer to periodically send the current routing table. Using a timer to send routing tables allows a routing node to send a routing table that does not reflect a new change in the network configuration. This timer adds to the slow convergence factor in distance vector routing. Triggered updates adds timers to each individual entry in the routing nodes routing table. This refresh timer is reset every time a packet matching the routing table entry passes through the routing node. If the routing node does not see a packet with the routing table entry network, it assumes that connectivity to the neighbor used to route traffic to the entry's network has failed. Each protocol uses a different length for this timer. A long timer allows the routing node to send a uninformed routing table to its neighbors. A short refresh timer does not take into account possible lost packets on the network. Lost packets can be delayed due to the network load. Triggered updates allows the distance vector routing protocol to send updates as soon as the node learns of them. In this way, convergence is faster and a more accurate representation of available routes is propagated through the

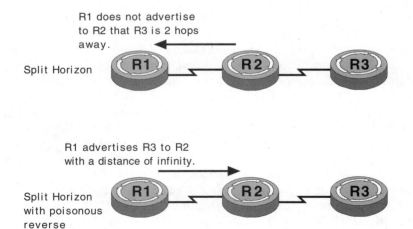

Figure 5.5   Diagram depicting the two forms of split horizon.

network. Triggered updates does not cure slow convergence but it does reduce the convergence time by reducing the time it takes to count to infinity.

The simplicity of distance vector routing algorithms has fostered many different routing protocols. The most popular of these distance vector routing protocols are Routing Information Protocol (RIP), originally developed for the BSD release of UNIX as part of the routeD program, and Interior Gateway Routing Protocol (IGRP), developed by the leading router vendor Cisco Systems.

5.2.1   Routing Information Protocol-1 (RIP-1)

In its first incarnation RIP was very basic. It provided a simple routing protocol with minimal configuration and processing overhead, which is quite suitable for a function of an operating system like UNIX. The RIP features and functions themselves were officially documented in the IETF RFC 1058 by Charles Hedrick in June 1988. RFC 1058 included RIP improvements for the use of split horizon and triggered updates. The version of RIP defined in RFC 1058 is known as RIP-1.

RIP-1 is an interior gateway protocol (IGP). IGPs are used for the exchange of information within a single network. These networks are called *autonomous systems* (AS). Figure 5.6 diagrams the RIP-1 message format. The command field is 8 bits in length. Though there are many values defined for the field implementors of RIP, consider only two values. A value of 1 indicates that this is a RIP request and a value of 2 indicates that this is a RIP response. The version field for RIP-1 is set to a 1. The version field is followed by a field that must contain all zeroes in the RIP-1 format. The address family identifier is a 2-byte field that originated from the protocols origin as a BSD-UNIX program, where the address is known as *socket address*. The field is 2 bytes in length to accom-

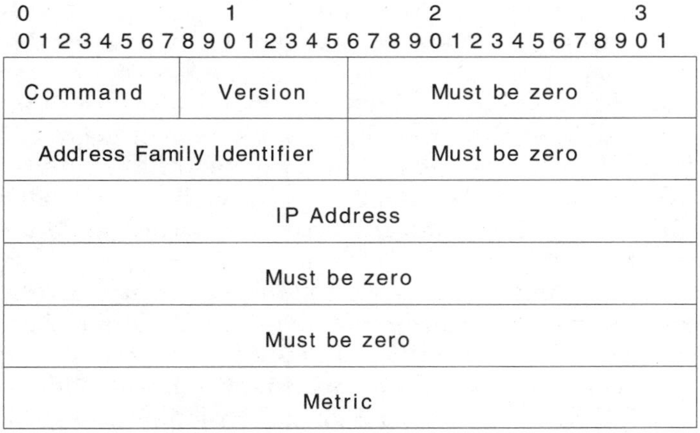

```
0                   1                   2                   3
0 1 2 3 4 5 6 7 8 9 0 1 2 3 4 5 6 7 8 9 0 1 2 3 4 5 6 7 8 9 0 1
```

Command	Version	Must be zero
Address Family Identifier		Must be zero
IP Address		
Must be zero		
Must be zero		
Metric		

Figure 5.6   Format of the RIP-1 message format.

modate large addresses that are used for Xerox Network Service (XNS) and X.25. However, RIP has been used only for IP and, hence, RIP implementations recognize only the reserved IP value of 2 and ignore all others. The next 2-byte field must contain all zeroes. This field is followed by the IP address.

The IP address field in the RIP-1 message format represents either a network, subnet, or host IP address. In RIP-1, the subnet mask is not passed in the message format. The routing node must analyze the IP address to determine its type. Recall that IP addresses are classified into three classes: A, B, and C. Each address class has a specific range. To determine the network address, the routing node must first determine the network part of the IP address field by inspecting the address and deciding where in the IP address class it belongs. Once this is determined, the subnet and host parts of the address are inspected. If the subnet and host fields are null or 0, the address represents a network entry; if it is not null or 0, the address is either a subnet or host entry. The RIP-1 code in the routing node analyzes the subnet and host fields by applying the defined subnet mask for use with this autonomous system. If the host field is null or 0, then the address is a subnet, otherwise it is an address for a specific host on the network.

RIP-1 identifies three types of reserved IP addresses. An IP address of 127.0.0.0 is reserved for a *loop-back* address to the routing node. This can be used by the routing node to determine network connectivity and congestion with the PING program. The *reserved* IP address of 0.0.0.0 is a default address when this AS connects to an external network. The final type is a *broadcast* address of 255.255.255.255. The value 255 requests all resources in the network, or subnet, to accept the packet and respond back in the case of an ICMP message.

The RIP-1 metric follows 8 bytes of zero. The RIP-1 metric uses the simplistic hop-count metric. The hop-count metric can be a value between 1 and 15, with 16 representing infinity. Should a routing entry be marked with infinity, the routing node determines that the network is unreachable and will eventually time out the entry. RIP-1 uses the standard default of 1 as the metric distance vector value for each hop. As the RIP-1 message format is reviewed, the routing node will modify its own routing table only after determining that the IP address field is a valid class A, B, or C; the network number is not 127 (the loop-back network for 127.0.0.0) or 0 (except for the default AS address of 0.0.0.0); that the host part of the address is not 255 and that the metric value is not larger than infinity or 16. If any errors are discovered in this validation check, the routing node will report it via ICMP.

At routing node initialization time or if the routing table has been manually flushed, the RIP processes send requests to each of its neighbors for a routing table update. This allows the routing node to set initial values for the routing table. The initial request to build the routing table specifies the default address of 0.0.0.0 and a metric of infinity. The receiving neighbor routing nodes will send a response containing the entire routing table. This RIP response message will vary for each interface (link) to its neighbor based on split horizon processing and subnet summarization. Once the routing node contains its completed table, normal 30-second and triggered update processes resume.

The RIP-1 message is supported on both point-to-point links and broadcast networks such as Ethernet and Token-Ring. The RIP messages are transported using the connectionless best effort User Datagram Protocol (UDP) on IP. The RIP-1 specifications dictate that the routing table be transmitted every 30 seconds to its neighbors. This message is considered a response message. Each message can be a maximum of 512 bytes in length. This maximum size will contain up to 25 entries. If the RIP routing table is greater than 25 entries, multiple RIP messages will be sent. If the update is sent because of a triggered update, only entries that have been changed since the last 30-second interval will be sent. The UDP source address is always the IP address of the sender.

The RIP messages are processed on UDP port 520 for sending and receiving. This socket address was important in its early selection because it provided system protection with BSD-UNIX. The use of port 520 allowed protection in a pure BSD-UNIX environment, since only privileged users (i.e., applications and end users) could send or receive on this port. In the LAN and remote access environments of today, any user that can send a UDP message on port 520 will be considered a neighboring routing node by the receiving routing node. RIP-1, because of its early roots in homogeneous BSD-UNIX environments, does not have built-in authentication.

5.2.2 Routing Information Protocol-2 (RIP-2)

Since RFC 1058 was accepted as the standard for RIP it has not been improved on until recently. This improvement is documented in RFC 1037, RFC 1388 by Gary Malkin and is referred to as RIP-2. RIP-2 defines improvements to RIP-1 in the areas of subnet masking, authentication, and support for multicasting.

RIP-2 provides much of its enhancements by utilizing the must be zero fields in the RIP-1 message format. As shown in Fig. 5.7, RIP-2 replaces these four fields with useful information. As in the RIP-1 message format, the command, version, address family identifier, IP address, and metric fields remain intact. Under RIP-2, the version field value is 2. The address family identifier has an added value to indicate the message as one for authentication.

In a routed network using the RIP-1 specifications, the subnet mask must be defined in all routing nodes, since the RIP-1 message format does not supply this information. Consequently, a RIP-1 network can properly interrogate addresses from its own network. In RIP-2, the subnet mask is passed in the RIP-2 message format. Passing the mask allows the RIP-2 routing node to support multiple networks each having different subnet masks. For instance, in Figure 5.7 a public class A network address of 10 is used. Routing nodes R1 and R2 use a subnet mask of 255.255.0.0 while R3 and R4 use 255.255.255.0 as

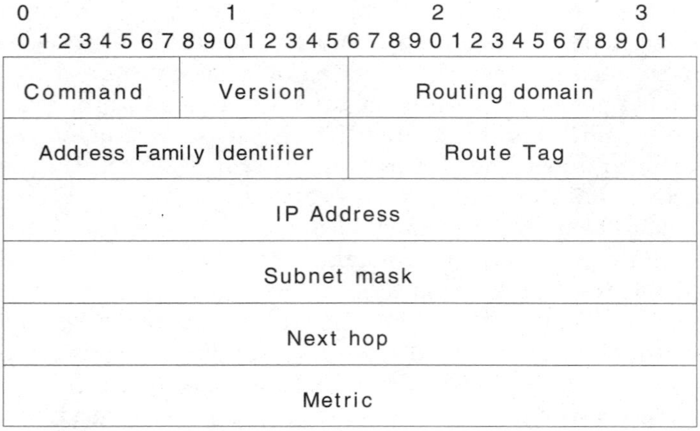

```
0                   1                   2                   3
0 1 2 3 4 5 6 7 8 9 0 1 2 3 4 5 6 7 8 9 0 1 2 3 4 5 6 7 8 9 0 1
```

Command	Version	Routing domain
Address Family Identifier		Route Tag
IP Address		
Subnet mask		
Next hop		
Metric		

Figure 5.7   RIP-2 message format.

their subnet mask. In a RIP-1 networking environment, R1 and R2 cannot transmit messages for stations on the 255.255.255.0 networks. Likewise, R3 and R4 cannot transmit messages for stations on the 255.255.0.0 subnets. RIP-2's inclusion of the subnet mask for the IP address allows the routing node to properly interpret the address so that the message can be delivered to the appropriate station. This support for carrying the subnet mask in the RIP message was spawned by the support for *variable length subnet mask* (VLSM) in OSPF.

RIP-1 routing nodes can be used along with RIP-2 messages because the RIP-1 code will ignore the four must be zero fields in the message when the version number is greater than 1.

RIP-2 implements authentication by having the first entry in the first packet be an authentication segment. The address field identifier is valued with 0xFFFF. The following field for the authentication segment is authentication type which indicates the type of authentication algorithm in use. The data needed for the algorithm follows. This authentication segment provides compatibility with RIP-1 because RIP-1 routing nodes will ignore the address field identifier since it is not set to 2 and process the remaining 24 entries.

Many of today's LAN environments provide for multiple autonomous systems sharing the same backbone. This is common with the use of FDDI or 100BaseT, and ATM as the backbone infrastructure. Figure 5.8 illustrates this topology. Routing nodes R1, R2, and R3 are a part of one AS, while R4, R5, and R6 are a part of a different AS. R4, however, knows of both networks and maintains a routing table for the two networks. It distinguishes these tables through the routing domain number assigned to each network. Routing nodes R1–R3 are associated with routing domain 100 and routing nodes R5 and R6 are associated with routing domain 200. The routing domain number is included by each router in the RIP-2 message routing domain field.

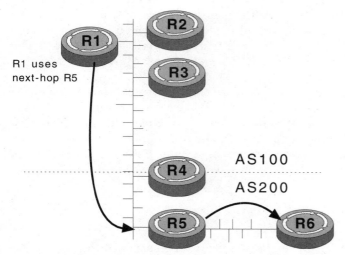

Figure 5.8   Diagram illustrating RIP-2's use of routing domain numbers and next hop.

Suppose R1 in domain 100 sends a packet destined for R6 in domain 200. R1 will send the packet to R4 since it is the nominal interface on the shared backbone to domain 200. R4 will forward the packet to R5 in domain 200. R5 will then forward the packet to R6. This routing is straightforward distance vector routing mechanics. The problem with it is that any packet from domain 100 to R6 will traverse the backbone twice.

RIP-2 employs the next-hop concept to relieve this excess on the backbone. R4 will include R5 as the next hop for R6 when advertising R6 to domain 100. The routing nodes in domain 100 will use the next-hop address (R5) instead of R4 to route packets to R6. The next-hop allows RIP-2 routing nodes to use a more efficient and direct route to destination nodes.

RIP messages are sent as broadcasts in the RIP-1 environment. This broadcast is on the MAC layer of the data link layer in the OSI Reference Model. Every adapter on the network will receive the broadcast on the MAC level and then interpret the frame for its usefulness at the station. This means that not only routers receive the RIP broadcasts but all the workstations and hubs on a shared-media environment.

RIP-2 uses the multicasting technique using a reserved IP address. IP class D address 224.0.0.9 is reserved for the RIP-2 router advertisement multicast address. To allow for compatibility with RIP-1 routing nodes, the RIP-2 specifications allow the network administrator to define to the RIP-2 routing node three modes of operations. These are:

1. Send RIP-1 packets in a broadcast mode.

2. Send RIP-2 packets in a broadcast mode.

3. Send RIP-2 packets in a multicast mode.

The first mode ensures that RIP-1 routing nodes will receive the routing advertisements. This mode is used at the onset of migrating from a RIP-1 to a RIP-2 environment. The second mode is used in a truly mixed RIP environment. The final mode of operation is when all the RIP-1 routing nodes have been migrated to RIP-2.

With all the improvements on RIP-1, RIP-2 still uses the basic hop-count algorithm to determine the best path between source and destination. This is due to the fact that RIP-2 must be backward compatible with RIP-1 routing nodes. The lack of incorporating bandwidth, delay, reliability, and load on the links still leaves the RIP distance vector algorithm with the possibility of selecting the least-optimal path between source and destination.

5.2.3 Interior Gateway Routing Protocol (IGRP)

RIP is used by all routing node vendors. It is an open standard that allows for any vendor's hardware to route with any other vendor's hardware. However, as we have discussed, RIP has some shortcomings. One of the first routing node vendors realized the RIP shortcomings and felt that it needed to provide its customer base with a more robust and tunable distance vector protocol. The company is called Cisco Systems. It developed an alternative to the open standard RIP because of the delay in updating the RIP protocol by creating what is known as Interior Gateway Routing Protocol (IGRP).

IGRP is a proprietary protocol. It is not an open standard and, hence, if it becomes the selected routing protocol for the network, you have locked your routing strategy into purchasing and maintaining Cisco routers. In the recent year, Cisco has begun marketing just its routing operating system to other vendors of network hardware as a means of providing some sort of openness and as a way for them to establish their routing operating system as the defacto standard for routing. The jury is still out on this matter, however, politics aside, IGRP does serve two purposes for networking engineers. First, it provides enhancements that cure some of RIP's ills and allows networking engineers to build large router networks with a robust routing protocol before the IETF developed the specifications for OSPF.

IGRP's robustness comes from the use of expanding the distance vector metrics to include four additional values for computation than just hop count. These are delay, bandwidth, reliability, and load.

Delay and bandwidth are determined either by the link type (e.g., Ethernet, Token-Ring, FDDI) or through network administrative definitions. Delay represents the total value of transmission delays of all the links in the path between the source and destination routers. The delay in IGRP is measured in units of 10 microseconds and expressed in 24 bits of the IGRP update message. IGRP sets the delay value to all 1s to indicate a destination is unreachable. The bandwidth metric is expressed by the number of seconds needed to transfer 10 billion bits on the link or the number of 10 millisecond time units needed to transfer a 10,000 bits message. Using a 24-bit value this allows for a bandwidth value (expressed in Kbps) to vary between 1200 bps and 10 gigabits/second (Gbps). The bandwidth metric in IGRP has the greatest effect on the optimal route decision because bandwidth is the most constraining piece of a network. Figure 5.9 illustrates the use of bandwidth with IGRP. Modifying the data rates to change optimal paths in an IGRP environment is a common routing-management technique.

Reliability and load are dynamic measurements determined by the router through link monitoring. Each is expressed as a 1 byte value with 255 meaning 100 percent. Reliability is determined through monitoring the error rates on the path. The resulting value indicates the probability of a packet reaching its destination on the path. The load is actually the utilization percentage of the link. For example, a load of 128/255 can be interpreted as a link utilization rate of 50 percent.

The load value is directly related to the bandwidth value. The network administrator may use an IGRP parameter on each link definition named BANDWIDTH. The value specified here overrides the default bandwidth associated with the link type. Increasing the BANDWIDTH parameter will change the algorithm to select the expected largest-throughput route. IGRP also employs a DELAY parameter on the link definitions. Increasing the DELAY parameter will change the algorithm to select what is perceived to be the shortest routes. Care should be taken when modifying these parameters because of their dynamic, potent, and direct influence on the best route selection process.

IGRP sends its routing table updates periodically. The default for IGRP is 90 seconds between routing table updates. As with RIP, IGRP employs the split horizon and triggered update techniques. However, it does not support split horizon with poisonous reverse. Instead, the earlier releases of IGRP used a path holddown technique. The latest releases of IGRP have replaced the path hold-down technique with route poisoning.

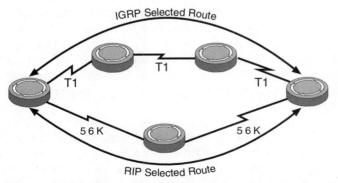

Figure 5.9 IGRP's use of bandwidth fir route determination versus RIP's use of hops.

Path hold-down technique is used by IGRP to avoid the construction of loops from a triggered update. Recall that a loop occurs when a router receives an old routing table update from a neighbor who has not yet updated its table for the failed path, causing a loop buildup in the network where some routers have the new table and some are sending the old table. The path hold-down mechanism reduces the loop buildup by prohibiting an update to the routing table for the downed destination for a period of time in the router detecting the failure. The default time is 180 seconds. This 3-minute hold-down ensures that the routing tables will all be updated properly. The downside to this is that the destination network will remain unreachable for a period of 3 minutes.

The latest versions of IGRP employ a mechanism for path hold-down called **route poisoning.** As the router receives an update from a neighbor with an increased hop-count, it will mark the route as unusable. The router will update the path as usable after it receives a follow-up update confirming the new hop count. The confirmation should happen on the periodic routing table update time of 90 seconds.

While IGRP has improved on the RIP distance vector protocol it still has a slow convergence time. IGRP may take as long a 3 minutes for the network to converge its routing tables. The slow convergence of distance vector protocols has lead to the development of a routing protocol that does not pass the entire table between neighbors, update the table, and then pass it on to the next neighbor. This new routing protocol enables each routing node to have a picture of the entire network and only updates the links between each neighbor and not the whole table. This allows for a faster convergence and lower bandwidth requirements for the routing information to be passed between routing nodes. The link state routing protocols provide a better solution to the slow convergence issue of distance vector routing protocols.

5.3   Link State

Link state routing protocols address the shortcomings of distance vector routing algorithms. This technology was first used to address routing issues in the ARPANET. Link state protocols exchange link topologies versus a distance vector protocol which exchanges distances to destinations. This topology exchange is performed by every routing node in the network, resulting in a network map. This map is considered to be distributed since each routing node has a copy of the network map. In fact, the network map is referred to as a link state database.

Link state routing protocol principles are simple in concept but may be complicated in implementation. In a distance vector routing protocol the routing node knows only of how far the destination is from itself. In a link state routing protocol the routing node can compute the exact shortest path throughout the network to the destination, based on the network map. Each network map is made up of a link state record. The link state record may contain the source node, destination node, interface identifier, the state of the link, and the cost. Using this information, each node can compute the shortest path to all other nodes in the network. Since all routing nodes have the same database, link state protocols inherently avoid looping.

The link state records are created from receiving *link state packets* (LSPs) from the routing node neighbors. But, before any routing node can receive the LSP, it must be aware that a neighbor is another routing node. Link state routing nodes accomplish this by sending a special identifying packet over the link. These identifying packets are sent on each point-to-point link and nonbroadcast networks. If the routing node is on a LAN it will send the identifying packet to a predefined group or a specific multicast IP address. The identifying packet will contain information about the greeting routing node. This information will contain the network mask of the link, a list of all known neighbors associated with the greeting router. The response is the same. In this way each neighbor router can learn of its immediate network connections.

The link state database is populated after the routing node contacts all its neighbors. But which comes first the chicken or the egg? That is, the LSPs are created based on the link state database and the link state database is created based on the LSP. This is known as recursion. In the case of link state protocols, the egg comes first; meaning the routing nodes will forward LSPs to all its neighbors as soon as:

1. A routing node discovers a new neighbor.

2. A link to a neighbor becomes inoperative.

3. The cost of a link is modified.

The sending of LSPs as soon as possible allows a link-state-based network to converge much faster than a distance-vector-based network. Link state protocols protect against a polluted database by providing a link state number and/or a time stamp on each LSP. This enables the receiving routing node to determine if it has already received this LSP. Another added protection to prevent erroneous databases and looping is the fact that the receiving router will not forward back an LSP to the sending neighbor. This algorithm is called the *flooding protocol*. The algorithm used by link state routing nodes using the flooding protocol is:

1. Receive the LSP and verify the checksum.

2. Search the database for the record.

3. If the record is not found it is a new LSP, add it to the database then forward the message to all known neighbors.

4. If the record is found, compare the link state number in the packet to the record. If the link state number in the packet is greater then replace the record and forward the LSP to the neighbors.

5. If the record is found and the link state number in the record is greater than the link state number in the packet, create an LSP from the record and send it only to the neighbor on the interface in which the original LSP was received.

6. If both numbers are equal, discard the LSP.

The link state or sequence number associated with each link state packet and record can become quite large as networks grow. The value for this number starts at 0 and is incremented by 1 with each link state change. The link state protocol dictates that this number will return to zero after reaching $2^{32} - 1$ or 4,294,967,295. Through the use of the flooding protocol, link state networks achieve a fast convergence of the routing tables, ensure a loopless environment, and allow for the complete path to be computed at the source routing node.

Link state protocols incorporate multiple metrics for computing the shortest path first. Link state algorithms use similar metrics, among which are throughput, delay, cost, and reliability. For each of the links out of the routing node several metrics must be documented and these metrics must be adhered to throughout the network to allow the routing nodes to compute different routing tables for each metric. Adhering to the used routing table metric is accomplished in a link state protocol by indicating the metric used in the LSP.

In robust networks there are many different available paths between each routing node. We have observed that RIP will arbitrarily choose a route based on the sequence in the routing table. Look at Fig. 5.10. In this figure, the path from R1 to R4 can be either through R2 or R3. Each of these paths are of equal cost, one hop from the destination. In a RIP environment, the first path found in the routing table, and only this one, from R1 to R4 will be used. This can lead to overloading links R1/R2 and R2/R4. In an IGRP environment, the path R1/R3 and R3/R4 will be used because of the higher bandwidth capacity for the R3/R4 link. Still, we see that only one path is chosen. The basic route decision process of distance vector algorithms makes poor use of network capacity.

Link state algorithms determines a faster and more efficient shortest path algorithm developed by E. W. Dijkstra. The algorithm has come to be known as

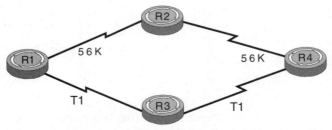

Figure 5.10 Diagram illustrating distance vector use of routing paths.

shortest-path-first (SPF). The SPF algorithm relies on several different databases. The first is the link state database, which contains the updated LSPs from each routing node. The second is the set of *evaluated paths* (PATH) for which this routing node has computed the best path to all other routing nodes. The PATH database entries consist of the node ID, path cost, and forwarding direction. A third database consists of the remaining optimal paths or a *tentative paths* (TENT) database to all the routing nodes in the network from this routing node. The final database is made up of the *ordered list of paths* (ORDERED) and is used as a forwarding database by this routing node, identifying the direction of the path.

The SPF algorithm for optimal path selection is selected as follows:

1. Initialize the PATH database to only this node. The TENT database is initialized with all other nodes. The ORDERED database contains the path for this node as its root. Each path in the ORDERED database has its cost equal to the metric value used for the link. The ORDERED database is then sorted in an ascending list with the root as its first entry. The root will have its cost and direction values set to 0.

2. If the ORDERED database is empty or the first entry has a metric value equal to infinity, then all the nodes in the TENT database are marked unreachable. The algorithm is complete.

3. For each LSP received, locate the shortest path in the ORDERED database for each interesting node indicated in the LSP. The interesting node will be the last node in the selected shortest path. If the interesting node is already in the PATH database, terminate the algorithm else the selected shortest path is optimal for the interesting node. The process moves the interesting node form the TENT to the PATH database.

4. To replace the entry in TENT for the interesting node, the process concatenates the selected shortest path and each of the links, starting from the interesting node. The new cost is the sum of the cost of the links in the shortest path selected and the metric of the link appended to the shortest path. This new path is inserted into the ORDERED database in ascending order. The algorithm returns to step 2.

The total number of paths available between any two nodes turns out to be the number of links in the network. The SPF algorithm sorts these paths to find the shortest path between the two routing nodes. Alternate paths to the destination, with almost equal costs, can be used in a link state network for providing simultaneous multiple paths between the source and destination. The alternate path is determined by examining the node prior to the interesting node (next-node) in the selected shortest path. If the cost between the source node and the node prior to the interesting node is lower, then the path to the next-node is marked as an acceptable alternate path to the destination.

There are three well-known link state routing protocols in use today. The OSI Intermediate System-Intermediate System (IS-IS), the published international standard for link state routing; the IETF Open Shortest-Path-First (OSPF) routing protocol forged by the Internet community; and finally, Enhanced IGRP, a proprietary link state protocol from Cisco Systems, based on providing the best of both distance vector and link state routing algorithms.

5.3.1   Intermediate System-Intermediate System (IS–IS)

The IS-IS link state protocol developed out of DEC Phase V DECNet. It was later accepted as the ISO standard for routing Connectionless Network Protocol (CLNP) packets for the OSI Reference Model.

As an international standard the IS-IS nomenclature is generic. In the OSI Reference Model there are systems. A router would be considered an *intermediate system* (IS) and a host is called an *end system* (ES). The notion of a network is called a *domain* and the function of routing in a network is referred to as *routing*. For clarity we will stay with the more familiar terms of routers, networks, hosts, and routing.

IS-IS divides the network into areas. Figure 5.11 illustrates the network hierarchy for IS-IS. In IS-IS these areas are referred to as *levels*. All the areas are connected with a common backbone area. The backbone area in IS-IS is known as level 2. The level 2 routers are all part of the same area. Connecting to level 2 routers are the subordinate level 1 routers. Level 2 routers manage the topologies of the level 1 routers. However, they are only concerned with connectivity to the level 1 router and not the links associated with each level 1 router. Level 1 routers keep track of all the links and nodes associated with level 1 routing. The hosts connected to a level 1 router are considered to be in an area. In IS-IS, at least one of the area's routers belongs to both level 1 and level 2 acting as a border router.

The level 1 routers learn of the hosts connected to the area supported by the level 1 router by using the End System to Intermediate System Routing (ES-IS) protocol. The ES-IS connections are noted in the link state records. Any packets destined for an area not managed by this level 1 router or another routing network are sent to the nearest level 2 router. This is usually the level 2 router directly attached to the level 1 router. Similarly, the level 2 routers will send packets to the nearest level 2 router, servicing the destined area for a packet.

IS-IS uses its own flavor of the Hello protocol to discover neighbors and to elect a designated and designated backup router on LANs. The IS-IS Hello packet contains:

1. Source identification (48-bit network layer address).
2. Circuit type characterizing the router as a level 1, level 2, or a border router.

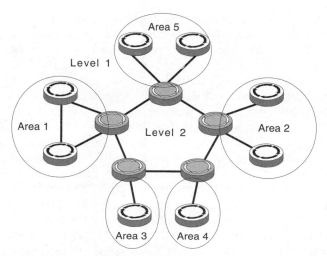

Figure 5.11   Logical view of IS-IS levels.

3. Priority code.

4. LAN identifier (7-byte field comprised of the designated router ID and a selector value assigned by the router).

5. Area address list to which the router belongs.

6. List of other router addresses connected to the LAN.

The designated router is determined by the router advertising the highest priority code in the IS-IS Hello packet. This value is defined by the router administrator. If more than one router has the same priority code, then the router with the largest source identification value becomes the designated router. The designated router sends the link state records detailing the link from the network to the other routers on the LAN. The nondesignated routers on the LAN advertise just the link to the network.

The hello packets in IS-IS have four different formats to describe: level-1 hellos, level-2 hellos, broadcast hellos, and point-to-point hellos. Point-to-point links do not negotiate a designated router. The hello packets are sent at regular intervals by the routers to determine link availability.

Flooding is the preferred protocol method in IS-IS for the passing of link state packets to each router in the network. Each router's link state records are flooded only within their area. Each record has an 8-byte LSP identifier (LSPID) made up of a 48-bit system identifier, a 1 byte pseudo-ID and an LSP record number. The pseudo-ID is used only by designated routers identifying a broadcast network. Information contained in a record may span multiple records. The first record in the sequence identifies the areas to which the router is a part. Successive LSP numbers relate the following records in the sequence. Each record is flooded independently into the area.

As each router receives an LSP from neighboring routers it compares the 32-bit sequence number in the LSP with the one found in the corresponding link state record. This sequence number can never be 0. If the new sequence number is larger or if the record is not in the database and the checksum field is valid, the LSP is added. The router then will send the LSP on to its neighbors and return an acknowledgment. The router will send its link state record to the sending neighbor should the received sequence number for a record, found in the database, be smaller than the sequence number in the LSP. Finding a matching sequence number and valid checksum in the database, the receiving router simply returns an acknowledgment to the sending neighbor. An invalid checksum indicates an error and the life of the link state record is expired.

A sending router determines LSP acknowledgment through the receipt of a sequence number message. Within this message is a set of record identifiers, sequence numbers, checksums, and lifetimes. On a point-to-point connection a sending router will continue to flood the network with the LSP until it receives a sequence number message back from its neighbor that contains the same identifier and sequence number or is replaced by a new value. Only designated routers on broadcast networks will send the sequence number message. If a nondesignated router on the broadcast network has a newer link state record it will then multicast the record onto the LAN allowing the designated router to update its own database.

The sequence number messages are also used for the exchange of records when a new adjacent router joins the network. In this case the message contains two fields that identify the starting LSP ID and the ending LSP ID. This range indicates to the neighbor the range of known links in its database. The receiving router compares this range with the link state records in its own database. Appended to the complete sequence number message is a link state entry describing each link state record known by the sending router. During adjacent contact the receiving router reviews these records and updates accordingly:

1. If the receiving router receives a link state entry whose sequence number is larger than the one found in its own database, it will update its database and flood the record to its neighbors.

2. If the receiving router receives a link state entry whose sequence number is lower than its own link state record, it will flood the network with its link state record.

3. If the receiving router finds a link state record in its database that falls within the range received from its neighbor but does not find a corresponding link state entry in the complete sequence number message, the receiving router will flood the network with each entry it has in that range but not found in the complete sequence number message.

4. If a link state entry in the complete sequence number message is not in the receivers database, it sends an acknowledgment for this entry back to the

sending router with a sequence number of 0. The 0 sequence number indicates to the original sending router a problem with the link state entry received by its neighbor and will broadcast to the network an LSP for that specific entry. This ensures that all routers will become aware of this new entry.

There may be a case where a router fails for a short period of time and receives its own link state packets flooded into the network prior to its failure. In such a case the router will receive the LSP, increase the sequence number, and flood the network with the corrected values. If in this scenario the router receives an LSP that it sent for a link that is no longer in the new database, the router will send this LSP immediately.

IS-IS has rather broad definitions. It was developed specifically for Connectionless Network Protocol (CLNP) in the OSI Reference Model. However, this protocol is not used by a majority of networks in the world. These networks utilize IP. The link state protocol developed for IP is Open Shortest Path First (OSPF).

5.3.2 Open Shortest Path First (OSPF)

The size and growth rate of IP networks warranted the IETF to develop a link state protocol. The result is published in the IETF RFC 1247. This IETF link state routing protocol standard has come to be known as Open Shortest Path First (OSPF).

OSPF is very similar to IS-IS. Both have their roots in link state algorithms, but OSPF borrowed many of its functions from IS-IS. A main difference between the two link state protocols is the network layer protocol in use. Quite naturally, OSPF uses IP as its network layer protocol. As such, the OSPF implementation uses IP addressing to provide many of its services. For example, the OSPF router identifier is an elected IP address associated with the router. Support for the designated router function on broadcast networks is used by the nondesignated routers, sending a multicast IP address of 224.0.0.6, which is the standard IP multicast address defined as *all-designated-routers*. Likewise, a designated router will use the multicast IP address 224.0.0.5 designated as *all-OSPF-routers* when flooding a broadcast network with link state information.

In addition to support for designated router and flooding, OSPF offers many other features that make it the preferred link state routing protocol:

1. Type of service routing.
2. Load balancing.
3. Partitioning large networks into smaller more manageable networks called areas.
4. Authentication for information exchange.

5. Host specific and network specific route support.

6. Designated router and backup designated router.

7. Flood protocol support.

8. Virtual links to noncontiguous areas.

9. Variable length subnet mask support.

10. Imports routing information from RIP and EGP networks.

Supporting these features requires that OSPF is a complex routing protocol and needs greater care than a distance vector configuration. To support the larger networks, OSPF divides a network into areas, as shown in Fig. 5.12, each identified with its own unique number.

The common network in OSPF is referred to as the backbone area. This is equivalent to the IS-IS level 2 network. Consequently, an OSPF backbone router is equivalent to an IS-IS level 2 router. An area number of 0.0.0.0 is always used for an OSPF backbone area. All other networks are simply considered areas and assigned unique numbers. Routers that function specifically within their area are called OSPF intra-area routers, which are IS-IS level 1 routers. In OSPF, a router that connects two areas is called an *area border router*. The notion of IP autonomous systems still exists with OSPF. Autonomous systems are connected using OSPF *autonomous system boundary* (ASB) routers. By partitioning the network into areas, OSPF limits the topology map

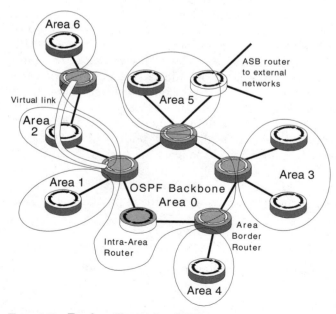

Figure 5.12   Topology illustrating OSPF networks.

required in each router. This has a positive impact on processing and memory requirements on each router and the amount of link state information being flooded into the network.

Every OSPF network must have at least one area with the 0.0.0.0 address denoting it as the backbone area. Each backbone router contains all the link state information and OSPF definition information for the entire network. This allows the backbone routers to distribute routing information between attached areas. For the most part, backbone routers are connected in such a fashion that they can form a contiguous network. In some instances, the selection of a backbone router may constitute its connectivity to the backbone through nonbackbone routers. In this type of situation a virtual link is defined between the backbone routers.

A virtual link is defined on the backbone pair but actually traverses nonbackbone routers. In order for these nonbackbone routers to deliver packets between the backbone routers on the virtual link they must be told to forward out-of-area packets to a backbone router that can then forward the packet to the destined backbone router.

Each router within the backbone provides routing functions within the backbone as well as to areas. OSPF routers responsible for routing within an area are called *intra-area* (IA) routers. Using the flooding protocol defined for link state algorithms, IA routers will send OSPF *link state advertisements* (LSAs) to only other IA routers found in the area. LSAs are equivalent to the IS-IS LSPs. If the IA router is on a broadcast link, it will also send LSAs, identifying all the routers on the broadcast network. Each IA router contains a network map of only the topology for that area.

OSPF connects areas through *area border* (AB) routers. Each AB router can connect two or more areas. Being on the border the AB router must maintain a database that reflects the topology of all the areas it interconnects. In addition, through the flooding of summary link state advertisements the IA routers learn of inter-area routes.

Connectivity to other autonomous systems is performed by OSPF *autonomous system boundary* (ASB) routers. ASB routers use external link advertisements when flooding information about the external networks connected to the OSPF network. These ASB routers also import non-OSPF routing information from such protocols like RIP, HELLO and EGP and then redistribute them as OSPF LSAs to the OSPF network.

The link state database has considerable growth when an OSPF network connects to an external network. This is due to the inclusion of the external records that describe the outside network. OSPF controls this through a final area called a *stub area* (SA). A stub area functions like any other OSPF area, except for the propagation of external routes. A stub area database contains only a default route to all the external routes. The stub area is usually a small OSPF area with one or two AB routers connecting it to the backbone area. Figure 5.13 diagrams stub areas. In order to maintain a small, link state database there are certain restrictions for a stub area:

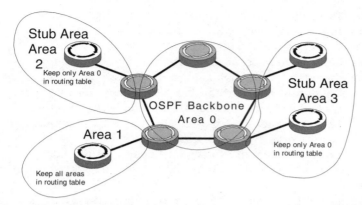

Figure 5.13   Diagram of stub areas in OSPF.

1. Stub areas cannot have an ASB router connecting to an external network.

2. Stub areas with multiple AB routers cannot choose the AB router when sending a packet outside of its area.

3. Stub areas cannot be used for configuring a virtual link.

In practice, stub areas function without a problem. However, there is often a need, due to network design requirements, to attach an external network to a stub area. An example would be the attachment of a small RIP network during a migration to OSPF. The OSPF committee researching this issue has come up with a concept called a *not-so-stubby area* (NSSA) shown in Fig. 5.14. The idea behind the NSSA is to allow the external routes to be replaced by a default route, except for selected external networks.

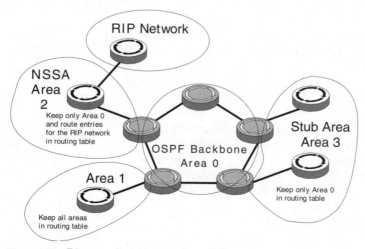

Figure 5.14   Diagram depicting a not-so-stubby area.

As in IS-IS, OSPF uses a Hello protocol to contact its neighbors. The main functions of this protocol is to verify link connectivity and the election of designated and backup OSPF routers. The activation of router interfaces causes the router to begin issuing hello packets. Each packet contains a priority field, designated router, backup designated router, and a list of neighbors. During router configuration definitions, the administrator assigns a value in the priority field (0–255) and indicates to the routing algorithm that the router can be either a designated, backup, or nondesignated router. Defining a 0 in the priority field denotes that the router sending this hello packet is not a candidate for either the designated or backup designated router.

Prior to electing the designated and backup designated routers each router must establish a two-way connection. This two-way connection between routers establishes them as being adjacent. In OSPF terms adjacent does not necessarily mean physical placement or physical connectivity. Each router determines its adjacency with the other routers by examining the neighbor list in the received hello packets. If the router finds its own router ID in the received hello packet neighbor list it can then consider the sending router an adjacent router. Otherwise the connection is considered one way and, therefore, the router cannot use the neighbor for routing or consider it in the designated router and backup designated router election process. The designated and backup router election process is as follows:

1. Each router will first transmit its hello packet with null values in the designated and backup ID fields of the hello packet. These fields contain the IP address of the router associated with the function.

2. A router will propose itself as a designated or backup router by placing its IP address in the appropriate field and then send its hello packet.

3. Each router interrogates the hello packet received from each neighbor. The router will keep a table identifying the neighbor's router ID, priority, and state of its relationship to the neighbor. Only adjacent neighbors can be elected as a designated or backup router.

4. The designated router is determined by the router ID sending hello packets with the highest priority. If there is a tie, the router with the higher router ID becomes the designated router.

5. The backup designated router is determined by the router ID sending hello packets with the highest priority. If there is a tie, the router with the higher router ID becomes the backup designated router.

The multicast IP address of 224.0.0.5 all-OSPF-routers is used to send the hello packets on point-to-point and broadcast networks. The router's IP address is used when the hello packet is used to contact a neighbor over a virtual link.

Once routers have become adjacent they must synchronize their databases. Each router goes through four states:

1. *ExStart.* Adjacency creation and the selection of the master.
2. *Exchange.* Topology database description.
3. *Loading.* The sending and receiving link state requests.
4. *Full.* Link state databases are completely exchanged and routing between the two routers can begin.

Data base synchronization is accomplished using the OSPF Exchange protocol. The first step after the creation of the adjacency is the selection of the master router. The router first to transmit in the exchange process becomes the master and the other router the slave. This protocol uses a *data description packet* (DDP). Each DDP sent from the master contains a list of records in its database and has a sequence number. The slave will respond to each DDP with an acknowledgment packet using the same sequence number received and include in this packet a data description record of its link records. During this exchange process, each router will process the link state record descriptions and compare the received link state advertisement against its own database, making a list of link state advertisements that are more up to date then in their own data base. Once the exchange process has completed, each router will issue link state requests to the other router for the most up-to-date instance of the link state advertisement. This database exchange process allows each adjacent router to have an identical topology map for routing calculation.

The SPF flooding protocol is used by OSPF to send out link state advertisements. OSPF has defined five link state types. These are:

1. Router links (type 1)
2. Network links (type 2)
3. Summary links for IP (type 3)
4. Summary links for boarder routers (type 4)
5. External links (type 5)

Router link advertisements are sent by all OSPF routers. Each advertisement describes the state of the router links in the area. Each advertisement describes the *type of service* (TOS) metrics to use when calculating routes using the link. Router link advertisements are flooded only within the area of the router.

Network link advertisements, like router link advertisements, are flooded only within the area of the router. The network link advertisement provides a list of all the routers that have formed an adjacency with the designated router on a broadcast and nonbroadcast network.

Summary advertisements are used by area border routers. Area border routers send summary links describing IP network summaries for each area border router and summary links describing routes to other area border routers. Each summary link contains a TOS metric list for use in route calculation.

External link advertisements describe routes external to this OSPF network. These advertisements are sent by AS boundary routers. The routes described with this advertisement are not comparable to the routes within the OSPF network. These advertisements include TOS metrics, however, they are not comparable to the metrics in the OSPF network.

The SPF algorithm uses the TOS metrics in its route computation. Each route is first computed for the default TOS 0. This default metric is normal service. There are a total of five TOS values that match the TOS field for IP. Figure 5.15 contains this list. OSPF contains several metrics for the specified TOS. Routers indicate their ability to participate in TOS routing by setting a support for TOS bit in the link state advertisement. Routers advertising lack of TOS support for links may result in unreachable destinations for some TOS routes. In this case, the metrics used are those for the default TOS 0. Each TOS can be assigned a metric based on bandwidth, delay, reliability, or cost. For example, bandwidth metric would be equal to 100,000,000 (100 Mb) divided by the speed of the interface, delay ends up being a function of the bandwidth, since link queues cause the longest delay; slower links have longer queues, reliability and cost can be defined from 0–65535, where 65535 is the most reliable and costly; cellular links, for instance, would have a high value for cost and a low value for reliability.

An OSPF configuration on a single router can involve specifying close to 2000 values. OSPF complexity is needed to support the large networks in place, supporting the Internet. However, some still believe in the virtues of a distance vector algorithm versus a link state algorithm. Cisco systems built extensions to their proprietary distance vector routing protocol IGRP with link state attributes and dubbed it Enhanced IGRP.

5.3.3   Enhanced-IGRP (E-IGRP)

Enhanced IGRP (E-IGRP) uses an algorithm that aims at removing transient loops. The algorithm is embedded in E-IGRP. Though this new approach to distance vector routing virtually eliminates transient loops, it does this by introducing transient unreachables. E-IGRP is based on the *diffusing update algorithm* (DUAL).

OSPF value	RFC 1349 TOS values	
0	0000	Normal service
2	0001	Minimize monetary cost
4	0010	Maximize reliability
8	0100	Maximize throughput
16	1000	Minimize delay

Figure 5.15   Table of TOS values.

Information on the distance from destination to the router's neighbors comes from the distance vector advertisements and the cost of the link used is defined locally. The router will select one of its neighbors as the next-hop to the destination. Passive state routers, routers with a stable version of the routing table, will evaluate the routing update, based on either the receipt of a new link cost or a distance vector change. If the new cost is lower, the router will direct traffic for the destination through the new lower-cost link (neighbor). A lower-cost route inherently means a shorter path and it is a premise of DUAL that loops cannot be created when using the shortest path. If however, the new cost of the link is higher and was received from the selected next-hop to the destination, the router will determine better alternative paths using the metrics defined in IGRP. In this case, the router will select a neighbor if its distance to the destination is shorter than the sending router's old value prior to the update. Finding no alternative paths the router will go into a diffusion computation. As part of this computation, the router sends a query update message to its neighbors, except for the original next-hop to the destination. The query includes the destination and the new distance, asking for a response from its neighbors on its neighbors new distance to the destination. Each neighbor first treats the query update as a normal update message, computing cost and distance. If the neighbors end up in passive state because they were not routing through the sending router, or the neighbor itself finds an alternate path, it will reply with the new routing table version. During this process the router receiving the original new update to the path freezes its routing table, thus preventing loops. As each neighbor goes through its computation it will propagate the update query to its neighbors, diffusing the new update through the network.

E-IGRP has incorporated five messages to provide for the diffusion update algorithm:

1. Neighbor discovery, using a Hello protocol.

2. Update, carrying passive router distance vector modifications.

3. Query, carrying distance updates of active routers and causing the diffusion of the update.

4. Reply, for query responses.

5. Requests.

The hello packets are similar to those used in OSPF. Each hello packet is multicast to all E-IGRP routers in the network. Each router sends the hello at regular intervals to also test for link connectivity. The update and query messages are transmitted with expected acknowledgments through multicasting. Replies and requests are unicast messages.

E-IGRP has also incorporated variable length subnet mask and support for CIDR. With extensions for external gateway route tag support and the ability to summarize routes and its ability to work with IGRP make it a formidable routing protocol.

5.4   Interdomain Routing

The ARPANET developed in the 1970s was the seed for today's Internet. As the ARPANET grew and expanded to include other internetworks and LANs, the exchange of the routing tables became more of a hindrance than a benefit. Management of an extremely large network, comprised of different hardware and software levels managed by different organizations and people, challenged the networks rigidity and flexibility. This led to the hierarchy of the Internet into autonomous systems divided into a core or backbone network through which stub networks could communicate. Figure 5.16 illustrates interdomain connectivity. The routers that connect the stubs to the core network are defined as exterior gateways exchanging routing information using interdomain protocols. These are Exterior Gateway Protocol and Border Gateway Protocol.

5.4.1   Exterior Gateway Protocol (EGP)

The first interdomain protocol used to provide autonomous systems routing through the Internet was Exterior Gateway Protocol (EGP). EGP borrowed many of the characteristics of distance vector protocols. Along with this, EGP inherited distance vector protocol shortcomings, namely loops and slow convergence.

The EGP function is quite basic. EGP not so much exchanges routing table information but more determines network reachability between not adjacent autonomous systems but rather two neighboring routers using IP. The EGP routers acquire neighbors through a simple two-way handshake. One router sends a neighbor request and the other can reply with a positive reply or refuse the handshake. When a successful request/reply exchange occurs, the routers are neighbors. This process under EGP is called *neighbor acquisition*.

Once EGP routers have become neighbors they perform a procedure that sends hellos at regular intervals. This process is known as *neighbor reachability*. The purpose of neighbor reachability is quite simply to verify link connectivity to the neighbor. Both routers may run the neighbor reachability protocol, but it is not a requirement.

The final stage in EGP is determining network reachability. This procedure facilities the exchange of network information between the EGP router neighbors. Each EGP router polls its neighbor at regular intervals for a list of reach-

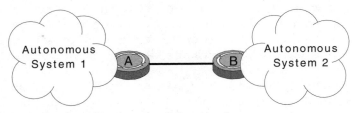

Figure 5.16   Interdomain connectivity example.

able networks. This list is used by each EGP router to update the routing tables within each EGP neighbor's autonomous system. The list is provided in a network reachability update message which is the response to the poll. The poll and a corresponding response contain the IP source network number of each EGP router. The list contains the distances to networks in the eternal network relative to the internal. A distance of 255 means that the network is unreachable.

Since EGPs inception in 1983 the Internet has grown to enormous proportions. This growth has stressed EGP to its limits. The answer to the stress: the innovation of path vectors. Path vectors are the foundation of the EGP successor Border Gateway Protocol.

5.4.2 Border Gateway Protocol (BGP)

Border Gateway Protocol (BGP) has had several iterations since its first version in 1989. BGP was developed to answer EGP's inheritance of distance vector routing loops and the unrealistic use of a link state algorithm for calculating vast numbers of links connecting autonomous systems found on the Internet. The developers of BGP employed a new routing algorithm called *path vector*.

For each routing update sent by BGP there is a list of all the autonomous systems used on the path from the source to the destination. This is similar to source route protocols. Duplicate AS entries in the list would imply a loop in the path and thus be in error. Each BGP router checks the route advertisement received for its own AS entry. If the router finds its own AS entry it will not forward the router advertisement, thereby avoiding a loop and the problem of counting to infinity. Not finding its own AS entry, the router will add its AS entry to the list and forward it on.

BGP utilizes TCP as its transport protocol. This alleviates BGP itself from any error-control processing, leaving BGP to concentrate on routing. BGP connections are established on the TCP port 179. As the BGP router makes a connection to its peer on this port, it will send an OPEN message. The OPEN message identifies the sending router's AS number, IP address, BGP version number, and a hold timer. During the initial connection establishment each router will verify the others BGP version. As of this writing, BGP has four different versions. Any vendor employing BGP must have a code to support each of these versions. If the versions are not the same, the connection will be broken. The routers will then reestablish the connection, using the lower version number. Each router will verify that the incoming AS number and IP address are valid for this network. The OPEN connection is considered established by the sending of keep-alive messages delayed no longer than the interval defined by the hold timer value.

BGP routers will send update messages after the open connection is established. The update message contains the list of autonomous systems for a single path. Each router will send an update message for each path it knows. Once routers have exchanged their routing tables, they will only send updates to each other and not whole tables. As the updates are received, each router will only place the shorter path in its routing table.

While path vectors make BGP very secure in protecting the network from routing loops and allowing the network to migrate from a hierarchical tree structure to a true meshed network, its use of listing each network in a path, both in its update messages and in its routing table, causes large routing messages and requires memory on each router. BGP-4 addresses this issue with the incorporation of Classless Interdomain Routing (CIDR).

5.4.3 Classless Interdomain Routing (CIDR)

In 1991 it became clear to the IAB that the rapid expansion and success of the Internet, due to its embrace by corporations and society, would find itself collapsing. The signs of this collapse were the depletion of class B addresses, routing table explosion, and the rapid deployment of registered IP addresses.

Each autonomous network attached to the Internet is advertised in routing tables. A network is assigned an IP address from one of the available IP address classes. As the IP network addresses were assigned and depleted, more and more class C addresses were being deployed. For example, one class B address would easily satisfy a network of 3500 hosts and require only one entry in the routing tables. Using class C network assignments, a 3500 host network would require 16 network addresses, and therefore, 16 entries in the routing tables. A means to allocate contiguous class C addresses but advertise them as being related with one routing table entry became the schema known as *classless interdomain routing* (CIDR). Figure 5.17 lists the contiguous class C address assignments for CIDR.

CIDR uses a concept similar to the network mask used to subnet IP networks into smaller ones. It summarizes contiguous class C addressing into a supernet. The approach is the advertisement of the class C address following a supernet network mask. Figure 5.18 lists the IAB assigned address allocations by regional area.

Network addresses required	Class C networks assigned
Fewer than 256 addresses	1 class C network
Fewer than 512 addresses	2 contiguous class C networks
Fewer than 1024 addresses	4 contiguous class C networks
Fewer than 2048 addresses	8 contiguous class C networks
Fewer than 4096 addresses	16 contiguous class C networks
Fewer than 8192 addresses	32 contiguous class C networks
Fewer than 16384 addresses	64 contiguous class C networks

Figure 5.17 Table of contiguous class C assignments.

Regional area	Class C address range
Multiregional	192.0.0.0–193.255.255.255
Europe	194.0.0.0–195.255.255.255
Others	196.0.0.0–197.255.255.255
North America	198.0.0.0–199.255.255.255
Central/South America	200.0.0.0–201.255.255.255
Pacific Rlm	202.0.0.0–203.255.255.255
Others	204.0.0.0–205.255.255.255
Others	206.0.0.0–207.255.255.255

Figure 5.18 Table of regional contiguous class C addresses for CIDR.

The mask identifies the IP prefix which matches the network number used in the IP address. CIDR identifies the longest match of the network portion of the IP address. For example, the IP address of 192.32.136.0 through 192.32.143.0 is represented by the mask 255.255.248.0 using CIDR. In this way, CIDR reduces the size of the routing tables on the Internet and provides for the allocation of IP registered addresses till 1999, when, at that time, IPv6 will be deployed to support the Internet for years to come.

5.5 Summary

We have seen in this chapter how routing protocols have evolved from static definitions to dynamic learning of network routes. The rapid growth of the Internet has led to just-in-time development of new architectures, routing protocols, and methodologies. The lessons learned in the growth and development of the Internet and IP prove their strength and flexibility for supporting current and future demands.

Asynchronous Transfer Mode (ATM)

ATM Concepts and Definitions

Asynchronous Transfer Mode (ATM) is a multiplexing and switching technology used to transport small fixed-length packets called *cells* over a high-speed network. It enables the integration and transport of data, voice, and video over the same high-speed network, supports different QoS levels depending on traffic types, and functions similarly over local and wide area networks. In this chapter we will introduce and explain the basic concepts and definition of ATM.

6.1 Requirements

Before proceeding into the basics of what ATM is and how it works, it might be helpful to discuss some of the driving forces behind its development and widespread acceptance. First of all, there is the simple fact that more bandwidth is always required and if it is available it will be used. Current switched or shared media technology in the LAN environment limits one to an economical maximum of 100 Mb. On the WAN side, it is typically whatever maximum-size channel one can carve out of either a private T1 or T3 TDM. Frame relay is available, but most carriers can only support up to a T1-size access rate. Whether one is discussing a typical desktop connection, a backbone LAN, or global internet backbone, it is perceived that more bandwidth is needed to move more information through the network. Users want it to support more, faster, and neater applications; carriers want more bandwidth to support more subscribers and users; vendors want it to provide to bandwidth-hungry customers and carriers and of course claim that they have the fastest on the market.

ATM offers a scalable range of speeds beginning at sub-T1 rates and increasing up to 622 Mb and beyond. Table 6.1 samples existing LAN and WAN technology bandwidths and where ATM fits.

Another requirement is to make intelligent use of the bandwidth that is available. Allocating a fixed-size chunk of bandwidth for a constant and predictable

TABLE 6.1 Bandwidth for LAN and WAN Technologies

Technology	LAN or WAN	Speed
T-1	WAN	1.5 Mb
Frame Relay	WAN	2.0 Mb
Ethernet	LAN	10 Mb
Token-Ring	LAN	16 Mb
ATM	Both	25 Mb
100 Anylan VG	LAN	100 Mb
Fast Ethernet	LAN	100 Mb
FDDI	LAN	100 Mb
ATM TAXI	Both	100 Mb
ATM OC3	Both	155 Mb
ATM OC12	Both	622 Mb

application, like voice, is fine. However, this may be suboptimal for a client/server LAN application that requires variable and bursty rates of bandwidth over a period of time. There is always the possibility that traffic bursts will exceed the peak fixed-bandwidth allocation or that bandwidth will go unused.

ATM makes efficient use of available bandwidth through a number of techniques, including statistical multiplexing, switched virtual connections, and rate-based flow control. All will be covered in more detail in subsequent chapters.

Support for real-time applications is another driving force behind ATM. The world of corporate and public communications is no longer limited to transaction-based text data or traditional voice calls. It now includes a mixture of both, along with video, packetized voice, real-time images, and video. Factor in the always increasing bursty LAN traffic and you now have a variable mix of application data each with its own QoS requirements. Those with very stringent delay and jitter requirements must be delivered through a network with some quarantee or they are all but useless. Figure 6.1 shows applications and their respective relative QoS.

Standards with the ability to design and build networks to open and accessible specifications is another requirement. The explosive growth of the Internet and TCP/IP can be partly attributable to the accessibility to TCP/IP standards documented in Request for Comments (RFC). The concept of open standards may seem like an anathema to private development and innovation, and to some degree it is. But open standards allows industry participation and competition, drives down the price of the basic network building blocks, and motivates product and functional differentiation, all within the framework of a common specification.

Network simplification is always in the forefront of a network manager's thoughts. Today, two different types of data networks must be designed, built, and managed: a local area network (LAN) that interconnects resources within a

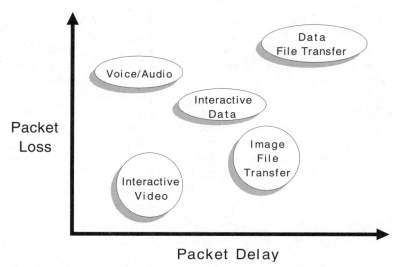

Figure 6.1 Applications and QoS.

campus and/or building topology and a wide area network that makes use of public carrier facilities to interconnect a collection of different campuses and/or buildings. Each requires its own and distinct set of design criteria, hardware and software costs, skills to operate and manage, and protocols. There is certainly overlap in some areas, for example, routers interconnect LANs over a WAN, but essentially they are two different network technologies. In addition, one may also have deployed separate but equally important voice networks that run parallel to the data networks. Add in video and one can see immediately the complexity of deploying and operating technically distinct but parallel networks.

A solution that reduces network complexity by merging both the LAN and the WAN into one network, that uses a single unified architecture, that enables both voice and data to share the same physical paths and use the same network hardware and software would seem to be very popular and marketable for all concerned.

And finally, what role have the vendors played in the momentum behind ATM? To answer this one might rephrase the question of What came first, the chicken or the egg? to What came first, the requirement or the technology?" The argument in the context of ATM could be made either way. But from the standpoint of the vendors who build and supply the hardware and software, there is both. Vendors see demand increasing from their customers for more bandwidth to support legacy and multimedia applications, to relieve LAN and WAN backbone congestion, to provide some network guarantees in performance for certain applications, and to do it all economically. Vendors also see an ability to manufacture and provide a new order of magnitude-faster network technology due to cheaper and faster chip sets, greater attachment/port densities (e.g., hubs, switches), and the fact that network processing takes place in firmware/microcode/hardware rather than software. There is an unprecedented momentum behind providing ATM equipment to the market as quickly as possible—even if it is perceived as immature or the standards are incomplete. Big players like Cisco, IBM, and Bay have committed hundred of millions of dollars to development and acquisitions. Venture capitalists are lining up to back small technology startups who may only have a ". . . statement of intention to design a prototype that will similate an anticipated emerging function. . . ."

Vendors see opportunity, and they have transformed their enthusiasm and optimism into products and strategies that customers are beginning to implement and believe in.

For these reasons and many others, ATM is and will continue to be a popular network technology and will successfully proliferate throughout public and private networks alike.

6.2   A Brief History

B-ISDN was first conceived in the 1980s as a broadband extension to the fixed-bandwidth, signal-based, digital integration services called ISDN. The idea behind ISDN was to provide an inexpensive and simple technique using the existing copper subscriber loop for transmitting digitized data and voice more reliably and at faster speeds into and through public digital networks. ISDN is limited to a maximum number of 64 Kb B-channels: basic service supports 2× B-channels plus a 16 Kb D-channel for signaling; primary supports 23× B-channels in the United States and 30× B-channels in Europe plus a 64 Kb D-channel. It was with commendable foresight that the standards bodies, influenced by the telecommunications carriers, saw a need to develop a standard that would support higher bandwidth than what was defined in ISDN Primary.

As ITU-T I.121 (revised, 1990) documents, B-ISDN was developed with the following in mind:

- Emerging demand for broadband services.
- Availability of high-speed transmission, switching, and signal processing technologies.
- Improved data and image processing capabilities.
- Integrate interactive and distribution services.
- Integrate circuit and packet transfer mode into one universal broadband network.
- Provide flexibility in satisfying the requirements of both user and operator.
- Need to cover broadband aspects of ISDN in CCITT recommendations.

Asynchronous Transfer Mode (ATM) was selected as the transfer mode for implementing B-ISDN for the following reasons:

- Flexible network access due to cell transport concept.

- Dynamic bandwidth allocation on demand.

- Flexible bearer-capability allocation and easy provision of semipermanent connections due to the virtual path concept.

- Independent of physical transport.

B-ISDN and ATM are two terms that are used interchangeably. Technically speaking, B-ISDN is a set of ITU-T standards that define broadband signaling, transport, and management of integrated services over a wide area network. ATM is the transport mode for B-ISDN networks.

In 1991, four vendors, Stratacom, Newbridge, Cisco, and NET formed the ATM Forum. The mission of the ATM Forum is to accelerate and facilitate the deployment of ATM technology by providing a set of interoperability standards. The ATM Forum is not a standards body but rather a consortium of vendors, carriers, customers, and other interested parties that produce implementation agreements based on international standards.

The ATM Forum has produced specifications for functions that have not been addressed by the international standards bodies and most likely never will be. These additional specifications are specific to data networking and the LAN environment and reflect the heavy data networking vendor presence in the ATM Forum. Also the LAN is where ATM is expected to be initially deployed. A few examples of ATM Forum specifications that are LAN influenced include:

- ATM LAN Emulation.

- Available Bit Rate services (ABR) for LAN-like data traffic.

- ABR rate-based flow control.

- Multiprotocol over ATM (MPOA).

Membership in the ATM Forum has exploded to over 800 members. On the upside, this represents an unprecedented opportunity for an entire industry including vendors, carriers, and customer to participate in the specification of new standards that will impact all concerned. On the downside, there may be too many hands in the pie. Each participant may have a separate agenda, and through the contribution process, politicing, lobbying, and the like, will attempt to shape the specifications and rulings in their own direction. It is hoped that technical common sense will prevail but there is the chance that decisions will be challenged and old arguments resurrected. Witness the rate-based versus credit-based flow control discussion as an example.

The ATM Forum is organized into a board of directors and underneath a technical committee, a market aware committee, and customer-drivern enterprise network roundtable. Figure 6.2 shows the organization of the ATM Forum.

The ATM Forum is an organization with global reach and an important mission. They recognize this and the urgency that all participants have in achiev-

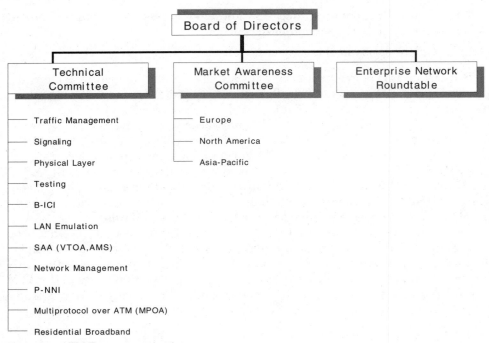

Figure 6.2　ATM Forum organization.

ing standardization on ATM as soon as possible. It is positive sign to see the ATM Forum converge with existing standards such as UNI 3.1 and ITU Q.2931 and incorporate work or at least agree on the spirit of work performed outside the forum. An example would be the liaisonal work performed between the IETF ION working group and ATM Forum MPOA working group. Figure 6.3 shows some of the key milestones that have been achieved in the history of ATM.

6.3　The Basic Components and Functions of ATM

Fundamental to an understanding of ATM is the following:

- ATM provides a connection-oriented service. This means that a path and connection must be set up between two ATM hosts before data is transmitted. This also means that, for the duration of the connection, data will traverse the same path. Connectionless service is supported but will flow over one or more preestablished paths.

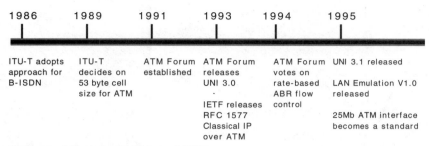

Figure 6.3   Milestones in history of ATM.

■ ATM uses virtual connections (actually called virtual channel connections) as the mechanism to connect and transport data between a source and destination. The virtual connection is dedicated to the source and the destination and cannot be shared by anyone else. One or more virtual connections can run over a single physical link.

■ ATM uses a fixed-length packet called a cell. The cell is 53 bytes long with 48 bytes of payload and 5 bytes of header.

■ ATM uses switches to interconnect ATM hosts and networks. Switches contain a routing table consisting of switch ports and connection identifiers (present in each cell header) that is built when a connection is set up. Cells are transported through the switch based on the connection identifier in the cell header.

■ ATM supports QoS. This means that an ATM network will provision or reserve resources that guarantee a specified minimum throughput, maximum delay, and maximum data loss for the duration of a particular connection. This QoS support on a per connection basis enables ATM to concurrently support any kind of traffic (i.e., data, voice, video) over a single network.

The asynchronism in ATM comes from the fact that cells can be transmitted from a source to a destination at any time and not at periodic time slots, as is the case in Synchronous Transfer Mode (STM). Multiplexing is part of ATM because, as mentioned, multiple virtual connections can run over the same physical link. In other words, cells from different sources running over separate virtual connections are multiplexed over a physical link. The connection identifier field in the header of each cell identifies which virtual connection the cell is associated with.

One can see how network integration can be performed in Fig. 6.4. Each application, be it bursty LAN data, a single 64 kb voice channel, or a variable bit rate video application, is allocated a virtual connection from a source to its partner application on a destination host. Information from these applications is segmented into cells which are then multiplexed over a single, physical

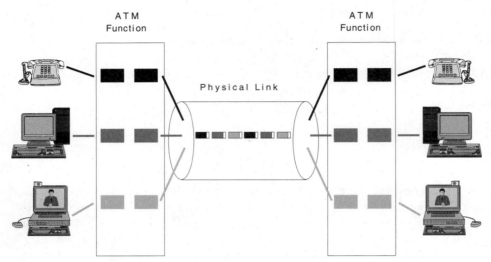

Figure 6.4 Data, voice, and video integration using ATM.

channel to the destination. At the destination, the cells are reassembled into frames or digital streams and passed up to the application (segmentation and reassembly, called SAR, is performed at two end-points of an ATM connection). Even though the cells are flowing over the physical link in an asynchronous manner, the applications themselves only see a dedicated point-to-point virtual connection with a dedicated amount of bandwidth and QoS.

6.3.1 Components

An ATM network consists of essentially four distinct physical components: hosts, switches, links, and a new one called edge devices.

An ATM host is charactersized by the following:

- Contains an ATM adapter.
- Attached to an ATM switch port over a physical link.
- Sends and receives ATM cells.
- Uses signaling to set up and tear down ATM virtual connections.
- Is the termination point for an ATM virtual connection.
- Contains an ATM adaption layer (AAL) that is both an interface to higher-layer application functions (e.g., data, voice, video) and lower-layer ATM functions.

In the discussions to follow and in general, an ATM host may also be referred to as an ATM end user, endpoint, end system, or DTE.

An ATM switch is characterized by the following:

- Contains two or more ATM ports.

- Attaches to ATM hosts and other switches over physical links.

- Transports cells from an input port to an output port, based on contents of identifier contained in cell header.

- Communicates using signaling with source host, destination host, and possibly other switches to set up a path and perform *connection admission control* (CAC). CAC is a function performed by an ATM network to decide if a connection and associated QoS can be accepted without affecting other connections.

- May monitor traffic at input port closest to source host to make sure it does not exceed agreed-upon traffic parameters determined at connection setup.

- May contain an ATM end-user function.

An ATM edge device is relatively new to the ATM lexicon but is very important because ATM will, for some time, coexist with non-ATM networks. An ATM edge device is positioned between an ATM network and a non-ATM network. It is characterized by the following:

- Performs all the functions of an ATM host/end user.

- Bridges and/or routes frames and packets between a legacy network such as a Token-Ring or Ethernet and an ATM network.

- Performs like-to-like networking of legacy frames and packets across an ATM backbone.

Physical links in an ATM network interconnect hosts, switches and edge devices to each other. They will employ some medium-specific encoding and framing to carry ATM cells.

6.3.2 Interfaces

ATM defines a number of different functional interfaces in a network. The interfaces are actually logical associations and functions that are performed between two adjacent entities. An entity is this case could be an ATM host, switch, or a separate ATM network.

Figure 6.5 shows the structure of an ATM network with the respective interfaces and components.

6.3.2.1 UNI. UNI stands for user network interface. It defines the procedures and protocols that enable an ATM host to connect to and function with an ATM switch. Logically, it is the boundary or demarcation line between an ATM end user (i.e., host, edge device) and the ATM network of which the adjacent switch is the entry point into. The UNI functions and protocols are comprehensive and have been defined in detail by the ATM Forum (UNI 3.0/3.1) and the ITU.

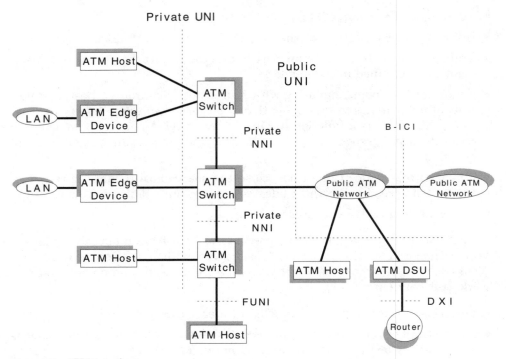

Figure 6.5 ATM interfaces.

Two UNIs exist: a private UNI, which is the interface between host and switch in a private network, and a public UNI, which is the interface between a host or network and a public network switch.

Without going into detail about the UNI (that has been covered ad nauseam in numerous references, including the ATM Forum's UNI 3.1 specification), it is simply a specification for the following functions between an ATM end user and network:

- Physical connection between the end user and switch, called the physical layer
- Performance of cell multiplexing/demultiplexing over the physical connection
- Signaling to a switch to establish a switched or dynamic virtual connection
- Managing end enforcing traffic between end user and switch
- Addressing ATM end users

Figure 6.6 illustrates the private and public UNI.

6.3.2.2 NNI. NNI stands for *network to network interface* and is defined as the interface between two adjacent ATM switches (or nodes). The private NNI is

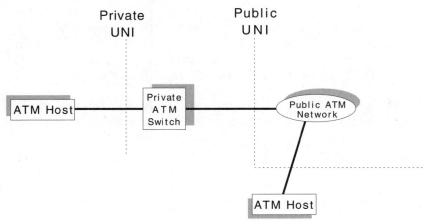

Figure 6.6   Private and public ATM UNI.

the interface between two switches in a private ATM network. The public NNI is the interface between two switches in a public network.

6.3.2.3   DXI.   DXI is the *data exchange interface* and is the interface that exists between a DTE, such as a router, and a DCE, such as a DSU. The DTE sends DXI-formatted frames of variable length to the DSU, which then segments the frames into cells and transports them across the ATM network. Figure 6.7 shows a router and ATM CSU connected over a DXI interface.

6.3.2.4   FUNI.   FUNI is relatively new and stands for *frame UNI*. Instead of segmenting data into cells at the end user or attached CSU, the ATM end user will transmit FUNI-formatted variable length frames into the ATM network. The adjacent FUNI ATM switch will then perform the necessary segmentation

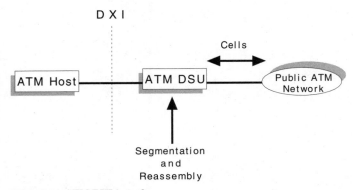

Figure 6.7   ATM DXI interface.

and reassembly (SAR) into cells. Because of the higher transmission efficiency (larger payload in relation to packet header), bandwidth is better utilized.

FUNI was designed as a means for ATM devices to more efficiently utilize slower-speed links such as T-1. The other alternatives are frame relay/ATM interworking and DXI. The FUNI interface is illustrated in Fig. 6.8.

6.3.2.5   B-ICI.   B-ICI or *broadband intercarrier interface* is a specification that enables two adjacent public ATM networks to interconnect and provide a set of end-to-end services. The end-to-end services that are defined include:

- Cell relay
- Circuit emulation
- Frame relay
- SMDS

6.3.3   Functions

The basic functions performed in an ATM network are simple. For ATM cells to be transported from a source to a destination over a virtual connection, two things must happen. First of all, a virtual connection must be set up. Second, the cells must be routed over that virtual connection.

A connection can either be permanent (similar to a leased line) or switched (dynamically set up on demand). The switched virtual connection is set up first by the ATM source host signaling to the adjacent switch that it wishes to establish a connection with an ATM destination host. This takes place over the UNI interface. Included in the signals sent from the ATM host to the adjacent switch are parameters for bandwidth, QoS, and the ATM address of the destination ATM host. This is illustrated in Fig. 6.9.

The ATM switch forwards this connection request through one or more switches until it reaches the destination ATM host who either accepts or rejects

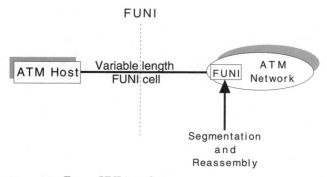

Figure 6.8   Frame UNI interface.

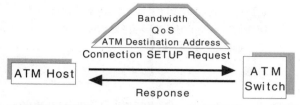

Figure 6.9   ATM host signals connection SETUP request to switch over UNI.

the request. While the connection request is being forwarded to the destination ATM host, the switches verify and allocate appropriate resources to support the requested parameters of the connection. If resources exist, then the ATM switches will accept the connection, allocate resources, and build routing tables. If not, then the switches will reject the connection setup request. The routing tables built for the connection contain entries that map an input port to an output port, based on a connection identifier contained in each cell.

A conceptual flow of the connection setup process is depicted in Fig. 6.10. ATM Host_A signals to the ATM network that it wishes to establish a connection with ATM Host_B, requiring specific traffic parameters, such as traffic descriptors and QoS. The ATM switches in the network then forward the connection request to the specified destination, verify that the network can support the connection with the associated QoS without impacting existings connections, and build routing tables. ATM Host_B receives the connection request and accepts or rejects the request. ATM Host_B will signal this information to the ATM network. The ATM network will, in turn, signal ATM Host_A with similar information.

Once the connection is set up, cells from the source ATM host to the destination ATM host follow the same path that was built at connection setup time. If any physical link is broken, then the connection must be rebuilt. The connection-

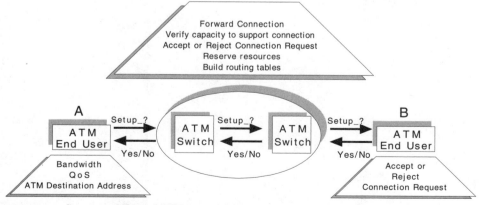

Figure 6.10   Conceptual flow of ATM connection setup.

oriented nature of ATM is not unique but is required so that the resources that were allocated at connection setup time in the path can be used to guarantee the QoS.

6.4   Cell Format

ATM uses a 53-byte cell to transport data: 48 bytes is payload; 5 bytes is header information. The choice of 48 bytes for payload was a compromise between various parties within the standards bodies. Voice proponents desired a small cell size because it would take less time to fill the cell with digitized voice samples and transport over the network. Data proponents desired a larger cell size because the transmission efficiency (ratio of payload to (payload+header)) could be maximized. The difference was split and 48 bytes was the result.

Two different formats for the cell header have been defined: one for the UNI and one for NNI. The difference is that 4 bits used for *generic flow control* (GFC) in the UNI cell header were reallocted to the virtual path identifier field in the NNI cell header. This makes sense, since, by definition, flow control is not performed over an NNI. Another advantage is that large networks of interconnected ATM switches can support more virtual paths (e.g., virtual private networks, VP cross-connects), thus making the switching of a large number of VCs more efficient. Figure 6.11 shows the format of a UNI cell header.

The definitions of the fields in the UNI cell header are:

- *Generic flow control (GFC).*   These four bits have significance only between the ATM end user and adjacent switch. The GFC was envisioned as a means for certain access mechanisms like DQDB to prioritize cells. The ATM Forum UNI 3.0/3.1 specifies that the GFC should be set to all zeros, x'0000'.

- *Virtual path identifier (VPI).*

- *Virtual connection identifier (VCI).*

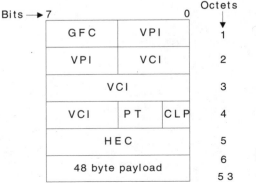

Figure 6.11   UNI cell header.

- *Payload type (PT).* A 3-bit field used to indicate whether a cell contains user data, OAM F5 related data, or traffic management info. Table 6.2 shows the possible values.

- *Cell loss priority (CLP).* One bit used to flag whether a cell is complient with traffic contract (CLP=0) or eligible to be discarded when congestion in network occurs (CLP=1).

- *Header error control (HEC).* Used by the ATM physical layer for detection/correction of bit errors in the cell header.

Figure 6.12 shows the NNI cell header. Again, the only difference being no GFC field and a larger VPI field.

6.5   ATM Connections

As shown, ATM end users transmit data to each other over a preestablished connections. These end-to-end logical connections can be permanent or switched. Permanent connections are provisioned manually (for example, an operator from a workstation configures parameters in the ATM end-user devices and switches to build a connection upon initialization) and generally stay active for a long period of time. Permanent connections should automatically reestablish themselves after a failure because the connection parameters have already been configured into the network. On the other hand, switched connections are set up real time, using signaling. Switched connections stay active until either a signal indicates that the connection should be terminated or the connection itself is broken. Switched connections are reestablished by the ATM end user who issues a connection setup request.

Connections can be point-to-point or point-to-multipoint. Point-to-point connections are used when data is exchanged directly between two, and only two, ATM end users. A point-to-multipoint connection is defined as a logical connection between a single root node (a node is an ATM end user) and multiple leaf nodes. When the root node sends data, a copy is received by all leaf nodes. Leaf nodes cannot communicate directly to each other. Point-to-multipoint connections, as shown later, play an important role in the ability for multicast and

TABLE 6.2   Payload Type Indicator (PTI) Values

PT encoding	Interpretation
_000_	User data cell, no congestion, SDU-type=0
_001_	User data cell, no congestion, SDU-type=1
_010_	User data cell, congestion, SDU-type=0
_011_	User data cell, congestion, SDU-type=1
_100_	Segment OAM F5 flow related cell
_101_	End-to-end OAM F5 flow related cell
_110_	RM cell (traffic management)
_111_	Reserved for future functions

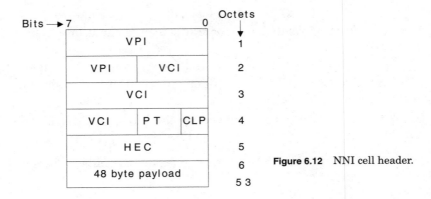

Figure 6.12 NNI cell header.

broadcast traffic to flow over a connection-oriented ATM network. Figure 6.13 shows a point-to-point and point-to-multipoint connection. Multiple ATM connections of either type can be defined and flow over a single physical link. The cell header shown in Sec. 6.4 contains two fields that identify which ATM connection the cell is part of: VPI or VCI.

6.5.1 Virtual connections

An ATM virtual connection is a logical channel between two ATM end users and is used to transport cells. Technically speaking, the standards documentation will refer to this end-to-end logical connection between two ATM end users

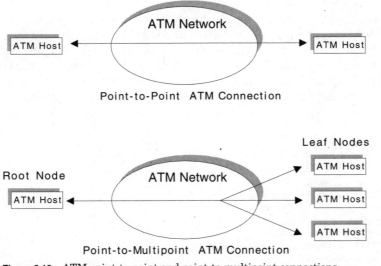

Figure 6.13 ATM point-to-point and point-to-multipoint connections.

as a *virtual channel connection* (VCC). A VCC is a concatenation of one or more *virtual channels* (VC). A virtual channel simply describes a unidirectional transport of ATM cells with a common identifier, VCI, in each cell. A *virtual channel link* (VCL) is a virtual channel between two points (e.g., host or switch) in a VCC where the VCI is assigned, swapped, or removed. Figure 6.14 shows the relationship between a VCC and a VCL.

The VCI in the cell header has meaning only for cells flowing over a virtual channel link. In other words, the VCI for cells flowing over a VCC may change as they pass through different switches.

An ATM VCC possesses the following properties:

- Originates or terminates in higher-layer functions
- Supports QoS
- Is switched or permanent
- Receives cells in order of transmission
- Is associated with a virtual path connection
- Can have unidirectional or bidirectional data flow
- Can have the same same (symmetrical) or different (asymmetrical) bandwidth in both directions
- Reserves or assigns certain VCI values for a specific function
- Assigns VCI values at the UNI by the network, the end user, negotiation by the end user and network, and standardization

6.5.2   Virtual paths

An ATM *virtual path* (VP) is a group of virtual channels. Each virtual channel is associated with a virtual path. Multiple VCs can be associated with the same VP. A virtual path runs over a *virtual path link* (VPL). A VPL is a virtual path between two points where the VPI is assigned, swapped, or removed. A virtual path connection (VPC) is a concatenation of one or more VPLs. Figure 6.15 shows the relationship between a VPC and a VPL.

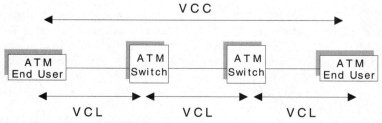

Figure 6.14   Relationship between ATM VCC and VCL.

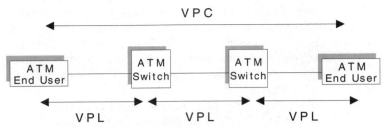

Figure 6.15 Relationship between ATM VPC and VPL.

An ATM VPC possesses the following properties:

- Originates or terminates in higher-layer functions
- Supports QoS
- Is switched or permanent
- Receives cells in order of transmission
- Some VCIs may lack availability for use within a VPC
- Can have unidirectional or bidirectional data flow
- Can have the same same (symmetrical) or different (asymmetrical) bandwidth in both directions
- Reserves or assigns certain VPI/VCI values for a specific function

The concept of virtual paths and virtual connections offers a flexible and robust mechanism for establishing and switching connections within an ATM network. Combined, there are 24 bits for the VPI/VCI at the UNI and 28 bits at NNI. Each VCC or VPC can have its own unique QoS. VCCs can be assigned permanently or dynamically. And virtual paths enable a large number of VCs to be transparently switched end-to-end over a single VP. VPs and VCs can be statistically multiplexed over a single physical link. Figure 6.16 illustrates the relationship of physical links, VPs, and VC.

6.6   Cell Routing

The routing of cells over an ATM network is based on the concept of *label swapping*. Label swapping is an internal routing technique used in other packet-switching technologies such as X.25 and frame relay. The function is simple: each packet contains a *logical connection identifier* (LCID). At each node or switch along a particular connection a routing table exists which maps the LCID and its input port to a new LCID and output port. This process continues until the packet reaches its destination.

Label swapping is an efficient technique for several reasons. The logic or cycles needed to extract and process the LCID need not be large because the

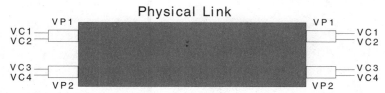

Figure 6.16 Relationship between physical link, virtual paths and virtual connections.

LCID itself is, typically, just a few bits long. Remember, there is no network address or end-to-end connection identifier to worry about. The routing function is typically performed in hardware or firmware in the switch, and it is basically the only function being performed by the node or switch. This will minimize the time spent in the switch, which is important for delay-sensitive traffic. In addition, the routing table is built either manually or by signaling before the first data packet comes along. In other words, one can say that all routing decisions in the network have been made before the first byte of user data flows. So, in keeping with the connection-oriented nature of the aforementioned technologies as well as ATM, a specific logical connection is already established and packets and cells can be transported and delivered in sequence over a predetermined path with minimal overhead and delay.

In ATM, the LCID is the combination of VPI and VCI fields in the cell header. Because there are two identifiers and two connection constructs within ATM, virtual path and virtual connection, two levels of switching can be performed.

The first is VP switching. In this case, a VP routing table is built and exists for each port or link in a VPC. Figure 6.17 shows a switch performing VP switching.

In this example, the switch contains four physical ports. There is one VP per port and one VP routing table with one entry per VP for each port. Shown is the VP routing table for Port_1.

As cells come in from Port_1, the VPI for each cell is examined and used to locate the appropriate entry in the Port_1 VP routing table. In this case, cells coming into Port_1 with a VPI=1 should be switched to Port_4 and changed to VPI=6. No changes were made to the VCI value at all.

The second level of switching which can be performed is VC switching. In addition to the VP routing table associated with each port, there is a VC routing table for each VP. Figure 6.18 extends our previous illustration to show both VP and VC switching.

Again, as cells come in from Port_1, the VPI for each cell is examined and used to locate the appropriate entry in the Port_1 VP routing table. Cells coming into Port_1 with a VPI=1 should be switched to Port_4 and changed to VPI=6. The VC routing table for VPI=1 cells is also examined. In this case, we see that cells coming in on Port_1 with VCI=21 should be switched to Port_4 and changed to VCI=51. A second entry in the VC routing table for VPI=1 cells

Port 1 VP Routing Table

Input VPI	1
Output Port	4
Output VPI	6
Output VCI	21, 22

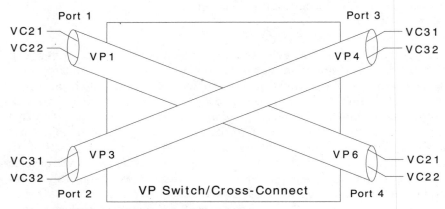

Figure 6.17 ATM virtual path switching example.

Port 1 VP Routing Table

Input VPI	1
Output Port	4
Output VPI	6
Output VCI	21, 22

Port 1 VPI=1 VC Routing Table

Input VCI	21	22
Output Port	4	4
Output VPI	6	6
Output VCI	51	52

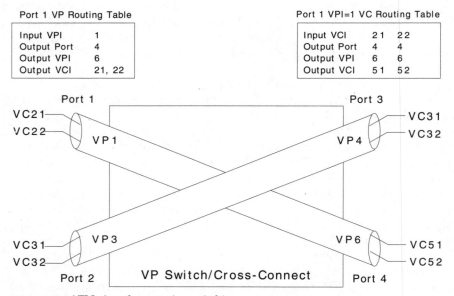

Figure 6.18 ATM virtual connection switching.

exists and indicates that VCI=22 cells should be switched to Port_4 and changed to VCI=52.

6.7 Summary

ATM is a cell multiplexing and switching technology designed to transport cells over a high-speed network. The need for high bandwidth, QoS support, network integration, and, to some degree, open standards and vendor enthusiasm are behind the growing popularity of ATM. An ATM network consists of ATM end users (hosts or edge devices) and switches interconnected by physical links. Functional interfaces, such as the UNI and NNI, have been defined to govern the behavior and protocols of the devices connected to those interfaces. ATM is a connection-oriented technology. This means that a path between any two ATM end users must be established before data can flow. ATM defines two levels of connections: virtual path and virtual connections. Cells are associated to a specific connection by the VPI and VCI fields in the cell header. Cells are switched through a contiguous series of switches using a label-swapping technique.

ATM Architecture

The architecture of ATM is based on the Broadband-ISDN Protocol Reference Model. It consists of control, user, and management planes for three distinct layers: the physical, the ATM, and the ATM adaptation layer. The physical layer defines how ATM cells are transmitted over a physical medium between two ATM entities. The ATM layer is positioned above the physical layer and below the AAL and is responsible for flow control, cell header generation, multiplexing/demultiplexing of cell streams, and VPI/VCI translation. The AAL sits on top of the ATM layer and maps higher-level services, such as voice and data, into the ATM layer.

7.1   B-ISDN Protocol Reference Model

Network architectures are sometimes defined within the context of a multi-layer protocol stack. Each layer in the stack performs a specific function and communicates with the layer above and below it. Although ATM is not viewed as a traditional protocol stack like OSI or SNA (this is probably open to debate from ATM purists), the architecture does make use of multiple functional layers. This is done for several reasons. Functions can be developed and enhanced without affecting other functions in the layers above and below. Communication with the layers above and below in the same host is kept simple and transparent. Interlayer communications between stacks on different hosts is performed on a peer basis. The multilayer approach also allows functions and protocols within a new technology like ATM to be categorized into a unified common reference model that standards can be developed for, vendors can comply with, and users can understand. Figure 7.1 depicts the multilayer approach to network architecture. Two hosts, Host_1 and Host_2 communicate over a physical network. Each functional layer communicates on a peer-to-peer basis with the corresponding functional layer in the other host.

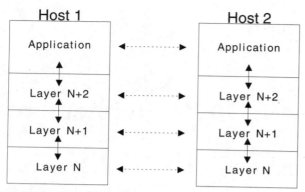

Figure 7.1   Multilayer network architecture.

The architecture of ATM is based on the Broadband-ISDN Protocol Reference Model that was developed in the ITU-T and documented in ITU-T Recommendation I.321. It is a multidimensional model consisting of a control, user, and management plane for three distinct layers: the physical layer, the ATM layer and the ATM adaptation layer (AAL). The physical layer defines how ATM cells are transmitted over a physical medium. The ATM layer is positioned above the physical layer and below the AAL and is responsible for flow control, cell header generation, multiplexing/demultiplexing of cells onto virtual connections, and VPI/VCI translation. The AAL sits on top of the ATM layer and maps higher-level services, such as voice and data into the ATM layer.

Figure 7.2 illustrates the B-ISDN Protocol Reference Model.

The *user plane* (U-plane) provides for the transfer of user data. It contains a physical layer, ATM layer, and several AALs that support different higher-level services, such as as voice and data. The U-plane is the ATM protocol layer and

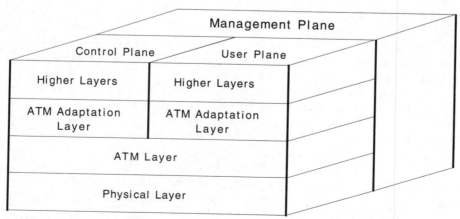

Figure 7.2   B-ISDN Protocol Reference Model.

function that supports application data transfer between two ATM end users. The *control plane* (C-plane) provides for the signaling and control functions necessary to establish a switched connection. The C-plane shares the physical and ATM layers with the U-plane and contains a separate signaling AAL and higher-level function. This is the portion of the ATM protocols and functions that support ATM SVCs and also takes place between two ATM end users. The *management plane* (M-plane) enables the U- and C-planes to work together and provides two types of functions: plane management and layer management. Plane management coordinates system-wide management functions and layer management performs functions specific to individual layers.

It is the C- and U-plane that generate the most interest when discussing ATM architecture. If one were to unfold and simplify this three-dimensional cube, it could look like Fig. 7.3. The C-plane is used strictly for setting up and tearing down connections, so its involvement, while short in duration, is nonetheless of great importance. As shown, it has its own signaling AAL. The type of AAL used in the U-plane depends on the higher-layer application in use. As mentioned, the C-plane does share both the physical and ATM layers with the U-plane, as well as some of the AAL function.

7.2 · Physical Layer

The *physical layer* (PHY) is responsible for the transmission of cells between two ATM hosts across a specific physical link. As defined in ITU-T I.321, the PHY layer consists of two sublayers:

- *Physical medium dependent (PMD).* The PMD sublayer, as the name implies, is dependent on the specific physical medium used. This function includes the insertion and extraction of bit timing information and any necessary line coding. The PMD sublayer views ATM cells as a continuous flow of bits with embedded timing information.

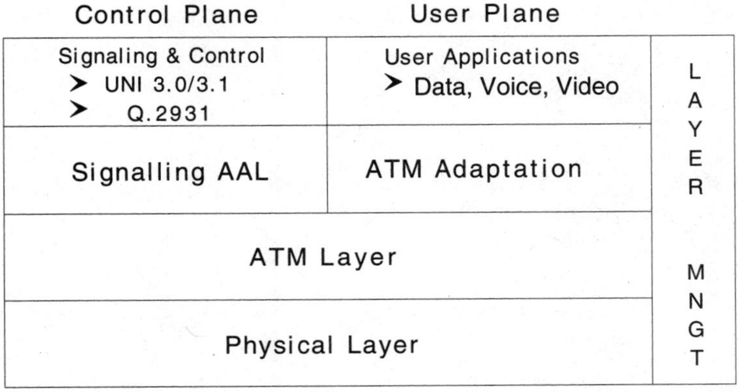

Figure 7.3 ATM multilayer architecture.

■ *Transmission convergence (TC).*   The TC sublayer sits on top of the PMD sublayer and below the ATM layer. It receives ATM cells from the ATM layer, packages them into a transmission frame (i.e., SONET frame), calculates the HEC field in each cell header, and sends them down to the PMD sublayer for transmission. On the receive side, cells are extracted and checked using the HEC field, and corrected if possible. If they cannot be corrected they are discarded. ITU-T I.321 specifies that the TC sublayer also performs cell-rate decoupling in which emtpy cells (VPI=0, VCI=0) are inserted or suppressed so that the cell flow rate between the PHY and ATM layers can match the speed of the physical medium. The ATM Forum on the other hand suggests that cell-rate decoupling take place in the ATM layer.

Figure 7.4 summarizes the functions performed by the PMD and TC sublayers of the ATM PHY layer.

7.2.1 ATM physical interfaces

Two levels of the UNIs have been defined: a public UNI and a private UNI. Distance between the ATM host and switch would be a key differentiator between the two and reflects, to some degree, whether a physical interface is supported over a public and private UNI. Some were designed to work over a WAN and as such are categorized as public UNI physical interfaces. Others were designed to work over short distances, such as between a workstation and a switch, and thus can be found working over private UNI connections. Because of the variation in distances involved, there may be more or less function performed by the TC sublayer.

The physical cabling used also may differ. Some of the physical ATM interfaces defined, such as Synchronous Optical Network (SONET), have been developed to exploit the growth and proliferation of the fiber-optical cable. This enables the error-free high-speed communications that ATM is expected to deliver. Others were designed to make use of the existing cable physical infrastructure such as telephone twisted pair UTP cable. Given the momentum

Physical Layer	T C	Cell Rate Decoupling HEC Header Processing Cell Delineation Transmission Frame Adaptation Transmission Frame Generation and Recovery
	P M D	Bit Timing Physical Medium

Figure 7.4   ATM physical layer functions.

behind ATM as an enabling high-bandwidth network technology, it is expected that even more physical interfaces will be developed.

A number of physical layer interface specifications have been released by the standards bodies, namely the ATM Forum and the ITU-T, to provide physical layer connectivity over the respective UNIs. ITU-T I.432 specifies ATM over 155.52 mb OC-3c SONET connections. The ATM Forum has added several more. Table 7.1 shows some of the physical ATM interfaces that have been standardized or under consideration.

7.2.2 ATM and SONET

ATM and Synchronous Optical Network (SONET) are two terms that are used often in the same context when discussing connectivity between ATM devices. ATM is a switching technology, SONET is a standard for the transport and management of information over various physical mediums between two entities. ATM and SONET are not competing technologies. SONET is one of several high-speed transmission technologies that ATM can and does make use of. Many ATM hosts and switches can be outfitted with SONET interfaces. ATM cells fit very nicely in SONET frames.

The basic SONET frame is 810 bytes and is sent every 125 microseconds. This translates to 51.84 Mbps, which is the minimum speed that SONET will operate. The SONET frame is called synchronous transport signal level 1 (STS-1) and is shown in Fig. 7.5. It can be conceptualized as being 90×9 bytes. Inside this structure is the synchronous payload envelope (SPE) which contains a pointer to the beginning of the virtual container. The virtual container is 87×9 bytes in size and contains ATM cells. The first three columns of every row consists of pointers and management information called *overhead*. It plays a

TABLE 7.1   The Physical Layer ATM Interfaces

Description	Rate in Mbps	Cell throughput in Mbps	Specification	Public/private UNI
ATM 25.6 Mb over UTP-3	25.6	25.6	ATM Forum	Private
51.84 Mb SONET STS-1 over UTP-3	51.84	49.54	ATM Forum	Private
TAXI 100 Mb over MMF	100	100	ATM Forum	Private
155 Mb FibreChannel over MMF or STP	155.52	150.34	ATM Forum	Private
155 Mb SONET STS-3c over SMF/MMF	155.52	149.76	ITU-T I.432	Public/private
155 Mb SONET STS-3c over UTP-3	155.52	149.76	ATM Forum	Private
155 Mb SONET STS-3c over Cat 5-UTP	155.52	149.76	ATM Forum	Private
DS-1	1.544	1.536	ITU-T G.804	Public
DS-3	44.736	40.704	ITU-T G.703	Public
E1	2.048	1.92	ATM Forum	Public
J2	6.312		ATM Forum	Public
E3	34.368	33.984	ATM Forum	Public
E4	139.264	138.24	ATM Forum	Public
ATM inverse multiplexing	N x DS1		ATM Forum	Private
622 Mb SONET STS-12c	622.08		ATM Forum	Public/Private

significant role in the management of SONET WAN connections. For SONET LAN connections, a portion of this overhead is unused, making it simpler to design and build interfaces. In either case the overhead portion can be subtracted from the total frame size and, thus, only 49.54 Mbps of payload can be carried by one STS-1 SONET frame. The more commonly used term for STS-1 is OC-1. OC-1 stands for optical carrier/channel-1.

Speeds greater than 51.84 Mbps can be accomplished by byte interleaving three OC-1 inputs into one OC-N frame where N stands for the number of OC-1 inputs. Thus, three OC-1 signals can be combined to make an OC-3 frame which supports 155.52 Mbps. The OC-3 frame is now 270 × 9 bytes. Subtracting out the overhead, the payload of the OC-3 frame is 261 × 9 bytes and contains three separate OC-1 SPEs, each 87 × 9 bytes. Another technique is to merge or frame align the SPEs of three OC-1 frames into a single larger SPE. This is called *concatenation* and is designated by adding the suffix "c" to the end of the OC-N or STS-N name. There is less overhead because only one SPE exists. The frame containing the single and larger SPE is called an OC-3c or STS-3c frame. This technique can be used to achieve speeds up to 2 Gbps (OC48) and beyond. Figure 7.6 shows an OC-3c/STS-3c frame.

SONET is the North American standard (ANSI) and Synchronous Digital Hierarchy (SDH) is the European (ITU-T) standard. The SDH hierarchy begins at 155.52 Mbps and is called the Synchronous Transfer Mode (STM-1). Table 7.2 shows the SONET/SDH hierarchy of speeds.

7.3 ATM Layer

The layer above the PHY layer in the ATM architecture is called the ATM layer. The ATM layer is independent of the PHY below it and the AAL above it. The ATM layer is responsible for a number of functions involving the contents

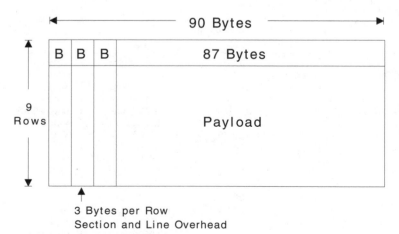

Figure 7.5   SONET STS-1 frame.

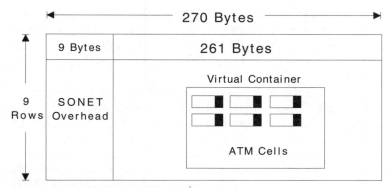

Figure 7.6   SONET OC-3c/STS-3c frame.

of the cell header, with the exception of the HEC field which is handled by the PHY layer. First of all, cell headers are generated and extracted by the ATM layer. In the transmit direction, a 48-byte AAL PDU* is passed down to the ATM layer which in turn generates and appends an appropriate cell header containing, among other things, the VPI and VCI fields. In the receive direction the cell header is removed and the ATM SDU is passed up to the AAL. Because of the presence of AALs, the function of cell header generation and extraction is performed only in ATM end users.

Another function performed by the ATM layer is cell multiplexing and demultiplexing. In the transmit direction, cells from individual virtual paths or virtual connections are combined into a noncontinuous cell flow which is then passed to the PHY layer for transmission. This multiplexing function enables the integration of cell flows from individual connections to be multiplexed over a single physical link. In the receive direction, the noncontinuous cell flow is demultiplexed into individual virtual paths or connections based on the contents of the VPI or VCI fields in the cell header.

---

* *Note:* The technical literature uses the terms Interface Data Unit (IDU), Service Data Unit (SDU) and Protocol Data Unit (PDU) to describe user data as it flows through the ATM layers. All three are frames of user information conforming to a specific architectural format. Keeping track of when a frame of user information is an SDU and when it is a PDU is really the job of the standards documentation. We advise the reader to consult the appropriate specification for more information. In the interests of simplicity we will use the following terminology: when the user information is at the AAL, it is a PDU. When it hits the ATM layer, it is an SDU. (We hope this simplifies things and does not offend the definition police.)

TABLE 7.2   SONET/SDH Speed Hierarchy

Frame and signal level	Bit rate	DS-0s	DS-1s	DS-3s
STS-1/OC-1	51.84	672	28	1
STS-3/OC-3/STM-1	155.52	2,016	84	3
STS-12/OC-12/STM-4	622.08	8,064	336	12
STS-48/OC-48/STM-16	2,488.32	32,256	1,344	48

The ATM layer performs VPI and VCI translation. This function will typically occur within switches or cross-connects. Based on the label-swap routine described in Chap. 6, the VPI and/or VCI field of each incoming cell is mapped to a new VPI and/or VCI and sent outgoing to an adjacent switch or host.

The ATM layer must also have the ability to discriminate, based on predefined fields in the cell header. This is so functions or conditions indicated by one or more predefined fields in the cell header can be performed or acted upon. An example would be the PTI field in the cell header as described in Chap. 6. The PTI enables the ATM layer to discriminate between cells containing user data and those containing nonuser data. Another example is the preassigned VPI and VCI values used to carry control and OAM information. For example, UNI signaling takes place over VPI=0, VCI=5. For any VPI the ITU-T has reserved VCI=0 thru 15 and the ATM Forum VCI=16 thru 31. Table 7.3 shows some of the preassigned VPI and VCI values.

Another very important function performed by the ATM layer is traffic and congestion control. Remember that each ATM virtual connection or virtual path has associated with it a QoS. This QoS is agreed upon by the ATM end user and network at connection establishment or subscription. The objective of this function is to support the QoS for each connection for the duration of the connection while protecting both the ATM end user and network from congestion. The ITU-T does specify that generic flow control (GFC) can be performed at this layer, however, it is the ATM forum that has broadened and expanded these capabilities. ATM layer traffic and congestion control functions include:

- *Connection admission control.* Actions performed at connection setup to determine if connection request should be accepted or rejected.

- *Usage parameter control (UPC).* Actions performed at network ingress to monitor and control traffic submitted to network by end user.

- *Priority control (PC).* Option to discard cells with CLP=1 if congestion occurs.

- *Frame discard.* Option for congested network to discard all cells associated with higher-level frame rather than individual cells.

TABLE 7.3   Preassigned VPI and VCI Values

Function	VPI	VCI
Empty	0	0
Metasignaling	0	1
F4 flow (segment)	0	3
F4 flow (end-to-end)	0	4
UNI signaling	0	5
SMDS	0	15
ILMI	0	16
LEC-to-LECS	0	17
PNNI RCC	0	18

- *ABR flow control.* Ability for end users to regulate traffic flow, based on network feedback so as to avoid congestion and allow fair access of all available bandwidth to participating end users.

Traffic mangement will be covered in more detail in Chap. 9.

And finally, from a management perspective the ATM layer performs several functions:

- Detecting, generating, and propagating virtual path or virtual connection failures at the public UNI through alarm surveillance.
- Verifying connectivity of at the VP and VC level.
- Discarding of invalid VPI and VCI values.

The management information is carried in OAM cells. Two management flows are supported and shown in Fig. 7.7.

- F4 flow provides segment or end-to-end VP connectivity and uses VCI=3 and VCI=4 values.
- F5 flow provides segment or end-to-end VC connectivity using PTI=4 and PTI=5 values in the OAM cells.

ITU-T I.610 and ATM Forum UNI 3.1 specifications discuss the ATM layer management in more detail.

As a requirement for keeping communications between layers simple, the ATM layer supports two primitives at the service access point between the ATM and PHY layers (PHY-SAP):

VP Level Service at UNI

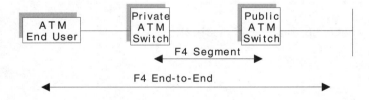

VC Level Service at UNI

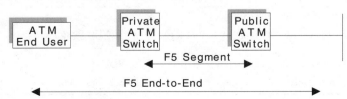

Figure 7.7 ATM layer OAM flows.

- PHY-UNITDATA.request. ATM layer transfers one cell to the PHY layer.
- PHY-UNITDATA.indication. ATM layer accepts one cell from the PHY layer.

For communications with the layer above, the AAL, two primitives at the ATM SAP are supported:

- ATM-DATA.request (ATM SDU, AUU, submitted cell-loss priority). One ATM layer SDU is received from AAL.
- ATM-DATA.indication (ATM SDU, AUU, received cell-loss priority, congestion indication). One ATM layer SDU is to be passed up to AAL.

Table 7.4 summarizes the possible values for the parameters associated with the AAL-ATM primitives.

In summary, the ATM layer is responsible for constructing and processing the cell header, forwarding the 48-byte payload to the next layer depending on the direction and traffic management.

Figure 7.8 summarizes the functions performed by the ATM Layer.

7.4   ATM Adaptation Layer

The ATM adaptation layer (AAL) sits on top of the ATM layer. Its primary purpose is to adapt the flow of information received from a higher-layer application like voice or data to the ATM layer. Because ATM was envisioned as a service to integrate many different kinds of applications, one adaptation technique would not suffice. For example, best-effort data traffic does not require synchronized clocking information, whereas voice most certainly does. Therefore, several service classes were defined, as well as the adaptation techniques or AALs to match and support them. In defining the service classes three criteria were established:

- Timing relationship between source and destination
- Bit rate
- Connection mode

TABLE 7.4   AAL ATM Primitive Parameters

Parameter	Meaning
ATM SDU	48 octets of ATM layer user data
AUU	ATM-user-to-ATM-user indicator, transported between ATM layers, value of 0 or 1
Submitted cell-loss priority	Indicates importance of requested transport of ATM SDU data
Congestion indication	Indicates received ATM SDU passed thru congested network node

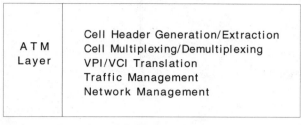

ATM Layer	Cell Header Generation/Extraction Cell Multiplexing/Demultiplexing VPI/VCI Translation Traffic Management Network Management

Figure 7.8   Functions performed by ATM layer.

The AAL service classifications are documented in ITU-T I.362 and shown in Table 7.5.

The AAL is comprised of two sublayers. The *segmentation and reassembly* (SAR) sublayer is responsible for first segmenting the higher-layer information field into a 48-byte cell at the AAL source and then reassembling the higher-layer information field from one or more 48-byte cells at the destination. The *common part convergence sublayer* (CPCS) function is dependent upon the higher-layers services that are using the AAL. It performs functions like padding and adding headers and trailers to the entire AAL frame before it is based to the SAR function below it.

Some other characteristics and functions common to all AALs are the following:

- AALs are located on ATM end users.

- AALs are dependent on the higher-layer application in use.

- Application data is passed from the higher-layer application to the AAL over an SAP in frame format. The frames may be up to 64 Kb in length.

- An additional layer of function called the *service specific convergence sublayer* (SSCS) may run on top of the CPCS depending upon the higher-layer function in use. An SSCS function is present for frame relay, SMDS, signaling and other special functions. Typically the SSCS will be null.

Figure 7.9 shows the structure of an AAL with its respective sublayers between two ATM end users.

TABLE 7.5   ITU-T AAL Service Classifications

	Class A	Class B	Class C	Class D	Class X
Timing between source and destination	Required	Required	Not required	Not required	User defined
Bit rate	Constant	Variable	Variable	Variable	User defined
Connection mode	Connection-oriented	Connection-oriented	Connection-oriented	Connectionless	Connection-oriented
AAL type	AAL1	AAL2	AAL 3/4 and 5	AAL 3/4 and 5	AAL0

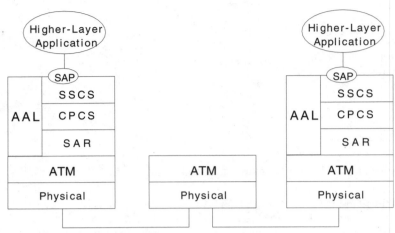

Figure 7.9 ATM adaptation layer structure.

7.4.1 AAL type 1

AAL1 supports class A traffic. Class A traffic is characterized by the following:

- A connection exists between the source and destination AAL1.

- Data is transferred between the source AAL1 and the destination AAL1 at a constant bit rate.

- Timing information is passed between the source AAL and destination AAL.

AAL1 typically supports applications that are delay and timing sensitive. Voice and real-time video fall into this category. If this data is not delivered to the destination at the same bit rate at which it was sent, or if it arrives too early or too late, then bits may be lost and transmission quality will suffer. AAL1 provides functions in the SAR and CS sublayers that can detect errors on the destination AAL1 and recover clock.

Information is passed at a constant bit rate from a higher-layer application to the AAL1 CPCS which then places it in 47-byte segments. The SAR sublayer then appends a 1-byte SAR PDU header. The SAR PDU header contains the following information:

- *Sequence number (SN).*   4 bits which are further subdivided into a *convergence sublayer indicator* (CSI) and a *sequence count* (SC). The CSI bit is service specific and can be used for techniques such as passing timing information from the source to the destination. The SC is a binary encoded sequence number that is passed between the source and destination AAL1.

- *Sequence number protection (SNP).*   4 bits which are subdivided into a 3-bit CRC and 1-bit parity field. The CRC and parity bits are used to validate the integrity of the SN field.

Figure 7.10 shows the format of an AAL1 SAR-PDU

7.4.2   AAL type 2

AAL2 supports class B traffic. Class B traffic is characterized by the following:

- A connection exists between the source and destination AAL2s.
- Data is transferred between the source AAL2 and the destination AAL2 at a variable bit rate.
- Timing information is passed between the source AAL2 and destination AAL2.

AAL2 is still under study within the standards bodies. In fact, it has all but disappeared from existing literature and product implementations. Two possible reasons are: first, the behavior of varible bit rate traffic is still being researched and second, AAL5, because of its simplicity and low overhead, seems to be the AAL toward which products are being developed.

7.4.3   AAL 3/4

AAL 3/4 supports class C or D traffic. Originally, AAL3 supported connection-oriented data traffic and AAL4 supported connectionless data traffic but they were later merged into a single AAL. AAL 3/4 supported traffic is characterized by the following:

- A connection may or may not exist between the source and destination AAL 3/4s.
- Data is transferred between the source AAL 3/4 and the destination AAL 3/4 at a variable bit rate.
- No timing information is passed.

AAL 3/4 supports two modes of operation: message mode service and streaming mode service. Message mode service is used to transfer one frame of information from a higher-layer application. Streaming mode is used to transfer one or more frames of information from a higher-layer application that may be separated in time. AAL 3/4 also supports assured and nonassured delivery. In the

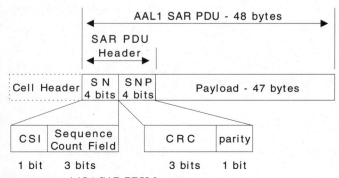

Figure 7.10   AAL1 SAR-PDU format.

former, retransmission in the case of errors detected in the data portion of the CPCS-PDU is performed by an SSCS. Currently, this is not implemented except in the Signaling AAL discussed later in this chapter. In the case of nonassured delivery all data, even error-detected data, is presented to the destination AAL, which in turn notifies the receiver of errors.

Information from the higher-layer application is passed down to an AAL 3/4 SSCS (which may be null) and then to the AAL 3/4 CPCS and formatted as shown in Fig. 7.11. The user information is padded out so that its length is in multiples of 4 bytes. The header and trailer are then appended. The AAL 3/4 CPCS-PDU header and trailer records contain the following information:

- *Common part indicator (CPI).* Specifies how other fields of the AAL 3/4 CPCS-PDU are to be interpreted.

- *Beginning Tag (Btag).* Number placed in Btag and Etag fields of header and trailer records that enables CPCS to check that PDU has been properly assembled.

- *Buffer allocation size indication (BASize).* Tells the receiver how much buffer space in reassembly buffers to allocate for the PDU at destination.

- *Padding.* 0–3 bytes used to pad user information so that it is a multiple of 4 bytes.

- *Alignment field (AF).* Extra byte added to 3-byte trailer record so that it can be processed by 32-bit processors.

- *End tag (Etag).* Matches Btag.

- *Field length.* Length of CPCS-PDU user data.

Next the AAL 3/4 CPCS-PDU is passed to the SAR sublayer which segments the CPCS-PDU into 44-byte segments. An SAR header and trailer are added to the 44-byte segments and it becomes an AAL 3/4 SAR PDU. The format for this shown in Fig. 7.12.

The header and trailer records of the AAL 3/4 SAR PDU contain the following:

- *Segment type (ST).* The 2-bit ST indicates where the individual segment belongs in the larger CPCS-PDU. The values for the ST are shown in Table 7.6.

- *Sequence number (SN).* 4-bit sequence number in modulo 16 used to number the SAR PDU.

- *Multiplexing identification field (MID).* 10-bit identifier used to identify to which larger CPCS-PDU the smaller SAR PDU belongs.

Figure 7.11   AAL 3/4 CPCS-PDU format.

Figure 7.12 AAL 3/4 SAR PDU format.

- *Length indication (LI).* 6-bit value which specifies how much data is in the variable part of the last SAR PDU. The last SAR PDU that is created from the CPCS-PDU may not contain 44 bytes of user information.
- *CRC.* 10-bit CRC used to detect errors in the SAR PDU.

AAL 3/4 provides a unique capability to multiplex cells from different frames over the same ATM virtual connection. This is performed using the MID field within the SAR header. The sending SAR assigns an arbitrary MID when it detects a BOM or SSM. All subsequent 44-byte segments belonging to the CPCS-PDU will use the same MID value until the SAR detects an EOM. The receiving SAR uses the MID value to reassemble the CPCS-PDU from SAR PDUs with the same MID.

The multiplexing capability of the AAL 3/4 enables ATM to provide a level of compatibility with Switched Multimegabit Data Services (SMDS). SMDS transports data traffic in 53-byte cells and is connectionless. Using AAL 3/4 along with an SMDS-specific SSCS, SMDS cells can be adapted to run over an ATM network.

7.4.4 AAL type 5

AAL5 supports the same AAL service classifications, class C and D, that AAL 3/4 supports. Again they are characterized by the following:

- A connection may or may not exist between the source and destination AAL 3/4s.
- Data is transferred between the source AAL5 and the destination AAL5 at a variable bit rate.
- No timing information is passed.

Like AAL 3/4, AAL5 supports both the message and streaming modes as well as assured and nonassured delivery options. Multiplexing is supported by

TABLE 7.6   Segment Type Values for AAL 3/4

_10_	Beginning of message (BOM)
_00_	Continuation of message (COM)
_01_	End of message (EOM)
_11_	Single segment message (SSM)

AAL5 but is performed at the SSCS sublayer rather than at the cell level via the MID field with AAL 3/4.

Information from the higher-layer application is passed down to an AAL5 SSCS (which may be null) and then to the AAL5 CPCS and formatted as shown in Fig. 7.13.

The user information is padded out so that its length is in multiples of 48 bytes. Only then is a trailer record appended. The AAL5 CPCS-PDU trailer record contains the following information:

- *CPCS user-to-user indication (CPCS-UU).*   Used to pass information from one CPCS to its partner CPCS.

- *Common part indicator (CPI).*   Current value of zero is used for boundary alignment but other uses are being studied.

- *Data length (Length).*   Tells how much of CPCS-PDU payload is data and how much is PAD. Also used to check on loss or gain of cells during transit.

- *CRC.*   32-bit CRC field used for validity check for the CPCS-PDU.

Next the AAL5 CPCS-PDU is passed to the SAR which segments it into 48-byte segments. There is no SAR header or trailer appended. When the 48-byte SAR PDU is passed to the ATM layer to have its 5-byte cell header added, the last segment of the original CPCS-PDU is marked as the end of message. This is performed by setting the SDU-type=1 in the ATM-DATA.request primitive.

The original designation for AAL5 was SEAL, which stands for simple and efficient AAL. It was felt by the designers of SEAL that data traffic (i.e., IP packets) did not require extensive AAL processing. Thus, SEAL, or AAL5, offers minimal processing at the AAL. For the following reasons AAL5 is by far the most widely implemented AAL in use today and most likely will stay so for the foreseeable future.

- *Error protection and frame integrity.*   AAL 3/4 performs error detection at both the SAR and CPCS sublayers. A 10-bit CRC is included in each 48-byte SAR PDU, and the segment type and sequence number is provided as a check for frame integrity before it is assembled. The CPCS uses the Btag and Etag fields to validate frame integrity. AAL5 uses a more powerful 32-bit CRC as well as a frame length field at the CPCS sublayer to detect errors and validate frame integrity. At the SAR sublayer the frame is assembled upon receipt of the last segment of the frame. AAL 3/4 checks for the integrity at

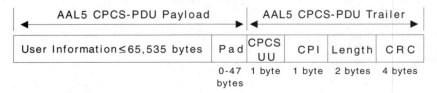

Figure 7.13   AAL5 CPCS-PDU.

the cell and frame level; AAL5 checks just at the frame level. This makes the AAL5 function less expensive to build and implement.

- *Available payload.*   Available payload for AAL 3/4 is 44 bytes of user information; AAL5 provides 48 bytes. A big difference when considering that a 53-byte cell already has incurred a cell tax of approximately 11 percent.

- *Processing overhead.*   No headers and trailers at the SAR sublayer in addition to a less powerful but suitable error-protection mechanism makes AAL5 much more attractive. Again, less overhead and less processing requirements lead to less expensive ATM equipment.

- *Standardization.*   All existing development and standardization work going on within the ATM Forum as it pertains to both data (MPOA) and in some cases nondata (MPEG2) has designated AAL5 as either the adaptation layer of choice or one to examine closely.

7.5 Signaling AAL

The signaling AAL (SAAL) provides a structured and reliable means to transport signaling traffic between two ATM end users. As part of the C-plane, it serves as the interface between higher-layer control and signaling functions such as UNI 3.1/Q.2931 and the ATM layer. Because ATM SVCs will not work unless the connection setup messages are delivered to the appropriate destination and the connection is built, it provides a highly reliable transport mechanism.

Figure 7.14 shows the structure of the SAAL.

The SAAL uses the common part (otherwise known as the CPCS) and SAR sublayer functionality provided by AAL5. The uniqueness of the SAAL is present in the SSCS. As shown, this contains two functions.

- *Service specific coordination function (SSCF).*   The layer is responsible for mapping the higher-layer application to the SSCOP.

- *Service Specific Connection-Oriented Protocol (SSCOP).*   SSCOP is a powerful connection-oriented data link protocol that provides a reliable trans-

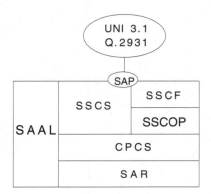

Figure 7.14 Signaling AAL structure.

port for signaling messages. It supports end-to-end error detection and correction, frame sequencing, and selective frame recovery.

7.6   Summary

The architecture of ATM is built on a multidimensional three-layer model. The PHY layer is responsible for physical transmission and interfaces. The ATM layer above it handles cell header processing, traffic, and network management. The next layer up, the AAL is responsible for adapting and interfacing the higher-layer applications to the ATM network. Several AALs, including one for signaling, have been defined because different applications require different functions from the ATM network.

ATM Signaling

ATM virtual connections are provisioned in one of two ways: (1) manually, using network management functions or, (2) dynamically. Dynamically built VCs are called *switched virtual connections* (SVC). Signaling is the technique used by ATM end users and networks to dynamically establish, maintain, and clear ATM SVCs. Signaling consists of the protocol and messages that are exchanged between ATM end users over the UNI. The messages contain information that is used by the ATM end user and the network to process the connection. SVCs offer the benefits of anytime-anywhere connectivity, efficient use of network resources (i.e., bandwidth), and automated administration.

8.1 Addressing

Before an SVC is established between two ATM end users, a series of messages is exchanged that contains information on bandwidth, QoS, and other connection-specific parameters. But for this exchange to even take place, the messages must be successfully routed from the source ATM end user (calling party) to the destination ATM end user (called party). To that end, each ATM end user must have a unique address. The ATM architecture indeed does specify a standardized addressing structure for both public and private ATM networks.

The address structure for ATM is characterized by the following:

- It is separate and unique from any higher-layer protocols and their associated address space that make use of an ATM network. In other words there is no correlation between the 32-bit IP address assigned to a TCP/IP workstation and the ATM address assigned to its NIC. However, as will be shown in Part 3, address mapping or resolution does need to take place for those higher-layer protocols to work properly over an ATM network just as address resolution between IP and MAC addresses on LANs needs to take place.

- Different address formats exist for both public and private ATM networks. This is a realization of the fact that public ATM networks like the telephone companies have their own internal addressing and routing mechanisms. Likewise, private ATM networks will want the flexibility to allocate addresses, as needed, according to their own internal policies. The two structures will of course interwork together.

- There is hierarchical structure. Call routing, administration, management, and overhead can be vastly simplified using a hierarchical addressing scheme as ATM allows one to do.

- It is scalable. An address space of 20 bytes is sufficient to ensure that one will never have to worry about an address space shortage—we hope.

For private ATM networks, the ATM Forum has defined three address formats for identifying ATM end users communicating over a private UNI. For public ATM networks and more specifically for identifying ATM end users communicating over a public UNI, the format specified in recommendation ITU-T E.164 is used. The three private ATM network address formats are shown in Fig. 8.1. They are modeled after the OSI *network service access point* (NSAP) address structure and are sometimes referred to in the literature as ATM NSAPs but in actuality are not OSI NSAPs. Again, ATM provides its own unique addressing structure that is used to define ATM end users only. Also note that there is an NSAP-style E.164 address format for private ATM networks. This was specified as an option by the ATM Forum so that private ATM networks could use E.164-style addressing. An example would be for an E.164-addressed private ATM network to obtain its network address prefix from its public ATM carrier, thus simplifying network administration.

All three formats shown consist of two parts: an *initial domain part* (IDP) and a *domain specific part* (DSP). The IDP consists of an *authority and format identifier* (AFI), which identifies the format and type of address in use, and an *initial domain identifier* (IDI). The values for the AFI are shown in Table 8.1.

The IDI can be either a 2-byte *data country code* (DCC) value as described in ISO 3166, a 2-byte *international code designator* (ICD) as maintained in ISO 6523 by the British Standards Institute, or an E.164 number.

The contents of the DSP is dependent on the format specified by the AFI value. Rather than duplicate the OSI NSAP format exactly, the ATM Forum combined the routing domain (RD) and AREA identifiers into one field called the *High-Order DSP* (HO-DSP). The field will be used to construct multilevel address hierarchies based on the application of a flexible prefix mask, similar in function to IP subnet masks. The End System Identifier (ESI) is a 48-bit field used to identify a specific host within an ATM subnet. Because of its length, the ESI could be matched up with 48-bit LAN MAC addresses that the existing Token-Ring and Ethernet devices use currently.

The ESI and SEL fields make up what is known as the user part of the address. Everthing else is known as the network prefix.

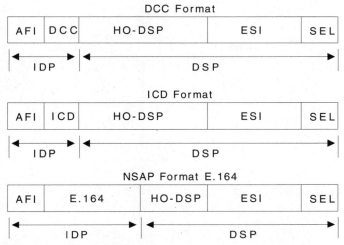

Figure 8.1 ATM address formats.

8.1.1 Address registration

Administration and configuration of 20-byte ATM addresses for end users could turn into a very tedious and error-prone task. Therefore, the ATM Forum has defined a technique for automatically registering an ATM address over the private or public UNI. This technique makes use of SNMP-based Interim Local Management Interface (ILMI) protocols to exchange address information between the ATM end user and switch. This allows an ATM end user to inform the ATM switch of its ESI address and in exchange receive the network prefix from the ATM switch across the UNI. This simple exchange is shown in Fig. 8.2

Address registration over the UNI is a technique for automatically configuring complete ATM addresses in end-user systems. At the same time, the ATM switch is provided with the ESIs for all end users attached to the switch. This information will be used by the ATM switches (via a switch-to-switch routing protocol) to properly route SVC requests from a source to the destination.

8.1.2 Anycast addressing

An *anycast address* is defined as a well-known group address associated with a particular service. This should be distinguished from a *multicast address,*

TABLE 8.1 Authority and Format Identifier (AFI) Values

AFI value	Format of IDI and DSP
39	DCC ATM format
47	ICD ATM format
45	E.164 ATM format

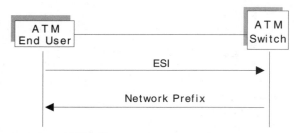

Figure 8.2 ATM address registration exchange.

which is an address associated with a group of end users (the option to dynamically join or leave the group may exist) and a broadcast which is a multicast address in which everyone is a member.

Anycast ATM addressing will be supported in the Signaling V4.0 specification. This will enable an ATM end user to request a connection with a particular anycast address. The first or nearest ATM end user (i.e., server) who has registered as an anycast server will respond. The calling ATM end user can then establish a point-to-point VC with that server. This obviates the need for manually configuring the location of servers or using special server location protocols. Candidates for ATM anycast addressing include ARP servers, NHRP servers, and the LAN emulation configuration server.

Anycast ATM address registration uses the same ILMI protocols as normal ATM address registration with the following exceptions:

- ATM end user, registering as an ATM anycast server, will use a service-dependent ATM group address as administered by the ATM Forum.

- ATM switch will use an ATM group address network prefix when registering the anycast server.

- ATM end user, registering as an ATM anycast server, will also supply a membership scope for the referenced anycast server. The purpose of the membership scope is to control, in the network and call routing hierarchy, where the anycast server will be advertised. In other words a connection request, which includes the membership scope, made to any anycast server outside the member scope will not be successful. There are sixteen levels of membership scope beginning with local network and going up to global.

8.2 ATM Signaling Messages

ATM signaling is a protocol used to set up, maintain, and clear switched virtual connections between two ATM end users over private or public UNIs. The protocol is, in fact, an exchange of messages that takes place between the ATM end user (caller or receiver) and adjacent ATM switch. The messages contain information that is used to build, maintain, or clear the connection. The messages themselves are segmented into cells at the signaling AAL and then transported over a standard signaling channel, VPI=0, VCI=5.

ATM signaling messages can be grouped into one of four functional categories: call establishment, call status, call clearing, and point-to-multipoint operations. Call establishment messages consist of the following:

- SETUP. Sent by calling, or source ATM end user, to network (defined here as nearest ATM switch connected to ATM end user over UNI) and from network (defined here as nearest ATM switch connected to destination ATM end user over UNI) to called, or destination ATM end user. Used to initiate connection setup. Contains information, such as destination ATM address, traffic descriptors, and QoS.

- CALL PROCEEDING. Sent by destination ATM end user to network and by network to source ATM end user to indicate that call establishment has been initiated.

- CONNECT. Sent by destination ATM end user to network and by network to source ATM end user to indicate that destination ATM end user accepts connection request.

- CONNECT ACKNOWLEDGE. Sent by network to destination ATM end user to indicate call is accepted. May also flow from source ATM end user to network maintain symmetrical call-control procedures.

- ALERTING. Sent by the destination ATM end user to the network and by the network to the source ATM end user to indicate that the destination ATM end user alerting has been initiated.

- PROGRESS. Sent by the ATM end user or the network to indicate the progress of a call in the event of interworking.

Figure 8.3 shows the flow of messages during connection setup for a point-to-point connection.

- STATUS. Sent by the ATM end user or network in response to a STATUS ENQUIRY message.

- STATUS ENQUIRY. Sent by the ATM end user or network to solicit STATUS message.

- NOTIFY. Sent by the ATM end user or network to indicate information pertaining to a call/connection.

Call clearing messages consist of the following:

- RELEASE. Sent by an ATM end user to request the network to clear the end-to-end connection or is sent by the network to indicate that the VCC is cleared and that the receiving ATM end user should release the virtual channel and prepare to release the call reference after sending a RELEASE COMPLETE.

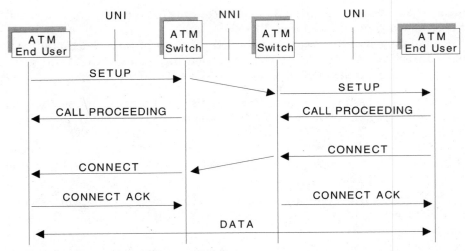

Figure 8.3   ATM connection setup message flow.

- RELEASE COMPLETE. Sent by an ATM end user or network to indicate that virtual channel and call reference have been released and that the entity receiving the message should release the call reference.
- RESTART. Sent by the ATM end user or network to request the recipient to restart the indicated virtual channel or all virtual channels controlled by the signaling channel.
- RESTART ACKNOWLEDGE. Acknowledges restart message and indicates restart is complete. Figure 8.4 shows the flow of messages for clearing a connection.

Point-to-multipoint connection procedures are well defined in the ATM Forum UNI 3.1 specification. Point-to-multipoint SVCs enable a single ATM end user to communicate with one or more ATM end users. Information flowing from the source ATM end user is replicated by the network, not at the

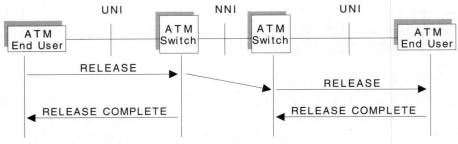

Figure 8.4   ATM connection release message flow.

source, and received by all destination ATM end users attached to the point-to-multipoint connection. The calling or source ATM end user is called the root, and the called or destination ATM end users are called leaves. Conceptually viewed, leaves are connected to the root in a tree structure.

The root establishes a connection to the first leaf using standard call-establishment messages as shown in Fig. 8.5. After that, additional leaves can be added or removed to the point-to-multipoint tree by the root. The leaves have the option of accepting the invitation and unilaterally removing themselves.

Point-to-multipoint messages consist of the following:

- ADD PARTY. Adds party (leaf) to an existing connection.

- ADD PARTY ACKNOWLEDGE. Acknowledges a successful ADD PARTY.

- ADD PARTY REJECT. Indicates that ADD PARTY request was unsuccessful.

- DROP PARTY. Drops or removes party (leaf) from an existing point-to-multipoint connection.

- DROP PARTY ACKNOWLEDGE. Acknowledges a successful DROP PARTY.

Figure 8.5 shows the messages required to be sent by the root to add a leaf (ATM_2) to an existing point-to-multipoint connection.

UNI 3.1 only allowed the root the option of adding leaves to an existing point-to-multipoint connection. This was deemed restrictive and would not provide the flexibility for applications to take full advantage of this capability. Therefore, UNI Signaling 4.0 added a capability for leaves to join a point-to-

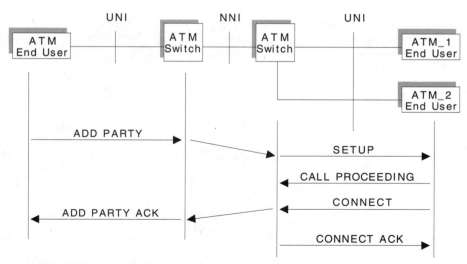

Figure 8.5 ATM point-to-multipoint connection flow.

multipoint connection without intervention from the root. This is called *leaf initiated join* (LIJ). LIJ is supported in one of two modes of operation:

- *Leaf-prompted join without root notification.*   In this mode a leaf generates and sends a request over the UNI to join a point-to-multipoint connection. The network handles the request and the leaf joins the connection without notifying the root. This is called a network LIJ connection.

- *Root-prompted join.*   In this mode the leaf generates and sends a request over the UNI to join a point-to-multipoint connection. This request, in turn, is forwarded up to the root which then invokes established procedures for adding a leaf to an existing connection. This is called a root LIJ connection.

Two new messages were added to support LIJ in UNI Signaling 4.0:

- LEAF SETUP REQUEST. Sent by leaf to initiate leaf-joining procedures.
- LEAF SETUP FAILURE. Sent to leaf by root or network to indicate failure to join the point-to-multipoint connection.

Figure 8.6 shows the flow of messages as a leaf (ATM_2 end user) joins an existing point-to-multipoint connection. Because the root is not notified as the leaf joins the existing connection, this is a network LIJ.

8.3   ATM Signaling Message Format

The format of an ATM signaling message as defined in Q.2931/UNI 3.1 is conceptually depicted in Fig. 8.7. Each message includes the following components:

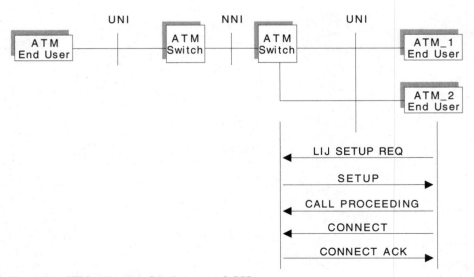

Figure 8.6   ATM point-to-multipoint network LIJ.

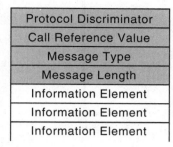

| Protocol Discriminator |
| Call Reference Value |
| Message Type |
| Message Length |
| Information Element |
| Information Element |
| Information Element |

Figure 8.7 ATM signaling message format.

- *Protocol discriminator.* Distinguishes messages for ATM end user-to-network call control from other messages.

- *Call reference value.* Associates message with connection at UNI. Local significance only.

- *Message type.* Identifies type of message as described in previous section.

- *Message length.*

- *TLV information elements.* Parameters associated with a particular message.

The presence of the first four components is mandatory in every message. A message will contain different *information elements* (IE) depending on the type of message. The IEs are *Type / Length / Value* (TLV) fields that contain information that is used by the ATM end user or network to process the connection.

8.3.1 Information elements

Table 8.2 describes most of the relevant IEs that have been defined in UNI 3.1 and UNI Signaling 4.0, and may be present (mandatory or optional) in ATM signaling messages:

TABLE 8.2 UNI Signaling Information Elements

Information element	Max length in bytes	Description
Cause	34	Why certain messages are generated and may provide diagnostic information.
Call state	5	Current status of call.
Endpoint reference	7	Identifies individual endpoints in point-to-multipoint connection.
Endpoint state	5	Indicates state of an endpoint (i.e., add party, drop party, etc.) in point-to-multipoint connection.
AAL parameters	20	AAL specific parameters such as CPCS-SDU size, AAL type.
ATM traffic descriptors	30	Forward and backward PCR, SCR, and burst sizes.
Alternative ATM traffic descriptors	30	Describes alternate ATM traffic-descriptor values and is used during negotiation of these values in UNI Signaling 4.0.

TABLE 8.2   UNI Signaling Information Elements (Continued)

Information element	Max length in bytes	Description
Minimum acceptable traffic descriptors		Describes minimum acceptable ATM traffic-descriptor values and is used during negotiation of these values in UNI signaling 4.0.
Connection identifier	9	VPI and VCI values.
QoS parameter	6	QoS class (0–4).
Extended QoS parameters	25	Indicates individual QoS values acceptable on a per-call basis. These include acceptable and cumulative forward and backward cell delay variation and acceptable forward and backward cell loss ratio.
Broadband high-layer information	13	Validates compatibility of high-layer informations such as ISO or vendor-specific protocols.
Broadband bearer capability	7	Indicates request for connection-oriented service that will provide interworking (i.e., DS1 emulation), ATM only, or VP service (for switched VPs). Also specifies CBR or VBR.
Broadband low-layer information	17	Validates compatibility of layer-2 and layer-3 protocols.
Broadband locking shift	5	Indicates new active code set.
Broadband nonlocking shift	5	Indicates temporary shift to specified code set.
Broadband sending complete	5	Indicates completion of the called party number.
Broadband repeat indicator	5	Indicates if IE is repeated in message and how they should be interpreted.
Calling party number	26	ATM address of source ATM end user.
Calling party subaddress	25	Used to convey a private ATM address across a public E.164 network.
Called party number	26	ATM address of destination ATM end user.
Called party subaddress	25	Used to convey a private ATM address across a public E.164 network.
Transit network selection	8	Identifies requested transit network.
Restart indicator	5	Identifies class of facility to be restarted, such as indicated VC or all VCs.
Narrowband low-layer compatibility	20	Q.2931-based IE used to validate low-layer compatibility for N-ISDN interworking device.
Narrowband high-layer compatibility	7	Q.2931-based IE used to validate high-layer layer compatibility for N-ISDN interworking device.
Notification indicator	5	Q.2931-based IE used to indicate information pertaining to a call.
Progress indicator	6	Q.2931-based IE used to describe an event which has occurred during the life of a call.
Narrowband bearer indicator		Q.2931-based IE used to indicate a requested circuit-mode N-ISDN bearer service to be provided by the network.
LIJ call identifier	9	Identifies point-to-multipoint LIJ call at root's interface.
LIJ parameters		LIJ parameters used by root to associate options with call at call setup.
LIJ sequence number	8	Used by joining leaf to associate SETUP, ADD PARTY, or LEAF SETUP FAILURE response message with corresponding LEAF SETUP REQUEST.
End-to-end transit delay	12	Q.2931-based IE used to indicate the maximum end-to-end transit delay acceptable on a per-call basis, and to indicate the cumulative transit delay actually experienced by a virtual channel connection. Equal

TABLE 8.2   UNI Signaling Information Elements (Continued)

Information element	Max length in bytes	Description
		to forward maximum cell transfer delay per traffic management V4.0 specification.
Extended end-to-end transit delay	12	Indicates backward maximum cell transfer delay.
Generic identifier transport	30	Used to indicate session and resource identifier for video-on-demand virtual connections.
Connection scope selection	6	Enables calling user to indicate to the network that the connection should proceed within the selected routing range. Used to limit search for anycast services.
OAM traffic descriptor	56	Provides information relating to the presence and handling of the end-to-end F5 OAM information flow for performance management and user-originated fault management associated with the user connection involved in the call.
ABR setup parameters	36	Specifies set of ABR parameters used during connection setup.
ABR additional parameters	14	Specifies additional ABR parameters.

8.4   UNI Signaling 4.0 Enhancements

ATM Forum UNI 3.0 provided not only initial signaling support for point-to-point and multipoint connections over the UNI but also documented traffic management, physical layer specifications, and network management connections. The signaling aspect of UNI 3.0 is based on ITU Recommendations Q.93B and Q.2100. UNI 3.1 is an upgrade to UNI 3.0 that was developed to align the signaling functions of the ATM Forum standard with those of the ITU and their Recommendation Q.2931. UNI 3.1 supports a new version of SSCOP which is based on ITU Recommendation Q.2100, Q.2110, and Q.2130. Because of this, UNI 3.0 and UNI 3.1 are not compatible even though there are no real functional differences between the two.

Rather than try to combine new functions in signaling, traffic management, physical layer support, and network managmenet into one mammouth document, the ATM Forum decided to break out these areas into their own separate specifications. Hence, there will not be a new UNI 4.0 specification commonly described in the literature and trade journals. What we will see from the ATM Forum are new specifications in the following:

- Signaling
- Traffic management
- Physical layer interfaces
- Network management

At the time of this writing UNI Signaling 4.0 was near completion. Much of the information from that specification was included in this chapter because it is felt by the authors that the function described will be standardized and released by the ATM Forum.

UNI 4.0 Signaling includes a number of significant functional enhancements over and above what is provided in UNI 3.0/3.1. Some have already been discussed, but it is helpful to review here the primary functional enhancements:

- *Leaf-initiated join.*   Allows end users to dynamically join existing point-to-multipoint connections.

- *Group addressing.*   Well-known functional addresses can be utilized to reduce signaling and configuration overhead.

- *Anycast addressing.*   Enables servers (and or services) to be assigned a well-known group address. The ability to control access to anycast servers is included using a connection/membership scope.

- *Proxy signaling.*   Used to support devices that do not support ATM signaling, such as residential broadband.

- *Switched virtual paths.*   ATM virtual paths can be dynamically provisioned. This will reduce administrative overhead in public and private networks.

- *Multiple signaling channels.*   This enable multiple ATM end users to share a single UNI interface or port on the switch.

- *Frame discard capability.*   Cells belonging to an entire frame can be discarded to prevent or relieve congestion.

- *Available bit rate (ABR) signaling for point-to-point connections.*   Parameters for ATM end users requesting ABR service can be signaled into the network.

- *Signaling of individual QoS parameters.*   Cell loss ratio, mean cell transfer delay, maximum cell transfer delay, and cell delay variation can be signaled into the network rather than just one QoS class.

- *Traffic parameters negotiation.*   ATM traffic parameters can be negotiated between ATM end users.

- *N-ISDN interworking.*   Enables interworking between narrowband and broadband ISDN networks.

Table 8.3 shows the new functions provided in the UNI Signaling 4.0, and whether the functions are mandatory (M) or optional (O) on both the ATM end user (terminal equipment) and switch (switching system).

8.5   Summary

ATM provides the capability for ATM end users to dynamically establish, maintain, and clear virtual connections and virtual paths. Point-to-point and point-to-multipoint connections are supported. Signaling is an exchange of

TABLE 8.3   UNI Signaling 4.0 Functions

Feature	Terminal equipment	Switching system
Point-to-point calls	M	M
Point-to-multipoint calls	O	M
Leaf-initiated join capability	O	M
Notification of end-to-end connection completion	O	M
ATM anycast capability	O	*
Multiple signaling channels	O	O
Switched virtual path (VP) service	O	O
Proxy signaling	O	O
Frame discard capability	O	†
ABR signaling for point-to-point calls	O	O
Generic identifier transport	O	O
Traffic parameter negotiation	O	O
Signaling of individual QoS parameters	O	O
Supplementary services	—	—
Direct dialing in (DDI)	O	O
Multiple subscriber number (MSN)	O	O
Calling line identification presentation (CLIP)	O	O
Calling line identification restriction (CLIR)	O	O
Connected line identification presentation (COLP)	O	O
Connected line identification restriction (COLR)	O	O
Subaddressing (SUB)	O	‡
User-user signaling (UUS)	O	O

* This feature is optional for public networks/switching systems and is mandatory for private networks/switching systems.

† Transport of the frame discard indication is mandatory.

‡ This feature is mandatory for networks/switching systems (public and private) that support only native E.164 address formats.

messages between ATM end users and the network over the UNI that accomplishes this. The messages contain information that is used by the source ATM end user, the ATM network, and the destination ATM end user to process the connection request.

ATM Traffic Management

ATM supports different service levels and QoS on a per-connection basis. To ensure that the performance objectives can be satisfied for both new and existing connections, ATM networks implement a number of different traffic and congestion control mechanisms called collectively in this chapter *traffic management*. Traffic management enables an ATM network to deliver QoS for individual connections, protects against conditions that could result in congestion and degraded performance, and provides new connections the opportunity to optimize available network resources.

9.1 Traffic Management in ATM Networks

ATM has the ability to support different types of applications over the same physical network infrastructure whether it be video, voice, data, or a combination. This is a very special ability because the demands made on network resources for different applications can vary significantly. For example, an electronic mail application places no boundary on how long a message takes to reach a destination. No real network resources other than whatever minimal bandwidth might be available at any point in time has to be allocated beforehand for it to work properly. It is connectionless and best effort in the purest sense. A real-time videoconference is another story. Not only does it require large and varying amounts of bandwidth, but the cells containing the digitized video image must reach the destination in a very short period of time. In addition, the application will not work if there is a large variation in the time between when back-to-back cells arrive at the destination. Very stringent demands are placed on the network to ensure that the real-time video application will work properly.

To successfully support the integration of different applications and QoS over an ATM network, several assumptions must be put forth and accepted by an ATM end user and the network. They are the following:

- There is available capacity within the ATM network to handle a new connection and its associated QoS without negatively impacting any other existing connections. If there is the possibility that an existing connection will be affected, then the new connection setup request is rejected.

- The ATM end user (application) and the network will come to an agreement at connection setup time on the characteristics of the traffic submitted to the network by the application. The characteristics (parameters might be a better word) include a maximum and minimum cell rate and QoS.

- The ATM network has the right to discard or tag cells that exceed the agreed-upon parameters made at connection setup time. This policing action is performed at the point where cells enter the network.

- The ATM network will provide fair and equitable access to ATM end users wishing to use unused network resources on a best-effort basis. However, if the ATM network detects congestion, then it can either discard cells or notify the ATM end user to slow down the rate of submitted traffic to the network.

These assumptions form the basis for the existing techniques used to manage traffic within an ATM network. The goals of traffic management pertaining to ATM are simple:

- Support multiple types of traffic at different speeds.
- Satisfy each application's QoS requirements on a per-connection basis.
- Maximize and optimize the utilization of network resources.
- Protect the ATM end user and the network in order to achieve network performance objectives.
- Minimize reliance on AAL and higher-layer traffic management schemes to reduce or eliminate congestion in an ATM network.

Technically speaking, the main goal of ATM traffic management is pure and simple: avoid congestion. *Congestion* in an ATM network is defined as a state in which the components of an ATM network, be it the switches, physical links, or hosts, are not able to meet the negotiated network performance objectives for the existing connections. Avoiding congestion is much easier said than done and solving this problem has been an intense area of study and debate for the last few years. The complexity arises because, as an integrated service, traffic introduced to the network can be unpredictable and will contend for the same network resources. One technique would be to allocate maximum bandwidth on a per-connection basis, but this could be wasteful and does not optimize network resources. Another technique would be to place buffers in the network switches, but the tradeoff could be increased latency, cost, and complexity. A third technique involves the network or destination ATM end user notifying the sending ATM end user to reduce the input cell rate when a congestion threshold is reached. And, of course, cells can be discarded at the network entry point if they portend congestion by exceeding a negotiated cell rate. There are other congestion-avoidance techniques that have been suggested and could very well be implemented in ATM networks. Fortunately, the standards bodies have decided on a foundation of basic traffic management functions that will be discussed in this chapter. They are documented in ATM Forum Traffic Management 4.0 and ITU-T Recommendation I.371.

Traffic management in an ATM network can be broken down into two areas: traffic control and congestion control. *Traffic control* is defined as the set of actions taken by the network to avoid congestion conditions. *Congestion control* is defined as the set of actions taken by the network to minimize the spread and duration of congestion. The specific technique used, under what traffic management area it falls, and where it is performed in the network is a function of the time needed to execute it. For example, checking to determine if a cell exceeds a maximum input rate of OC3 is performed at the network ingress switch and should be executed in less than 3 microseconds (one cell transmitted at 155.52 Mb takes 2.73 microseconds). Another example would be end-to-end flow control. This function can be performed within the duration of a round-trip between the source and the destination.

The chart in Fig. 9.1 lays out possible traffic and congestion control schemes and the scale in time in which they are executed. Most traffic and congestion control takes place at the network ingress or entry point to the ATM network. This prevents congestion by discarding or marking traffic that can lead to congestion situations. Given the potential input rates and the variation in traffic types, it is easy to see why traffic management is such an important and complex function in ATM networks.

Traffic Control and Congestion Control Technique	Time frame
Traffic policing Traffic shaping Cell discard Frame discard Buffer management	Cell/PDU input rate
Network feedback	Round-trip propagation delay
Connection Admission Control	Connection setup
Network Engineering/Design	Long term

Figure 9.1 Traffic management functions.

9.2   Traffic Management Definitions

Resources are allocated at connection setup time and traffic management is performed for the duration of the connection, based on the quantity and quality of the traffic submitted to the network. ATM defines a set of traffic and QoS parameters which are used to capture the characteristics of an ATM connection.

9.2.1   Traffic parameters

The traffic parameters defined are:

- *Peak cell rate (PCR).*   Specifies the maximum rate that cells can be introduced into the network over a virtual connection.
- *Sustainable cell rate (SCR).*   Specifies average rate over time that cells can be introduced into the network over a virtual connection.
- *Maximum burst size (MBS).*   Specifies the amount of time the virtual connection can accept traffic at the PCR.
- *Minimum cell rate (MCR).*   Specifies the minimum cell rate that the network must guarantee for a virtual connection.

9.2.2   Traffic descriptors

Traffic descriptors is another term for traffic parameters. ATM defines two types of traffic descriptors: source and connection. A *source traffic descriptor* is a set of traffic descriptors used during connection setup time to capture the characteristics of the connections requested by the source ATM end user.

A *connection traffic descriptor* specifies the traffic characteristics of the connection. A connection traffic descriptor will include the source traffic descriptors, the *cell-delay variation tolerance* (CDVT), and the conformance definition. The CDVT is a measurement on the variation in cell-arrival times and the conformance definition is used by the traffic policing function to verify compliance and maintain network performance objectives. The connection traffic descriptors are used by the CAC to allocate resources at connection setup time and by the traffic policing function during the course of the connection to check on the compliance of cells entering the network.

9.2.2.1   CDVT.   As mentioned, the CDVT is the upper bound on the variation in actual versus expected cell arrival times. This variation can be caused by queuing and delay as cells from different connections pass down through the ATM layers (AAL, ATM) and are multiplexed onto a single physical interface. A variation that is too big may cause problems, particularly for applications which depend on the cells arriving back-to-back in a predictable manner. The concept of CDVT is illustrated in Fig. 9.2.

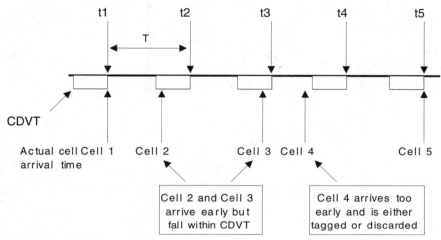

Figure 9.2   Cell-delay variation tolerance.

9.2.2.2   Conformance definition.   The conformance definition is simply a test that is run against each cell as it enters the network. A *conforming cell* is one that passes the test and is emitted into the network. A *nonconforming cell* is one that fails the test and may either be discarded before it enters the network or is tagged as being nonconforming (using the CLP bit) and then emitted into the network. The test is not so strict that only conforming cells will make it. In reality, a compliant connection will consist of both conforming and nonconforming cells.

The test is actually an implementation of the Generic Cell Rate Algorithm (GCRA) that is documented in ITU-T Recommendation I.371. The more common term for the GCRA is *leaky bucket*. The term leaky bucket is used because, conceptually, it could be pictured as a bucket with a fixed-size hole at the bottom. Cells fill up the bucket and are then leaked into the network. If there is any overflow, then those cells are considered nonconforming.

The GCRA uses a combination of PCR and CDVT or SCR and MBS as parameters to test for traffic conformance. One or more leaky buckets with different parameters may be placed in a series to test for traffic conformance. Cells marked with their CLP bit equal to zero or one (CLP 0+1) hit the leaky bucket that is located, typically, on the ingress switch. They can be optionally tagged (CLP bit changed from zero to one), discarded, or passed to a second leaky bucket. CLP=1 cells pass through the second leaky bucket unchanged and are admitted to the network. Only the CLP=0 cells are checked for conformance or nonconformance.

Figure 9.3 depicts the GCRA implemented at the network ingress. Cells are submitted to the network. If they exceed the PCR or the CDVT, they are either discarded or marked. CLP=0 cells then flow to the next bucket where

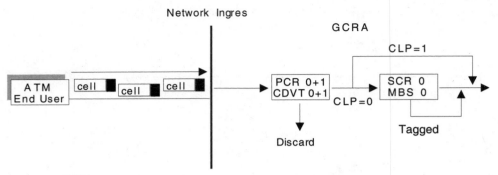

Figure 9.3   GCRA.

SCR and MBS are tested. These cells are possibly marked and then emitted into the network.

9.2.3   Quality of service

QoS is a measurement on the delay and dependability that a particular connection will support. QoS is used by the CAC to allocate resources at connection setup time and by traffic management to ensure that the network performance objectives are met. Six parameters are specified, the first three of which can be negotiated using UNI 4.0 Signaling at connection setup time:

- *Peak-to-peak CDV.*   Specifies variation in cell transfer delay.
- *Maximum cell transfer delay (maxCTD).*   Specifies end-to-end cell transfer delay.
- *Cell loss ratio (CLR).*   Lost cells/total transmitted cells.

The remaining three are nonnegotiable:

- *Cell error ratio (CER).*   Errored cells/(successfully transmitted cells+errored cells).
- *Severely errored cell block ratio (SECBR).*   Severely errored cell blocks/total transmitted cell blocks.
- *Cell misinsertion rate (CMR).*   Misinserted cells/time interval.

Further information on these parameters is available in the UNI 4.0 and Traffic Management 4.0 documents from the ATM Forum.

9.2.4   Traffic contract

An ATM end user will request a connection by signaling or subscription. Along with this connection request comes source traffic descriptors, CDVT and QoS parameters which characterize quantity and quality of the traffic to be transported over the connection. The ATM network uses this information to set up the connection and police the traffic as it enters the network. This implicit agreement between the ATM end user and the network which consists of traffic descriptors, QoS, CDVT, and a conformance definition make up what is called the *traffic contract*. Simply put, the ATM network will support the connection and associated QoS as long as the ATM end user stays within the agreed-upon parameters. Figure 9.4 depicts the concept of the ATM traffic contract.

9.3   ATM Service Architecture

The ATM Forum has defined a service architecture consisting of five ATM layer service categories that relate traffic and QoS parameters to network behavior. They are:

- Constant bit rate (CBR)
- Variable bit rate—real time (VBR-rt)
- Variable bit rate—non-real time (VBR-nrt)
- Available bit rate (ABR)
- Unspecified bit rate (UBR)

9.3.1   CBR

CBR service is used for applications and connections that require a fixed and consistent quantity of bandwidth. Bandwidth and resources on a CBR connection is established and fixed at the PCR for the duration of the connection. This is required if the source emits cells at a sustained PCR for the duration of the

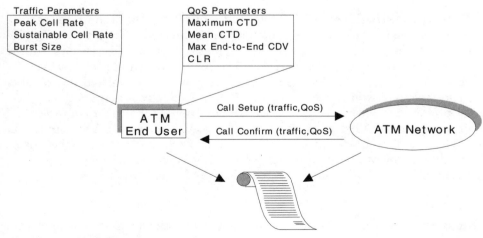

Figure 9.4   ATM traffic contract.

connection but could prove wasteful in bandwidth and resources otherwise. A source may send data up to the PCR for any length of time. CBR service is used to emulate high-speed leased lines like T1 upward and to support real-time applications that require a small network delay and cell delay variation.

9.3.2   VBR-rt

VBR-rt service is used for applications and connections that require a small and controlled network delay and CDV but whose bandwidth requirement may vary during the life of the connection. VBR-rt connections are characterized by PCR, SCR, and MBS. Cells can burst up to the PCR for a period of time but on average will be emitted at the SCR for the duration of the connection. Cells exceeding the maxCTD are of no use to the application using the VBR-rt service. The variation in the cell input rate enables multiple VBR-rt sources to be statistically multiplexed over the same physical connection to maximize network resources. Examples of VBR-rt applications are desktop videoconferencing and voice.

9.3.3   VBR-nrt

VBR-nrt service is used for applications and connections that are insensitive to network delay and whose bandwidth requirements may vary. VBR-nrt connections are characterised by PCR, SCR, and MBS. The variation in the cell input rate enables multiple VBR-nrt sources to be statistically multiplexed over the same physical connection to maximize network resources. Examples of VBR-nrt applications are any VBR applications that can operate without a maximum network delay and where the network can benefit from statistical multiplexing. These could be airline reservation systems and frame relay interworking.

9.3.4   UBR

UBR service is strictly for applications and connections that require no service guarantees. No traffic or QoS parameters are applied on a UBR connection. No traffic contract per se exists. Applications making use of UBR service will be delay and loss tolerant. UBR sources can transmit up to link access speeds for however long that bandwidth is available. Any cells transmitted in excess of the available bandwidth will result in cell loss. Typically, it is up to the higher-layer protocols to recover (e.g., TCP). UBR is a popular choice for running LAN applications over ATM because it is simple and mirrors LAN application behavior—no foreknowledge on traffic rates or QoS, random transmissions at full available bit rates, and a reliance on higher-layer services for error recovery. Examples of UBR applications are file transfer and E-mail.

9.3.5   ABR

ABR service is designed for applications and connections whose cell input rate may vary depending on feedback provided by the network. This feedback, or rather control information, is conveyed to the ABR source in *resource management* (RM) cells. RM cells contain information about network conditions (e.g., congestion) and based on this information, the ABR source will increase or decrease its cell input rate. An ABR connection is characterized by a PCR and an MCR; however, the maximum input cell rate achieved by an ABR source may be less than the PCR, depending on network feedback. ABR applications are delay and loss tolerant. ABR sources can expect fair access to any available bandwidth at any point in time. ABR service is unique because of the flow control mechanism which provides a minimum amount of bandwidth to all ABR sources that behave and adjust according to network feedback. ABR is intended as the optimal ATM service for data networking applications because of the flow control and fair-access mechanisms. ABR flow control will be discussed in more detail in Sec. 9.5. Examples of ABR applications are LAN traffic and file transfer.

9.3.6   ATM layer service attributes

Table 9.1 shows ATM layer services along with their specific attributes relating to traffic and QoS.

9.4   ATM Traffic Management Mechanisms

The purpose of traffic management is to optimize network resources, provide QoS for existing connections, and avoid or limit congestion. To that end, the standards' bodies have specified a number of different traffic management functions that can be implemented. Some are simple and can be applied to all

TABLE 9.1   ATM Layer Service Parameters

Attribute	CBR	VBR-rt	VBR-nrt	UBR	ABR
Traffic parameters					
PCR and CDVT(pcr)	specified	specified	specified	specified*	specified[†]—note 3
SCR, MBS, CDVT(scr)	n/a	specified	specified	n/a	n/a
MCR	n/a	n/a	n/a	n/a	specified
QoS parameters					
peak-peak CDV	specified	specified	unspecified	unspecified	unspecified
maxCTD	specified	specified	unspecified	unspecified	unspecified[‡]
CLR	specified	specified	specified	unspecified	
Flow control					
closed loop	unspecified	unspecified	unspecified	unspecified	specified

* Used either in CAC and UPC or informational purposes only.

[†] Represents maximum cell rate that ABR source may ever send. The actual maximum cell rate will be determined by network feedback.

[‡] CLR is low for ABR sources which adjust cell input rate according to feedback.

ATM services; others are more complex and service specific. But they have all shown to be effective and are therefore critical to the successful operation and function of an ATM network. The traffic mechanisms are:

- Connection admission control (CAC)
- Usage parameter control (UPC)
- Selective cell discard
- Traffic shaping
- Explicit forward congestion indication (EFCI)
- Resource management using virtual paths
- Frame discard
- Generic flow control
- Forward error correction
- ABR flow control

9.4.1   CAC

CAC is the procedure that decides if a connection is established or rejected. CAC uses the connection traffic descriptors and requested QoS as input into its algorithm. If capacity is available, the requested QoS can be met and other existing connections and their agreed-upon QoS will not be impacted, then the connection is accepted. If any of these three preconditions are not met, then the connection request will fail. CAC determines which traffic parameters will be required by the UPC function and the allocation of network resources. CAC is performed by every switch along the path from the source to the destination in an ATM network.

CAC does not name a specific calculation for network resource allocation needed to support a connection and meet the QoS. That is left up to the switch-specific CAC algorithm. One technique would be to allocate bandwidth based on the PCR for each connection. Depending on the traffic type, this could prove suboptimal and lead to a rapid depletion in available network capacity. Another technique is to exploit the bursty nature of many ATM applications and allocate only the minimum amount of bandwidth and resources needed to meet a particular QoS. This technique, called *source equivalent capacity,* or *equivalent bandwidth* in some quarters, makes much better use of network resources, but again is only effective when the ratio of PCR to SCR is greater than one.

9.4.2   UPC

UPC is defined as the set of actions taken by the network to monitor and control traffic. UPC is also called *traffic policing* and as the name implies, this function polices the traffic as it is submitted to the network. UPC checks on the validity of the VPI and VCI, enforces the traffic contract, and if necessary will tag or discard any cells that violate the conformance definition. UPC must act in a matter of individual cell time and must not disrupt the flow of traffic.

The UPC function is usually placed in the ingress switch of the network and is implemented using single or dual leaky buckets. Whether one or two leaky buckets is used depends on the traffic type and conformance definition. For example, a switch will police a CBR connection using a single leaky bucket (GCRA(1/PCR, CDVT)) whereas a VBR connection will use two (GCRA(1/PCR, CDVT), (1/SCR,MBS))

9.4.3 Selective cell discard

A congested network component may discard cells that are nonconforming or if CLP=1. This protects cells with a value of CLP=0.

9.4.4 Traffic shaping

Traffic shaping alters the characteristics of cell traffic to achieve better network efficiency and still meet the QoS requirements. Examples of traffic shaping functions include PCR reduction, burst-length reduction, CDV removal, and cell spacing. All of these have the effect of changing the traffic characteristics and introducing some nominal amount of latency. However, the cell sequence integrity and QoS objectives are maintained for the connection.

Traffic shaping is optional and can be performed anywhere in the network. One strategy involves placing the shaping function at the network ingress. This may have the effect of smoothing out the traffic by reducing the PCR and CDV, and thus the total network allocation of resources. Another strategy is to place the shaper at the egress of the network. This enables the shaper to cancel out any accumulated burstiness or CDV. This would provide an improved QoS for the traffic presented to an ATM end user or over a public UNI to a public ATM network. A traffic shaping function at the network egress is shown in Fig. 9.5.

9.4.5 EFCI

The PTI field of the cell header contains a congestion notification function. If cells pass through a congested-network component on their way to the destination, then these bits may be turned on to indicate congestion. This happens in the forward direction only. It is up to the end systems to react to this congestion indication. One technique available in ABR flow control enables backward compatiblity with older switches. If the switch turns on the EFCI bits in any of the data cells, then the ABR destination will return an RM cell with a congestion notification which will instruct the ABR source to reduce its cell input rate.

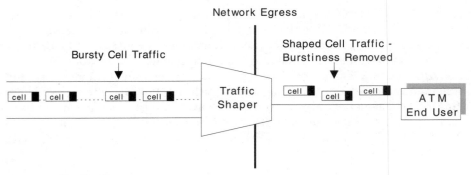

Figure 9.5 Traffic shaper.

9.4.6 Resource management using virtual paths

Proper and effective management of ATM virtual paths can be used to maximize network resource allocation and reduce the chance of congestion. Remember that a VP is a collection of one or more VCs. All traffic management functions can be performed at the VP rather than the VC level. This can simplify many of the traffic management functions and make better use of network resources. This flexibility is further enhanced in UNI Signaling 4.0 with the availability of switched virtual paths (SVP). For example, an SVP could be established during off-hours to support a site backup where multiple VCs may be required.

9.4.7 Frame discard

ATM handles congestion by dropping cells. These cells may be part of different AAL PDUs (packets). If that is the case, then the higher-layer protocols like TCP at the source may retransmit the entire frame, which means a new AAL PDU and more cells. This amplifies the congestion situation. Frame discard enables cells to be dropped for the entire AAL PDU. This is achieved by examining the ATM SDU type in the ATM cell header. If one cell is dropped, then the switch drops all cells until it sees the end-of-frame indicator in an ATM cell header. Another name for this technique is *early packet discard* (EPD) and will be examined more closely in Sec. 9.6.1.

9.4.8 Generic flow control

The four GFC bits in the header of the UNI cell are used to indicate two classes of traffic: controlled and uncontrolled. Controlled traffic is subject to congestion control mechanism while uncontrolled is not. Just about all implementations today specify traffic as uncontrolled, leaving traffic and congestion control to mechanisms other than GFC. This technique is documented in ITU-T Recommendation I.150 and I.361.

9.4.9 Forward error correction

Cell loss can result in degraded performance or even an aggravated congestion situation. FEC is a technique which enables frames to be recovered from lost or corrupted cells. FEC is implemented at the SSCS level as shown in Fig. 9.6. A source higher-layer service passes data down to the FEC SSCS where it is then passed over the ATM network to the destination. The destination FEC SSCS recovers from any bit errors, cell, or frame loss and then presents the data to the higher-layer service. FEC is suitable for both real-time VBR video, where data loss can be damaging, and to an ABR ATM LAN data, where reliability and performance are important.

9.5 ABR Flow Control

Applications like video and voice that make use of CBR and VBR connections know beforehand how much bandwidth they will require to operate effectively. This information in the form of traffic parameters and QoS is used to reserve resources and build a connection dynamically or by subscription. The same cannot be said for data networking applications, particularly those that run on a LAN. They will use whatever bandwidth is available on a first-come-I-want-it-all basis. This type of traffic can be characterized by the following:

- Transmissions are bursty.

- The cell input rate of a source will vary over time.

- Variable length frames of sizes are considerably larger than 53-byte cells.

- It is delay and loss tolerant.

- It is bandwidth greedy, using whatever bandwidth is available at the time.

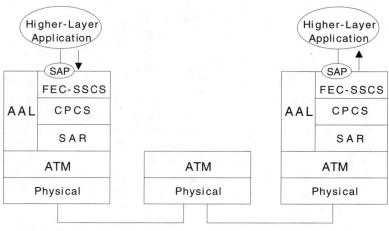

Figure 9.6 Forward error correction.

- It is transported in connectionless layer-3 datagrams independent of the link-level operations (e.g., ATM, Ethernet).

- It is the most popular and fastest-growing type of traffic in networking. Witness the Internet and the growth of corporate global data networking.

- They can increase or decrease their transmission rates based on changing network conditions.

The ATM Forum has specified a new service class, *available bit rate* (ABR), which most accurately reflects the behavior of LAN traffic. However, reflecting on its greedy and unpredictable nature, introducing LAN traffic onto ATM networks could be problematic. Network resources could be underutilized. Worse yet, congestion could reduce application throughput for LAN traffic to a fraction of its minimum levels. LAN applications expect fair or deterministic access to bandwidth, and that could be undermined if one user grabs all of it. And due to the statistical multiplexing nature of ATM, the service guarantees provided for CBR and VBR traffic could be impacted if a burst of ABR traffic is allowed to flow unchecked into the ATM network. Some level of control for ABR traffic then is required.

9.5.1   Closed loop congestion control

Congestion control can be performed in open loop or closed loop systems. *Open loop* congestion control is when the network takes a unilateral action to avoid or relieve a congestion condition without notifying or involving the traffic source. This is the case with applications using CBR and VBR service. CBR/VBR sources establish a traffic contract with the ATM network and begin transmitting at an agreed-upon cell input rate. The network, unbeknownst to the source will tag or even drop cells to control congestion. CBR/VBR sources will continue to transmit at the cell input rate whether congestion is present or not. It should be pointed out for clarity that CBR/VBR sources would not be able to adjust their cell input rates even if the network tried to tell them.

In a *closed loop,* the traffic source will modify its cell input rate as a result of feedback received from the network (destination included). Two notification techniques can be used: BECN and FECN. *Forward explicit congestion notification* (FECN) is a method that enables network components (e.g., switches) to signal congestion in either data or control cells as they flow from the source to the destination. FECN really only serves as a signal to the destination to take some action (notify traffic source). An FECN indicator (EFCI is PTI field) is supported in the ATM cell header. *Backward explicit congestion notification* (BECN) flows in the opposite direction and can be sourced directly from the point of congestion. When a network resource detects congestion, a notification is sent back to the traffic source. Based on that information, the traffic source will either increase or decrease the rate of input into the network. This is illustrated in Fig. 9.7.

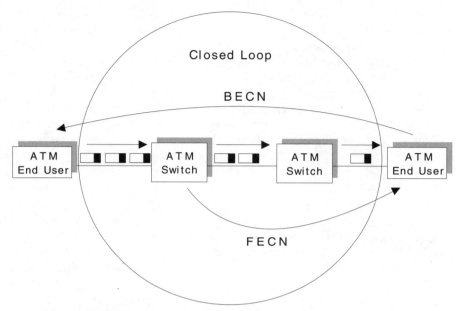

Figure 9.7   Closed loop congestion control.

The type of feedback received from the network can be binary (bits flipped to indicate congestion, increase/decrease rate) or explicit. If it is explicit, then it could be a new cell input rate as computed by the network or it could be the exact number of receive buffers available in the adjacent switch. The size of the feedback loop can be end to end or hop by hop. The smaller the feedback loop the quicker the traffic source can be throttled back. The tradeoff is that resources are required to close a loop (e.g., send BECN) and that the BECN messages still have to flow over what may be a congested path back to the source. A network can be segmented into a series of concatenated closed loops with each loop supporting a different feedback scheme and policy which could be based on the type of network in the loop.

There are two flavors of closed loop congestion control for ABR service: rate based and credit based. The rate-based scheme enables a source to adapt its specific cell input rate based on feedback from the network. The credit scheme is a link-by-link approach that enables a sender to transmit cells if and only if there are available buffers (credits) in the receiver switch. The number of available buffers is conveyed to the upstream neighbor via feedback.

The choice of which is better has been a topic of discussion and debate for several years now. On the WAN side, the rate-based solution is better because the switches do not require a potentially large (bandwidth/propagation delay) buffer requirement, is backward compatible with older switches using EFCI, and enables public carriers to better manage usage/billing by explicitly controlling the rate of usage. On the LAN side the credit is better because it provides zero cell loss, transmits at full link speed immediately, and is simple to implement in the end stations. A solution incorporating a choice of both schemes was rejected because it would require different techniques to be supported by vendor and the standards and would violate the concept of seamless ATM LAN/WAN integration.

The traffic management subworking group voted overwhelmingly, in the fall of 1994, to standardize on a rate-based solution. From the ashes of defeat the credit scheme was resurrected by several vendors and reissued under the name of *quantum flow control* (QFC).

9.5.2   Rate-based congestion control

The ATM Forum selected a rate-based scheme as the basis for ABR flow control. Some remaining details are still being worked out, but the framework which we will call *explicit rate* (ER) flow control is in place.

ER flow control uses binary or explicit feedback from the network to set the optimal and congestion-free cell input rate at the source. The basic function is as follows:

- The ABR source generates a *resource management* (RM, PTI=6) every N (e.g., 32) cells. Included in this cell is the cell input rate at which the ABR source is transmitting.

- At any point of congestion along the way, to and including the destination, the RM cell can be marked to indicate congestion in a link or switch, or the switch can calculate and place in the RM cell a new explicit cell input rate at which the source should transmit.

- The RM cell is returned to the source that adjusts the cell input rate upward or downward.

ER introduces a function called *intelligent marking*. It factors in the current cell input rate at the source and an estimation calculated by each intermediate switch of the optimal bandwidth for each VC passing through the switch. Based on these two values, an RM cell returned to the source may contain a new explicit cell input cell rate. Fairness may be enforced because the switches can compute the maximum congestion-free rate for an ABR source, based on the source VC's *current cell rate* (CCR) and available network capacity. This concept is illustrated in Fig. 9.8.

ER provides the flexibility to configure multiple feedback loops between the actual endpoints of the VC. Specifically, a *virtual source* (Vsrc) and *destination* (Vdst) can be placed in the network to initiate and terminate separate feedback loops. This shortens the feedback loop, thus providing a faster response to potential congestion conditions. This also enables separate network types (e.g., LAN, WAN, public carriers) to implement their own flow control policies. Fig-

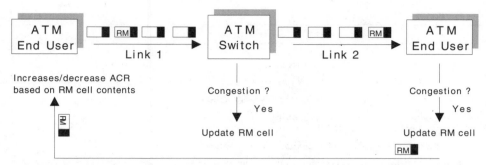

Figure 9.8   ER flow control.

ure 9.9 depicts three separate ER feedback loops configured over an ATM network. The middle loop consists of a public ATM carrier network.

The basic parameters specified at connection setup time for ABR service are shown in Table 9.2. A set of parameters is mandatory and should be signaled at connection setup time. An additional set is optional.

Resource management (RM) cells are used to communicate feedback information between ABR sources, destination, and switches. The RM cell contains fields that are marked or updated by intermediate switches as it is forwarded through the network. The RM cell is turned around by the ABR destination and returned to the source. The source, in turn, then adjusts its ACR based on the contents of the returned RM cell.

The contents of the 53-byte RM cell are described in Table 9.3.

Despite the almost unanimous vote for the rate-based scheme in the ATM Forum, it has not been an easy task to finish the specification. There is the issue of the numerous parameters that must be configured and perhaps tuned, in both the ABR source and the switches. This leads to additional cost and complexity in the ATM end-user adapters and the switches. Cell loss is another issue. ABR service is intended to carry bursty LAN traffic whose frames are typically much larger than individual cells. Any cell loss results in a lost frame which must then be retransmitted by the higher-layer protocol. The time it takes an RM cell to

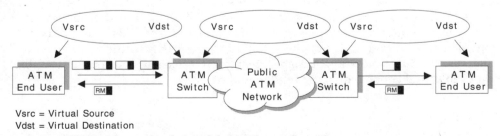

Vsrc = Virtual Source
Vdst = Virtual Destination

Figure 9.9   ER virtual source and virtual destination configuration.

TABLE 9.2   ABR ER Parameters

Parameter	Description
Mandatory	
PCR	Peak cell rate—cell input rate source may never exceed.
MCR	Minimum cell rate—minimum cell input rate that source is guaranteed.
ICR	Initial cell rate—cell input rate at which source should send after idle period.
RIF	Rate increase factor—used to calculate increase in cell input rate upon receipt of RM cell, additive increase rate (AIR)=PCR*RIF.
RDF	Rate decrease factor—used to calculate decrease in cell input rate.
TBE	Transient buffer exposure—negotiated number of cells that the source should send during start-up periods.
FRTT	Fixed round-trip time—sum of the fixed and propagation delays from the source to the furthest destination and back.
Optional	
Nrm	Maximum number of cells a source may send for each forward RM cell.
Trm	Provides an upper bound on the time between forward RM cells for an active source.
CDF	Cutoff decrease factor—controls the decrease in ACR associated with CRM.
ADTF	ACR decrease time factor—time permitted between sending RM cells before the rate is decreased to ICR.
Other	
ACR	Allowed cell rate—current cell input rate that a source is allowed to send.
CRM	Missing RM cell count—used to limit number of forward RM cells which may be sent in the absence of received backward RM cells.
TCR	Tagged cell rate—limits the rate at which a source may send out-of-rate forward RM cells.

propagate back to the source almost guarantees that some cells will be lost due to congestion. Another drawback is that it is only first supported under UNI Signaling 4.0, thus leaving legacy UNI 3.0/3.1 ABR sources with no option. Although simulations of ER behavior have shown it to be stable with a quick ramp-up time, it still remains to be seen if it can adequately and fairly control a large number of bursty ABR sources in a production network.

In defense of explicit rate flow control, the ATM Forum is working hard to simplify its operation and reduce the complexity. The rate-versus-credit debate forced the rate proponents to aggresively identify and fix any deficiencies. It is backward compatible with older switches and the Vsrc/Vdst capability will enable private and public networks to flow control ABR traffic at the network ingress. By the time the final specification is released, it should be stable, workable, and capable of being implemented.

9.5.3   QFC flow control

The decision in the ATM Forum to proceed with a rate-based solution did not sit well with the credit-scheme folks, many of whom are ATM LAN equipment

TABLE 9.3 RM Cell

Field	Octet	Description
Header	1–5	Cell header with PTI='110'
ID	6	Protocol ID
DIR	7	Direction, 0=forward, 1=backward
BN	7	BECN, BN=1 indicates network or destination generated RM cell
CI	7	Congestion indication, CI=1 indicates congestion and cause's source to decrease ACR
NI	7	No increase, used if switch detects impending congestion condition
RA	7	Request/acknowledge per I.371, not used in ATM Forum ABR specification
Reserved	7	
ER	8–9	Explicit cell rate
CCR	10–11	Current cell rate, CCR=ACR when source generates RM cell
MCR	12–13	Minimum cell rate
QL	14–17	Queue length, not used in ATM Forum ABR specification
SN	18–21	Seq. number, not used in ATM Forum ABR specification
Reserved	22–51	
Reserved	52	
CRC-10	52–53	

vendors, who had a working implementation in place. Therefore, a consortium of vendors, led by DEC and Ascom Nexion, was formed and the credit scheme was published under the name *quantum flow control* (QFC). QFC is a classic credit-based flow control mechanism. It operates under the basic premise that a sender cannot transmit any cells to a receiver unless there are available buffers in the receiver. It operates on a link-by-link basis, so the feedback loop is small and operates with a link-speed propogation delay. Other characteristics of QFC include:

- Guarantees zero cell loss due to network congestion.

- Instantaneous access to available network bandwidth.

- Supports ABR service over point-to-multipoint connections (ER only offers a framework for future study in TM 4.0).

- Configures automatically.

- Has compatibility with UNI 3.0/3.1 (requires additional code point in BBC information element).

QFC utilizes per-VC accounting to ensure fairness. Every VC is allocated a specific amount of send buffer space (credit balance) that determines how much data can be received by the downstream receiver on the link. When the sender transmits N cells to the downstream receiver, the credit balance is decremented by N. When the adjacent receiver forwards the cells over the next link, a credit is returned to the sender and the credit balance is incremented. The credit flow control technique showing two links is illustrated in Fig. 9.10.

The model for a QFC implementation consists of a logical link, the transmitter, and the receiver. There are several counters and variables used within the

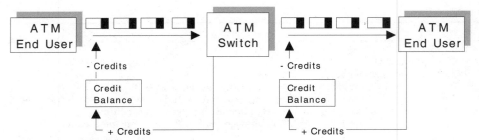

Figure 9.10   Credit flow control.

QFC protocols which keep track of the number of cells forwarded and received on a connection and link basis. A *connection* is defined as a VP or VC, and a *link* connects a transmitter to the receiver. The following are especially important because they determine if the receiver has available resources to buffer cells from the transmitter and thus guarantee zero cell loss due to congestion.

- *TxCounter(VC or link).*   The number of cells transmitted on the connection or link to the receiver.

- *BSU_Fwd_Count(VC or link).*   Value received in control message from receiver that represents how many cells have been forwarded (passed on to the next hop) by the receiver at the time the message was created. Separate values for VC and link resources are used.

- *Limit(VC).*   Maximum number of cells allocated at the receiver for a connection.

- *BSL_Limit(link).*   Maximum number of cells allocated at the receiver for all connections flowing over a link.

The counters at the transmitter are updated by buffer state control messages received from the transmitter. The QFC protocol reference model as well as the cell transmission decision criteria are shown in Fig. 9.11.

ABR flow control is critical to the successful operation of ATM multiprotocol networks. The ER rate-based scheme has been selected by the ATM Forum and will be released as a standard. However ER is complex and work remains to simplify and stabilize it before vendors can safely implement it. QFC is technically elegant and simpler but does not enjoy industrywide acceptance or at least it has not been acknowledged. It remains to be seen how this most interesting debate is settled.

9.6   UBR Congestion Control

The potential and importance of supporting LAN traffic over ATM networks and the absense of an ABR flow control standard have forced vendors and developers to look elsewhere for a solution. The obvious alternative would be to

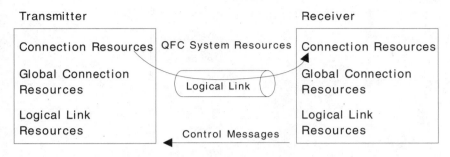

TxCounter - BSU_Fwd_Count <= Limit
(connection buffers available for VC or VP at receiver)

TxCounter(link) - BSU_Fwd_Count(link) <= BSL_Limit(link)
(shared buffer pool for link not exhausted at receiver)

Figure 9.11 QFC protocol model and cell transmission criteria.

support LAN traffic as UBR or best effort. Essentially, that is how it is supported today. Throughput and reliability tend to be very good over lightly loaded networks.

However in the face of potential or current congestion conditions, UBR performances degrade rapidly. The problem is this: there is no flow control or feedback, so UBR sources will transmit up to PCR (if available) and will continue to do so, congestion or no congestion. Cells will be discarded due to switch buffer overflow, thus rendering an entire packet useless even though some cells survive. The destination AAL will not be able to reconstruct the packet. The surviving cells from the corrupted packet continue to fill up links and buffers in the network. Meanwhile, the higher-layer protocol (e.g., TCP) at the UBR source recognizes that a packet has been lost and retransmits the packet (segmented into more cells at the SAR) into the network. This compounds the congestion problem.

9.6.1 Early packet discard

A simple solution to relieve this congestion condition is to discard the surviving cells from the lost packet. This technique is called *early packet discard* (EPD). To avoid congestion, a switch maintains an EPD buffer threshold which is a percentage of the all the buffers in the switch. When the EPD threshold is exceeded, the switch will drop all remaining cells making up the AAL5 PDU until the last cell. It knows that it has reached the last cell of the AAL5 PDU by looking a the PTI field of the cell header. The operation of EPD is shown in Fig. 9.12.

Simulations of UBR with EPD congestion avoidance, sufficient buffers, and per-VC processing have yielded good performance with fair access. UBR has nowhere near the complexity of ABR, and EPD is easily able to be implemented. In addition, UNI 4.0 UBR sources can signal their desire for EPD support at connection setup time using the frame discard code point.

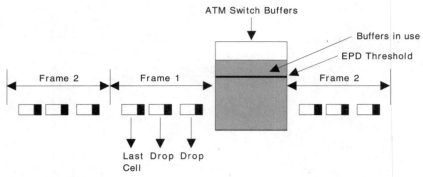

Figure 9.12   EPD.

9.7   Summary

Traffic management is required in ATM networks to preserve the performance and QoS objectives of existing connections, utilizing the five ATM layers services: CBR, VBR-rt, VBR-nrt, ABR, and UBR. It maximizes network resources and protects both the network and the ATM end users from degraded service. Traffic management consists of traffic control, which attempts to avoid congestion, and congestion control, which attempts to minimize its severity. Traffic and congestion control techniques include CAC, UPC, traffic shaping, ABR flow control (rate and credit), and UBR EPD.

PNNI

PNNI is a switch-to-switch protocol developed within the ATM Forum to support efficient, dynamic, and scalable routing of SVC requests in a multivendor private ATM environment. PNNI phase I consists of two protocols: routing and signaling. PNNI routing uses a hierarchical topology-state protocol to disseminate topology and resource information among participating switches or groups of switches. PNNI signaling uses the topology and resource information available at each switch to construct a designated transit list which determines the path the SVC request will traverse to meet the requested QoS objectives and complete the connection.

10.1 PNNI Requirements

It is envisioned that ATM will grow and evolve into large networks consisting of dozens if not hundreds of switches connected by high-speed links. Many hundreds and thousands of SVC requests will be submitted to the network and the network will be expected to forward each individual request to the right destination, establish a path, allocate resources, and guarantee a QoS. Selecting the right path that optimizes network resources and meets the QoS objectives will be a challenging task as the network grows in size. The network itself may be made up of a mixture of ATM switches from different vendors. Different groups or organizations each with its own set of policies and procedures may control different domains of switches along the path. Normal network dynamics, such as changing traffic loads, and unavailable resources will alter the working network topology at any point in time. Simply administering this process would seem an insurmountable task.

The ATM Forum recognized these problems and decided that a dynamic interswitch protocol was needed. Much like a routing protocol used by routers to exchange reachability information, this interswitch protocol would enable

ATM switches to exchange information about the network topology, available resources, and QoS capabilities. This interswitch protocol would need to possess the following properties:

- *Scalable.*   It must support small to very large networks of ATM switches.
- *Simple to install and configure.*   This is especially true for small networks. As soon as two switches are connected, they should exchange topology information and then be able to route SVC requests with minimal if any configuration.
- *Provide efficient routing of SVC requests through the network while supporting QoS.*   The best path that will meet the QoS objectives in the SVC request should be computed and then the SVC request forwarded along that path.
- *Enable both source or transit policies to be administered.*   Different switch domains may have different policies based on security, usage, traffic types, and so on.
- *Multivendor.*   The protocol must be supported by a network of multivendor switches but must allow enough latitude for individual switches to perform certain functions (e.g., route computation, CAC).

Designing a protocol to meet these requirements was not an easy task. Coordination to support QoS in particular was required between the UNI signaling and traffic management subworking groups. As it was it took the PNNI subworking group well over two years to complete the specification.

10.2   PNNI Concepts

PNNI stands for Private Network Node Interface or Private Network-to-Network Interface. The two names reflect the dual usage and self-similarity of its behavior, as will be illustrated. PNNI is a switch-to-switch protocol developed within the ATM Forum to support efficient, dynamic, and scalable routing of SVC requests in a multivendor environment. PNNI phase I consists of two protocols:

- *Routing.*   PNNI routing is used to distribute information on the topology of the ATM network between switches (network node) and groups of switches (network-to-network). This information is used by the switch closest to the SVC requestor to compute a path to the destination that will satisfy QoS objectives. PNNI supports a hierarchical routing structure that allows it to scale to large networks.
- *Signaling.*   PNNI signaling uses the topology and resource information available at each switch (node) to construct a source-route path called a *designated transit list* (DTL). The DTL lists the specific nodes and links the the SVC request will traverse to meet the requested QoS objectives and complete

the connection. Crankback and alternate routing are also supported to route around a failed path.

One of the important design criteria behind PNNI was to implement, where appropriate, existing mechanisms to provide a desired function or operation. Therefore, PNNI makes use of several techniques that have been previously implemented in other internetworking protocols. They are:

- Link-state routing
- Hierarchical routing
- Source routing

Indeed, PNNI is a routing protocol and therefore requires a routing algorithm. One choice was distance vector, which is used in routing protocols such as RIP. This was deemed unworkable immediately because it is not scalable, is prone to routing loops, does not converge rapidly, and uses excessive overhead control traffic. The other choice was link-state routing. This was chosen because it is scalable, converges rapidly, generates less overhead traffic, and is extensible. Extensible means that information in addition to the status of links can be exchanged between nodes and incorporated into the topology database.

Figure 10.1 shows the concept of link-state routing used in PNNI. Each ATM switch exchanges updates with its neighbor switches on the status of the links, the status and resources of the switches, and the identity of each other's neighbor switches. This information is used to build a topology database of the entire network. Each ATM switch in the group will have an identical copy of the topology database. If a change in topology occurs (e.g., link is broken), then only that change is propagated between the switches.

PNNI is a topology-state protocol. ATM switches (nodes) include information on the links and nodes in the status update messages sent to neighboring switches. The nodal information may include data about switch capacity, QoS, and transit time. This information is important because SVC requests are routed over a path that must meet its QoS objectives.

PNNI must be scalable and to achieve this it implements a hierarchical routing structure. In a hierarchical routing structure topology and addressing information about a group of nodes is summarized and presented as a single node in the next level up in the hierarchy. The single node then advertises the summarized information about the group of nodes it represents one level below. The single node also behaves as if it was an actual ATM switch. This serves the purpose of limiting the amount of information about a group of nodes that is advertised. Considering the volume of information about connections in an ATM network, this could be massive. *Topology aggregation* as this process is called reduces complexity. But because the information advertised at the next level is summarized, some degree of accuracy is sacrificed. The concept of a routing hierarchy is shown in Fig. 10.2.

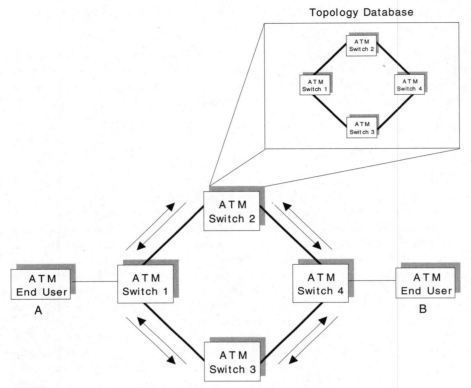

Figure 10.1 Concept of link-state routing.

The third technique that PNNI makes use of is source routing. Source routing enables the first switch in the SVC request path to compute the entire path, based on its knowledge of the network. Because QoS metrics are advertised and contained in the topology-state database, the first switch should have a pretty good idea about what path to take. Intermediate switches along the path do not need to perform any path computations. They just need to perform CAC and forward the SVC request by following the information in the source-route path. And finally, source routing prevents loops. Any possibility of a routing loop when attempting to satisfy an SVC request would be catastrophic.

10.3 PNNI Routing

To best illustrate the functions of the PNNI protocol a sample routing hierarchy is shown in Fig. 10.3. The PNNI specification defines the following:

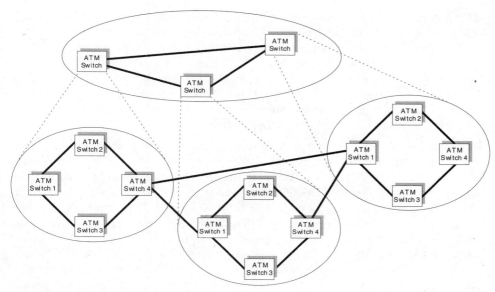

Figure 10.2   Multilevel routing hierarchy.

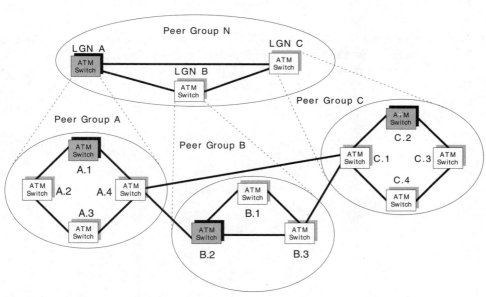

Figure 10.3   PNNI routing hierarchy.

- *Peer group.*   A peer group is a collection of nodes that maintains an identical topology database and exchange topology and resource information with each other. Members of a peer group discover their neighbors using a hello protocol. Four different peer groups: A, B, C, and N are depicted in our sample routing hierarchy. Peer groups A, B, and C consist of real ATM switches connected by physical links. Peer group N consists of three *logical group nodes* (LGN). The LGNs are summarized representations of the peer groups of actual switches they represent below them.

- *Peer group identifier.*   Members of the same peer group are identified by a common peer group identifier. The peer group identifier is derived from a unique 20-byte ATM address that is manually configured in each switch. The peer group identifier consists of two components. The first is a manually configured bit mask up to 13 bytes (104 bits) in length. This component is the address prefix as shown in Fig. 10.4. The second component is a 1-byte level indicator. This is used to determine how many bits in the address prefix are significant or, in other words, what level in the hierarchy the peer group is in. PNNI uses the address prefix to advertise reachability to end systems and achieve scaling by performing address summarization. This addressing structure is hierarchical in that the peer groups further down the hierarchy will have a greater number of significant bits in common than those peer groups higher up.

- *Logical node.*   A logical node is any switch or group of switches that runs the PNNI routing protocol. As an example, all members of PG A and the node above it, LGN A, are logical nodes.

- *Logical group node (LGN).*   An LGN is an abstract representation of a lower-level peer group for the purposes of representing that peer group in the next higher-layer peer group. In Fig. 10.3 LGN A represents PG A, LGN B represents PG B, and LGN C represents PG C. Even though an LGN is not a real switch but a logical representation of a group of switches, it still behaves as if it was a real ATM switch.

- *Parent peer group.*   This group contains an LGN representing peer group below it. PG N is a parent peer group.

- *Child peer group.*   Child peer group contains a node that is part of an LGN in the next higher-level peer group. Peer Groups A, B, and C are child peer groups in Fig. 10.3.

Figure 10.4   PNNI address format.

- *Peer group leader (PGL).*   Within the peer group, a PGL is elected to represent the peer group as a logical group node in the next higher-level peer group. The PGL is responsible for summarizing information about the peer group upward and passes higher-level information downward. In Fig. 10.3, each of the peer groups has a PGL shaded in grey. They are nodes A.1, B.2, C.2, and LGN A.

- *Hello protocol.*   This is a standard link-state procedure used by neighbor nodes to discover the existence and identity of each other.

- *Border nodes.*   A border node is a logical node which has a neighbor that belongs to a different peer group. This is established when neighbor switches exchange hello packets. The links connecting two peer groups are called *outside links*. In Fig. 10.3, nodes A.4, B.2, B.3, and C.4 are border nodes.

- *Uplinks.*   An uplink is a logical connection from a border node to a higher-level LGN. The existence of an uplink is derived from an exchange of hello packets between border nodes. The other members of the peer group are then informed about the existence of the uplink. An uplink is used by the PGL to construct a logical link between LGN in the next higher-level peer group. Figure 10.5 shows two uplinks from PG A to LGN B and LGN C.

- *Logical link.*   A logical link is a connection between two nodes. Logical links interconnect the members of PG N in Fig. 10.3. Horizontal links are logical links that connect nodes in the same peer group.

- *Routing control channel.*   VPI=0, VCI=18 is reserved as the VC used to exchange routing information between logical nodes. An RCC that is established between two LGNs serves as the logical link information needed by

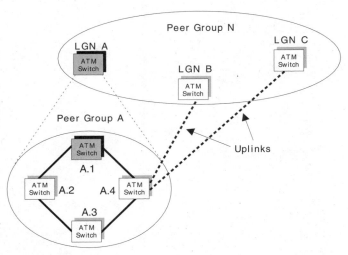

Figure 10.5 PNNI uplinks.

LGNs to establish the RCC SVC between other nodes in the peer group and is derived from the existence of uplinks.

- *Topology aggregation.*   This is the process of summarizing and compressing information at one peer group to advertise into the next higher-level peer group. Topology aggregation is performed by the PGLs. Links can be aggregated such that multiple links in the child peer group may be represented by a single link in the parent peer group. Nodes are aggregated from multiple child nodes into a single LGN.

- *PNNI topology-state element (PTSE).*   This unit of information is used by nodes to build and synchronize a topology database within the same peer group. PTSEs are reliably flooded between nodes in a peer group and downward from an LGN into the peer group it represents. PTSEs contain topology-state information about the links and nodes in the peer group. PTSEs are carried in PNNI topology-state packets (PTSP). PTSPs are sent at regular intervals or will be sent if triggered by an important change in topology.

- *Upward and downward information flow.*   Figure 10.6 shows the information flow during this process for PG A and LGN A. The PGL in A, A.2, is responsible for producing information about PG A, summarizing it and then representing A as a single LGN in PG N. This is the upward flow. Note that no PTSEs flow upward. PTSEs flow downward and horizontally from the PGL. This provides the nodes in PG A with visibility outside its peer group and enables them to intelligently route an SVC request. External visibility for nodes in a peer group is limited to knowledge about uplinks to other LGNs.

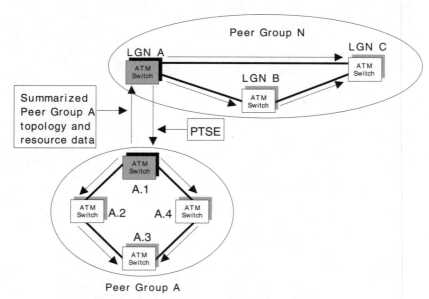

Figure 10.6   PNNI upward/downward information flow.

10.3.1   PNNI peer group generation process

The process of building PNNI peer groups is recursive—that is, the same process is used at each level in hierarchy. The exceptions are (1) the lowest-level peer groups because the logical nodes representing actual switches can have no child nodes and (2) the highest-level peer group because there is no parent to represent it. Generally speaking, though there is no difference in the protocol behavior because, as specified, a logical node performs the PNNI functions. And a logical node can be a real ATM switch or a summarized version of a collection of switches called a *logical group node*.

The recursive process of building a PNNI routing hierarchy is summarized in Table 10.1

10.3.2   Topology-state parameters

As mentioned, PNNI is a topology-state protocol. This means that logical nodes will advertise link-state and nodal-state parameters. A link-state parameter describes the characteristics of a link and a nodal-state parameter describes the characteristics of a node. Together these form topology-state parameters which are advertised by logical nodes within their own peer group.

Topology-state parameters are metrics for attributes. A topology-state metric is a parameter whose value must be combined for all links and nodes in the SVC request path to determine if the path is acceptable. A topology-state attribute is a parameter that is considered individually to determine if a path is acceptable for an SVC request. Topology-state attributes can be further subdivided into two categories: performance related and policy related. Performance-related attributes measure the performance of a particular link or node. Policy-related attributes provide a measure of conformance level to a specific policy by a node or link in the topology.

Table 10.2 shows the topology-state parameters supported by PNNI and an explanation of each follows.

TABLE 10.1 PNNI Peer Group Generation Process

Step	PNNI procedures
1	Exchange hello messages with physical peer switches
2	Determine peer group membership
3	Flood topology-state PTSEs in peer group
4	Elect peer group leader
5	Identify uplinks (if any)
6	Build horizontal links between LGNs
7	Exchange hello messages with adjacent logical nodes
8	Determine peer group membership
9	Flood topology-state PTSEs in peer group
10	Elect peer group leader
11	If highest-level peer group, then process complete
12	Return to step 5

- *Cell delay variation (CDV).* Expected CDV along the path relevant for CBR and VBR-rt traffic.

- *Administrative weight (AW).* Link or nodal-state parameter set by administrator to indicate preference.

- *Cell loss ratio (CLR).* Describes the expected CLR at a node or link for CLP=0 traffic.

- *Maximum cell rate (MCR).* Describes the maximum link or node capacity.

- *Available cell rate (ACR).* Measure of effective available bandwidth of the advertiser.

- *Cell rate margin (CRM).* Measure of difference between effective bandwidth allocation and the allocation for sustainable cell rate (SCR).

- *Variance factor (VF).* Relative measure of the square of the CRM normalized by the variance of the aggregate cell rate.

- *Branching flag.* Used to indicate if a node can branch point-to-multipoint traffic.

- *Restricted transit flag.* Nodal-state parameter that indicates whether a node supports transit traffic or not.

10.3.3 Generic connection admission control (GCAC)

CAC is the function performed by ATM switches that determines whether a connection request can be accepted or not. This is performed by every switch in the SVC request path. But CAC is not standardized, so it is up to the individual switch to decide if a connection request and its associated QoS can be supported.

PNNI uses information stored in the originating node's topology database, along with the connection's traffic characteristics and QoS requirements, to compute a path. But again, CAC is a local switch process that the originating node cannot realistically keep track of. Therefore, PNNI invokes a *generic connection admission control* (GCAC) procedure during the path selection process, which provides the originating node with an estimate of whether each switch's local CAC process will accept the connection.

TABLE 10.2 PNNI Topology-State Parameters

Metrics	Performance/resource attributes	Policy attributes
Cell delay variation	Cell loss ratio for CLP=0	Restricted transit flag
Maximum cell transfer delay	Maximum cell rate	
Administrative weight	Available cell rate	
	Cell-rate margin	
	Variance factor	
	Branching flag	

10.4   PNNI Signaling

The signaling component of PNNI is used to forward the SVC request through the network of switches until it reaches its destination. PNNI signaling makes use of the network topology, resource, and reachability information provided by PNNI routing to progress an SVC request through the network. It is based on UNI 3.1/4.0 signaling but has been enhanced with several extensions specific for the PNNI environment. Whereas UNI signaling can be asymmetrical, PNNI signaling is symetrical. This makes sense, because this is a switch-to-switch signaling protocol rather than an end-user-to-switch protocol. PNNI signaling supports new capabilities present in UNI 4.0 and TM 4.0: specific QoS parameters, ATM anycast addressing and scoping, and ABR. Additionally, PNNI uses two other techniques, designated transit lists (DTLs) and crankback with alternate routing, to successfully complete the SVC request and connection setup.

10.4.1   Designated transit lists

PNNI uses source routing to forward an SVC request across one or more peer groups in a PNNI routing hierarchy. The PNNI term for the source route vector is *designated transit list*. A DTL is a vector of information that defines a complete path from the source node to the destination node across a peer group in the routing hierarchy. A DTL is computed by the source node or first node in a peer group to receive an SVC request. Based on the source node's knowledge of the network, it computes a path to the destination that will satisfy the QoS objectives of the request. Nodes then simply obey the DTL and forward the SVC request through the network.

A DTL is implemented as an information element (IE) that is added to the PNNI signaling messages SETUP and ADD PARTY. One DTL is computed for each peer group and contains the complete path across the peer group. In other words, it is a list of nodes and links that the SVC request must visit on its way to the destination. A series of DTLs is combined into a stack with the lowest-level peer group on top of the stack and the highest-level peer group at the bottom. A pointer is also included to indicate which node in the DTL the SVC is currently visiting. When the pointer reaches the end of a DTL, the DTL is removed from the stack and the next DTL in the stack is processed. If the SVC request enters a new lowest-level peer group, then a new DTL will be generated by the ingress switch and placed at the top of the DLT stack for processing.

As an example, suppose User A wishes to establish an SVC with User C as shown in Fig. 10.7, and for policy reasons the SVC request can only traverse the path shown. So the SVC request is signaled across the UNI to node A.2. Node A.2 knows that User C is reachable through LGN C and that LGN C is reachable through LGN B. Node A.2 constructs two DTLs, one to provide a path across PG A and another across PG N. The SVC request is forwarded. Not shown but included is a pointer that indicates which node in the DTL is currently being visited. When the last node in the DTL is reached, node A.4, it is removed and the next DTL in the stack is processed.

When the SVC request reaches node B.2, a new DTL (B.2, B.3) is popped on top of the stack. Node B.2 simply adds a DTL that enables the SVC request to traverse PG B. When the SVC request reaches the end of the current DTL (B.2, B.3), it is removed and the next one in the stack is processed. When the SVC request reaches node C.1, a new DTL (C.1, C.2, C.3) is popped on top and the call is forwarded to the destination.

10.4.2   Crankback and alternate routing

Nodes that generate DTLs (A.2, B.2, C.1 in the previous example) use information in the topology and resource database that may change while the SVC request is being forwarded. This may cause the SVC request to be blocked. Short of going all the way back to User A and attempting to reestablish the connection, PNNI invokes a technique called *crankback with alternate routing*.

When the SVC request cannot be forwarded according to the DTL, it is cleared back to the originator of the DTL with an indication of the problem. This is the crankback mechanism. At that point a new DTL (alternate route) may be constructed that bypasses the nodes or links that blocked the SVC request but which must match the higher-level DTLs which are further down in the DTL stack. If no path can be found, then the request is cranked back to

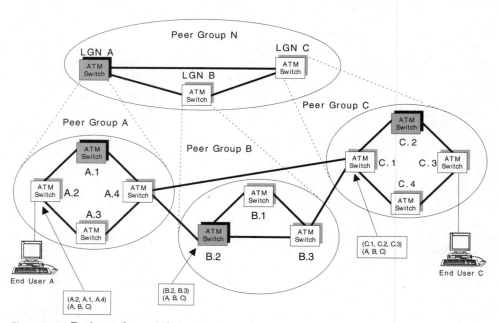

Figure 10.7   Designated transit lists.

the previous DTL originator. If the DTL originator is the original source node, then the crankback message is translated into a REJECT and User A must attempt another connection request.

In our example, suppose the port on node B.3 that connects the link to node B.2 experienced congestion while the SVC request was being forwarded. Node B.3 would realize, after running CAC, that the SVC request could not be satisfied over this port. A crankback message would then be sent back to node B.2 indicating a problem with the specified port on node B.3. Node B.2 would then recompute a new DTL as shown and forward the SVC request around the failed resource. This is illustrated in Fig. 10.8.

10.5   Interim Interswitch Protocol (IISP)

The Interim Interswitch Protocol (IISP), released in 1995, was developed by the ATM Forum as an interim solution until PNNI phase I is completed. Originally called PNNI phase 0, IISP is a very simple signaling protocol for interswitch communications. It is based on UNI 3.0/3.1 signaling and uses manually configured address prefix tables in each switch to route SVC requests from an origin switch to a destination switch. There is no scalability or QoS support; however, it is a clean and simple technique for supporting multivendor SVC request routing in small networks.

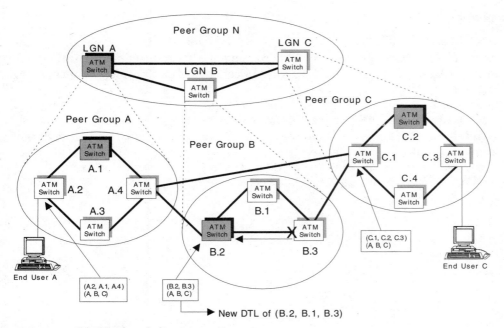

Figure 10.8 Crankback and alternate routing.

10.6 PNNI Routing Extensions

PNNI phase I was designed to support signaling and routing of SVC requests through a network of ATM switches. However, PNNI can be extended to support not only the routing of SVC requests but also the routing of layer-3 packets such as IP. Two proposals are now in the works to extend the capabilities of PNNI to support IP routing. They are:

- *PNNI augmented routing (PAR).* With PAR, IP routers and ATM switches separate routing protocols (e.g., OSPF for IP and PNNI for ATM). However, routers attached to the ATM network would also run PNNI. This would enable routers attached to the same ATM network to locate each other and set up SVCs. PAR enables ATM-attached routers to "bootstrap" a series of interrouter SVCs over the ATM network, thus removing the requirement to preconfigure ATM information in the router. It would also provide ATM-attached routers, which would presumably be backbone routers, with information about the QoS capabilities of the ATM network.

- *Integrated PNNI (I-PNNI).* I-PNNI is a single routing protocol that is used between IP routers and ATM switches. Routers and switches exchange topology information about the entire network. This enables end-to-end routing to be based on a single network topology, supports QoS (since PNNI advertises QoS attributes) routing, and requires only one routing protocol to be configured and managed.

10.7 Summary

PNNI is a switch-to-switch protocol developed within the ATM Forum to support efficient, dynamic, and scalable routing of SVC requests in a multivendor private ATM environment. PNNI phase I consists of two protocols: routing and signaling. PNNI routing uses a hierarchical topology-state protocol to disseminate topology and resource information among participating switches or groups of switches. PNNI signaling uses the topology and resource information available at each switch to construct a designated transit list which determines the path the SVC request will traverse to meet the requested QoS objectives and complete the connection. PNNI routing can be extended to support IP and other layer-3 routing protocols.

Multiprotocol Networking and ATM

Chapter 4

IP over ATM: Intra-Subnet

In Part 1 we reviewed the state of current internetworking technology to date. Bridging, switching, and routing of different protocols with the emphasis on TCP/IP were covered. In Part 2 we introduced ATM. ATM is a network architecture that enables information to be transported in small packets called cells over preestablished connections. In Part 3 we turn our attention toward the integration of these two important technologies. More specifically, what are the techniques and protocols used to transport connectionless layer-3 packets over a connection-oriented ATM-based switch fabric.

TCP/IP is the defacto standard for internetworking heterogeneous network hosts and applications. ATM has emerged with the ability to integrate not only TCP/IP data traffic but other forms of information including voice and video.

In this chapter we will review techniques for supporting unicast and multicast IP traffic running over ATM in a single subnet environment. Classical IP and ARP over ATM or RFC1577, as it is generally referred to, is a technique for supporting IP over ATM in a single *logical IP subnet* (LIS). An LIS is a group of IP hosts that share a common IP network number and subnet mask, and who communicate with each other directly using ATM connections. IP multicast over ATM enables IP multicast transmissions over an ATM network through the use of a *multicast address resolution server* (MARS) and ATM point-to-multipoint connections. A MARS resolves the IP group address with the ATM addresses of the group members.

11.1 IP over ATM Considerations

One of the benefits of IP is that it can run over any physical network. Ethernet, FDDI, Token-Ring, X.25, Frame Relay, fibrechannel, async, and so on—just about any physical network out there today and ones not even thought of will support IP. And of course ATM is no exception. Indeed, the first implementations of IP over ATM treat ATM as just another data link protocol. While acceptable to do so, viewing ATM from the perspective of TCP and IP as just another data link protocol may not do either TCP/IP or ATM justice. As we have shown, ATM is much more. It has its own addressing structure and hierarchical routing function, uses signaling to set up and tear down connections with a specified traffic contract and QoS, and for better or worse is universally acknowledged as a viable technology to carry data from the worldwide carrier all the way down to the residential setup box. On the other hand, TCP/IP is a connectionless network protocol designed to forward data packets on a hop-by-hop basis, network to network, independent of the underlying physical media. It defines a robust and flexible set of host and network behaviors that enable it to adapt to dynamic network conditions. TCP/IP is supported on just about every network device and is universally accepted as the data networking protocol of choice. Its basic mechanisms have changed little over the years and that stability as well as its ability to run on any platform have contributed to its widespread deployment.

But TCP/IP does lack some important capabilities. It is a data network protocol only. Yes, one can support voice and video using TCP/IP, but only in very carefully controlled network configurations with more than sufficient bandwidth. The MBONE is an example of this. It lacks an ability to provide QoS for those applications that are delay and jitter sensitive. These are areas that are currently being worked on within various groups of the IETF (Integrated Services, RSVP), but it will be some time before these standards are complete and solutions are deployed. But assuming that it will be possible to create an integrated services internet, TCP/IP will still need to coexist and work harmoniously with ATM. TCP/IP can immediately benefit from scalable bandwidth in the LAN environment, lower latency, and perhaps more cost-effective bandwidth in the WAN environment, and from the efficiences of scale when integrating all traffic types in any network environment. The ATM service layers and QoS mechanisms defined in ATM are also areas from which TCP/IP can learn.

So for the purposes of the remainder of this book and because we believe that both solutions are viable and necessary, we will "punt" on the TCP/IP versus ATM polemic and assume that TCP/IP and ATM work together.

The basic considerations of addressing, packet encapsulation, address resolution, and broadcast/multicast support apply to the single or intra-subnet environment for supporting IP over ATM.

■ *Addressing.*   IP and ATM have different address structures. Two address models exist: peer and separated. The peer model supports an algorithmic translation of the IP address to an ATM address and vice-versa. One address scheme to administer would be desirable, but it requires that a host perform this function, thus requiring a change in host behavior. There is also the issue of mobility and consistency across address hierarchy bounderies. The separated model keeps the IP and ATM address spaces separate. A dynamic mapping or association of an IP address with an ATM address is required.

- *Packet encapsulation.*   IP has no knowledge of the underlying data link it is running over. IP packets are encapsulated in Ethernet frames when running on an Ethernet, Token-Ring frames when running on a Token-Ring, and so forth. ATM uses AAL5 or AAL 3/4 for data. AAL5 contains less overhead than AAL 3/4 but does not support a multiplexing of cells from different AALs on same VC.

- *Address resolution.*   For shared media LANs like Ethernet and Token-Ring, IP uses ARP to resolve an IP address with the associated MAC address. ARP uses the broadcast support of the underlying shared media to accomplish this. ATM does not support broadcast and an ATM network uses ATM addresses. A mechanism is required to help resolve an IP address with the associated ATM address similar to what ARP does with MAC addresses.

- *Broadcast and multicast.*   IP multicast enables one or more senders to send packets to multiple destinations by addressing them to a group address. Broadcast could be considered a varient of multicast in which IP packets are sent to all stations on the network. ATM does not have an inherent broadcast or multicast function.

In the sections to follow we will see these specific issues addressed.

11.2   Classical IP and ARP over ATM

Classical IP and ARP over ATM was the first and perhaps most natural implementation of IP over ATM. As alluded to earlier, the classical IP model positions ATM as a replacement for the wires or LAN segment connecting two workstations on the same subnet. IP routers are still required to interconnect two or more IP subnets. Indeed the classical model purposely limits ATM to intra-subnet connectivity.

The components and operation of classical IP and ARP over ATM are contained in a series of RFCs issued by the IETF Internetworking over NBMA (ION) working group. The RFCs describe an encapsulation technique, ATMARP service, UNI signaling flows, and default MTU size. Without fully exploiting the capabilities of ATM, they have provided developers and vendors with an initial and stable set of guidelines for deploying IP over ATM.

11.2.1   RFC1483

RFC1483 defines two techniques for encapsulating routed and/or bridged packets in ATM AAL5 cells. The first technique is called LLC/SNAP encapsulation. As the name suggests, an LLC/SNAP header is prepended to each packet to identify which protocol is contained in the payload. The LLC/SNAP header consists of a 3-byte LLC, a 3-byte OUI field, and a 2-byte PID field. It is the PID which distinguishes one protocol from another. A value of 0x0800 specifies IP, 0x0806 is ARP, 0x809B is Appletalk, 0x8137 is IPX, and so on. Additional PIDs can be found in RFC1700. Figure 11.1 illustrates LLC/SNAP encapsulation for an IP packet.

Because of the presence of the LLC/SNAP header it is possible but not required to support multiple protocols over the same VC. This can reduce or conserve the number of ATM VCs required in a multiprotocol environment.

The second technique described in RFC1483 is called VC multiplexing or "Null" encapsulation. This differs from LLC/SNAP encapsulation in that the VC is terminated directly at a layer-3 endpoint. In other words, the AAL endpoints of an RFC1483 VC-multiplexed connection would be the layer-3 protocol entities. This means that a VC will carry one protocol only. In a multiprotocol environment, this scheme would use additional VCs.

In terms of selecting one over the other, the LLC/SNAP technique is the default method for classical IP and ARP over ATM. The UNI signaling required to initiate an LLC/SNAP encapsulated SVC is defined in RFC1755. The important advantage is that multiple protocols can share a VC thus limiting the number of VCs required in an IP and multiprotocol environment. On the other hand, it does use an additional 8 bytes per AAL frame. One also requires an LLC/SNAP entity to be present at each endpoint to demultiplex the frames and pass them up to the higher-layer protocol. VC-based multiplexing is a more efficient from a pure VC perspective. And because a single protocol is mapped to a single VC it may be easier to perform filtering and/or authentication on a per-protocol basis.

RFC1483 PVCs between two routers is an effective technique for utilizing ATM, gaining some of the advantages of higher bandwidth and supporting IP as well as other protocols. It effectively functions as a leased line. This is shown in Fig. 11.2.

11.2.2   RFC1577

RFC1577 formally defines the classical IP and ARP over ATM protocol. Its development by the IETF ION working group was motivated by a desire to introduce ATM technology with as little disruption and change to the existing IP model as possible. Hosts on a subnet are still assigned an IP address and physical layer address (ATM in this case). When communicating with another

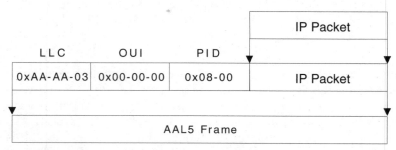

Figure 11.1   RFC1483 LLC/SNAP encapsulation.

RFC1483 ATM PVC

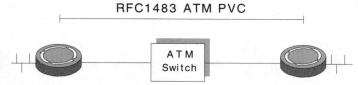

Figure 11.2   RFC1483 PVC between two routers.

host on the same subnet using ATM, it is necessary to resolve the destination IP address with the ATM address of the endpoint. And of course when traversing subnet boundaries, it is necessary to first pass through a router which can continue to implement any filtering, access, or security policies that currently exist. Classical IP over ATM supports unicast communications only.

The characteristics of the classical IP model are the following:

- The same *maximum transmit unit* (MTU) size of 9180 octets is used as a default for all VCs on a subnet. With 8 bytes of LLC/SNAP header that makes the default AAL5 frame size equal to 9188 bytes. However, as specified in RFC1626, it is possible to negotiate the MTU size during connection setup.

- LLC/SNAP encapsulation of IP packets in AAL5 cells as described in RFC1483 is used.

- IP addresses are resolved to ATM addresses by use of an ATMARP service within the LIS. The scope of the ATMARP service is limited to the LIS, just as the scope ARP is limited to a single subnet.

- A single LIS can support many hosts and routers with the same IP network and subnet mask. Communications between any two members of the LIS takes place over an ATM PVC or SVC.

- The traditional IP model is unchanged.

11.2.2.1   RFC1577 configuration requirements.   RFC1577 limits connectivity to point-to-point connections between two ATM-attached IP hosts on the same LIS. To that end, the following configuration requirements must be met:

- All LIS members must use the same IP network/subnetwork number and subnet mask.

- All LIS members are directly attached to the same ATM network.

- IP hosts outside the LIS are accessed by a router.

- All LIS members must use ATMARP and InATMARP in conjunction with an ATMARP server entity to resolve IP and ATM addresses when using SVCs.

- All LIS members must use InATMARP to resolve VCs to IP addresses when using PVCs. An ATMARP server entity is not required when using PVCs.

- All LIS members must be able to communicate with all other LIS members using an ATM PVC or SVC. This implies that the underlying ATM fabric can be fully meshed.

The following ATM parameters must be configured for each member of the LIS:

- *ATM hardware address.* This is the ATM address of the individual IP host.
- *ATMARP request address.* This is the ATM address of the ATMARP server for the LIS. If the LIS is using only PVCs, then this requirement may be null.

11.2.2.2 ATMARP. IP communications on any subnet operates over two planes of addressing: IP and whatever data link protocol or media is in use. A dynamic binding or mapping between the known destination IP address and the unknown or unresolved media-specific address is required and typically this has been performed by ARP for shared media LANs and InverseARP for point-to-point connections like Frame Relay. ATMARP is based on ARP but has included extensions to operate over a nonbroadcast unicast ATM network. A PVC may exist between two members of an LIS without knowing what the IP address is at the other end. This situation is resolved by use of the InverseAT-MARP (InATMARP) protocol which is similar to InverseARP except that extensions have been added to support nonbroadcast unicast ATM networks.

The unique component of the classical IP model is the ATMARP server. This is a special member of the LIS whose primary purpose is to maintain a table or cache of IP and ATM address mappings. At least one ATMARP server must be configured for each LIS, along with a specific IP and ATM address. A single ATMARP server may service more than one LIS as long as it is IP and ATM addressable within each LIS. An ATMARP server learns about the IP and ATM addresses of specific members (IP clients) of the LIS through the use of ATMARP and InATMARP messages exchanged between the ATMARP server and LIS members. And finally, an ATMARP server can run on an IP host or router. Figure 11.3 shows an LIS with 2 IP clients and a stand-alone ATMARP server.

The ATMARP protocol is composed of five unique message types. Table 11.1 summarizes these messages and includes the important fields in each message.

11.2.2.3 Registration. IP clients must first register their IP and ATM addresses with the ATMARP server. This is performed by the IP client who initially establishes an SVC with the ATMARP server. The IP client is able to do this because it is configured with the ATM address of the ATMARP server. Next the ATMARP server sends out an InATMARP request. The purpose of this message is to obtain the IP address of the client. The client returns an InATMARP reply which will contain both the IP and ATM addresses of the client. The ATMARP server checks its existing table and if there are no duplicates, time-stamps the entry and adds it to the table. This entry is valid for a minimum of 20 minutes. The IP client may

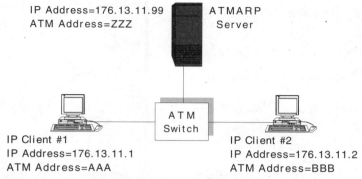

IP Address=176.13.11.99   ATMARP
ATM Address=ZZZ   Server

IP Client #1
IP Address=176.13.11.1
ATM Address=AAA

ATM
Switch

IP Client #2
IP Address=176.13.11.2
ATM Address=BBB

Figure 11.3   Classical IP LIS with ATMARP server.

issue its own InATMARP request to the ATMARP server to obtain its IP address. The registration process flow for IP Client #1 is shown in Fig. 11.4. Of course IP Client #2 will register its own address with the ATMARP server once it is initialized.

11.2.2.4   Address resolution. If IP Client #1 wishes to communicate with IP Client #2 and a connection already exists, then packets will immediately flow over that connection. IP Client #1 may contain the ATM address of IP Client #2 in its own ARP cache and if so, then it can immediately set up an SVC to IP Client #2. However, if a connection does not already exist and IP Client #1 does not know the ATM address of IP Client #2, then the ATMARP process is invoked.

IP Client #1 sends an ATMARP request to the ATMARP server that contains the source IP address, destination IP address, and source ATM address. If the ATMARP server contains an IP/ATM address entry for IP Client #2, it will return that information in an ATMARP reply message. IP Client #1 then knows the ATM address of IP Client #2 and can set up an SVC. If not, then the ATMARP server will return an ARP NAK message.

The process of ATMARP address resolution is shown in Fig. 11.5.

TABLE 11.1   ATMARP Messages

ATMARP message	Description
ATMARP request	Sent from IP client to server to obtain destination ATM address, contains the client's IP address, ATM address, and the destination's IP address
ATMARP reply	Response from server to IP client with destination ATM address, contains the client's and destination's IP and ATM addresses
InATMARP request	Sent from server to IP client over VC to obtain IP address, contains the client's ATM address and the ATMARP server's IP and ATM addresses
InATMARP reply	Response from IP client over VC with IP address, contains the client's and server's IP and ATM addresses
ATMARP NAK	Negative response to ATMARP request sent from server to IP client

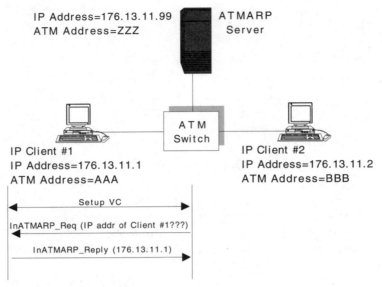

Figure 11.4   RFC1577 address registration process.

11.2.2.5   Classical IP over ATM enhancements.   Improvements to the classical IP over ATM operation are being studied. One area that is under consideration is the registration process. Currently the ATMARP server uses InATMARP messages to retrieve the IP address of the IP clients. But consider the case where the ATMARP server runs on a router that supports many workstations, some sup-

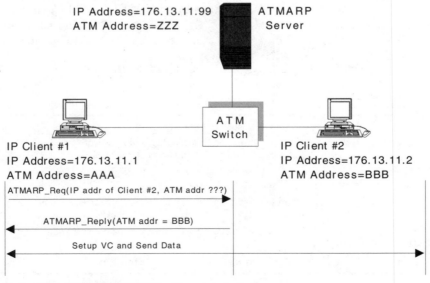

Figure 11.5   RFC1577 ATMARP address resolution.

porting IP, others supporting IPX and Appletalk. By definition, the ATMARP server will issue InATMARP requests to all stations on the LIS even if they do not support IP. This is an unnecessary use of router and workstation resources. Registration of IP client addresses with the ATMARP server could be just as easily performed during the first ATMARP request sent from an IP client. This change is expected to be implemented in the follow-on to RFC1577.

Another process under study is how to remove the single ATMARP server per LIS restriction. A single ATMARP server per LIS is in fact a single point of failure. A means of supporting multiple synchronized ATMARP servers would remove this limitation and provide a more robust and scalable implementation. Server synchronization messages would flow over a VC(s) established between the two or more ATMARP servers. In designing a server synchronization protocol several issues must be considered:

- Existing IP clients must be able to use the ATMARP multiserver service but are limited to connecting to one server only.

- New IP clients (those supporting the RFC1577 follow-on) should be able to use any server in the ATMARP multiservice.

- ATMARP requests should be allowed to arbitrarily flow to any ATMARP server and not to one particular server.

- Server-to-server to synchronization flows must be minimal.

- ATMARP multiserver service must scale.

- Utilize existing techniques where appropriate.

Work has begun on the Server Cache Synchronization Protocol (SCSP) that will address the issues associated with supporting a multiserver service for ATMARP. More generally, the intent of SCSP is to provide a means by which multiple server entities can synchronize their contents and transparently service a specific group of clients. In addition to ATMARP, SCSP could support a multiserver service in NHRP MARS and LAN Emulation.

11.2.3   RFC1626

Some applications, such as NFS, function quite well with larger MTU sizes. It is also desirable to minimize IP fragmentation where possible to enhance performance. RFC1209 defines a default MTU size of 9180 bytes for SMDS. This seemed like a reasonable value for a similar cell-switched technology, ATM, so the value of 9180 bytes was also chosen for ATM.

As defined in RFC1626, two IP clients connected via a PVC must default to the MTU size of 9180 bytes unless there is some agreement beforehand to use a smaller or larger MTU size. In an SVC environment, two IP clients will attempt to negotiate the MTU size during call setup. The source IP client will include either the default MTU size or some MTU size in the forward and backward maximum CPCS-SDU size fields of the AAL parameters information element in the SETUP message. The destination IP client will either agree to support the MTU size contained in the SETUP message and return that value in the CONNECT message or deposit a smaller MTU size in the CONNECT message and return it to the source IP client. A larger value can also be negotiated in which case both the source and destination IP clients will agree to perform some IP fragmentation. If either the source or the destination has a problem with the MTU size, then an error message will be generated and then connection will fail.

To ensure that the largest possible MTU is used along a routed path, all routers and hosts that support RFC1577 operations should implement the path MTU discovery mechanism specified in RFC1191 and RFC1435. The purpose is to ensure that router resources are not wasted due to unnecessary IP fragmentation. Given that routers have to work hard enough as it is when attached to an ATM network, reducing the need for IP fragmentation can only help and certainly not hurt.

11.2.4   RFC1755

RFC1755 defines the UNI 3.1 signaling procedures that are used in classical IP and ARP over ATM implementations. ATM signaling procedures were covered in Chap. 8 and RFC1755 makes use of the same. However, whereas UNI 3.1 states that the AAL parameters and *broadband lower-layer information* (B-LLI) are optional, RFC1755 requires that they be mandatory. This is because RFC1577 end users (IP clients and ATMARP servers) make use of specific AAL functions and parameters that must be defined at call setup.

RFC1755 describes the information elements (IEs) that should be included in the SETUP/CONNECT messages between two RFC1577 end users in an SVC environment. One group of IEs, AAL parameters, and B-LLI is concerned with endpoints. Another group of IEs (traffic descriptors, QoS, and broadband carrier) have ATM network significance.

11.2.4.1   Endpoint IEs.   AAL parameters and B-LLI are used by RFC1577 end users. The information contained in the AAL parameters includes the AAL type, maximum CPCS-SDU sizes, and the fact that null SSCS should be used. Table 11.2 shows a sample group of AAL parameters.

LLC/SNAP encapsulation is specified in the B-LLI IE. B-LLI is the only IE contained in UNI 3.1 that designates layer-2 and layer-3 endpoints. Table 11.3 shows the fields contained in the B-LLI IE that could be used to specify LLC/SNAP encapsulation between two RFC1577 end users. Including the layer_2_id and user_information_layer is sufficient for specifying LLC/SNAP encapsulation between two endpoints. If one wished to have an LLC/SNAP-encapsulated VC support IP, only then all four fields would be specified. If one wished to set up a null VC connection between two endpoints as defined in RFC1483, then only the layer_3_id and ISO/IEC fields would be required.

TABLE 11.2   AAL Parameters

aal_type	5 AAL5
fwd_max_sdu_size_id	140
fwd_max_sdu_size	65,535 max MTU size, could also be default size of 9188
bwd_max_sdu_size_id	140
bwd_max_sdu_size	65,535 max MTU size, could also be default size of 9188
sscs_type identifier	132
sscs_type	0 null SSCS

TABLE 11.3   B-LLI Parameters

layer_2_id	2
user_information_layer	12 lan_llc-ISO 8802/2
layer_3_id	3
ISO/IEC TR 9577 IPI	204 0xCC, specifies IP

11.2.4.2   ATM network information elements.   The second group of IEs defines the traffic and QoS parameters for the IP over ATM connection that will be placed over the ATM network. Specifically, the IEs that are utilized are the traffic descriptors (PCR, SCR, MBS), broadband bearer capability (BCOB-X which stands for best-effort is used in most cases), and QoS (class 0). It is up to whoever establishes the connection to use whatever combination of parameters is required to support the IP over ATM connection. RFC1755 suggests a number of different combinations that will support both best-effort and CBR connections. Chapter 8 provides more detail on ATM UNI Signaling.

The follow-on to RFC1755, which is underway, will take into account some of the new capabilities available in UNI Signaling 4.0. These include ABR support, traffic parameter negotiation, and frame discard support.

11.3   IP Multicast over ATM

Multicast is the most efficient way to send information from one host to multiple hosts. The sending host uses a special group address to address and then send the information to the receiving hosts or members of the group. The sending host uses a single send operation and the network, through a variety of techniques, forwards the group-addressed information to the members of the group. The most widely used implementation of the multicast is a MAC-level broadcast that occurs on shared media LANs like Token-Ring or Ethernet. A single copy of the broadcast packet addressed to x'FFFFFFFFFFFF' is sent by the sending host to all members on the LAN.

IP uses the class D address space to address packets to one or more members of a multicast group. RFC1112 defines a group membership protocol called the

Internet Group Management Protocol (IGMP). Hosts and routers exchange IGMP messages. The routers use the results of this message exchange along with a multicast routing protocol (e.g., MOSPF) to build a delivery tree from the source subnetwork to all other subnetworks that have members of the multicast group.

As described in Chap. 8, ATM supports point-to-multipoint VCs between a single sender called the *root* and multiple receivers called *leaves*. In UNI 3.1 the root is responsible for adding the leaves and thus must have knowledge of the leaf's ATM address. In UNI 4.0 it will be possible for a leaf to unilaterly join an existing point-to-multipoint connection. But the unidirectional point-to-multipoint VC is the only way to support multicast transmissions over an ATM network.

ATM has no knowledge of the IP layer or the class D address space and vice-versa. Therefore, as is the case in the unicast environment, a mapping must occur between the IP (multicast group address) and the ATM addresses of the one or more members of the IP multicast group. The multicast address resolution server (MARS) provides this capability by serving as a central registration and distribution entity for IP multicast group membership and address resolution. The MARS will be described in more detail later.

11.3.1 VC mesh versus multicast server

A *cluster* defines a set of ATM hosts that participate in an ATM level multicast. Two models exist for supporting an ATM level multicast. The first involves an ATM host establishing a point-to-multipoint VC with other ATM hosts that are members of a specific multicast group. This is called a VC *mesh*. If all hosts on the cluster wish to transmit and receive within the same multicast group, then there will be one point-to-multipoint VC originating from each host. The second involves the use of a *multicast server* (MCS). An ATM host(s) sends data directly to the multicast server over a VC that in turn retransmits out over a point-to-multipoint VC to members of the multicast group. The two models are illustrated in Fig. 11.6.

Both models will achieve the same result, but there are tradeoffs. It can be visually confirmed that a VC mesh will require many more VCs and that this will extract a toll in network resource consumption. More buffers, switch control blocks, and UNI signaling overhead will be required to support multicast traffic. Of course, a VC mesh offers optimal performance and leverages the switch fabric so that the multicasting is performed at the cell level. This could be a big advantage where performance for multicast applications such as real-time distance learning is key.

On the other hand, an MCS is easy to manage and conceptualize. There are fewer VCs required to support a multicast group. Any changes in group membership would only impact the point-to-multipoint VC from the MCS. Since

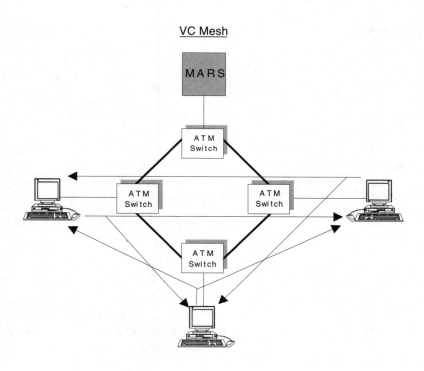

Figure 11.6 VC mesh and multicast servers.

VCs are expensive (e.g., over a WAN), an MCS might be a better fit. Of course, one will note that performance can be an issue. A sending host forwards multicast traffic over a VC to the MCS where it must be reassembled into an AAL frame before it is transmitted back out into the network by the MCS. The latency and delay associated with this indirect route could be unsuitable for certain applications. However, for policy and control reasons, an MCS offers the best solution because all multicast traffic must flow through it.

Both models are applicable depending on the network's available resources, the cost of VCs, the performance requirements, security, and control. Both will be implemented in ATM networks.

11.3.2 MARS

The MARS is used to support IP multicast over an ATM network. Generally speaking, it can be viewed as an analog to the ATMARP server that supports multicast address resolution. IP hosts attached to an ATM network utilize the MARS to track and disseminate information about multicast group membership. IP multicast senders may query the MARS when multicast address needs to be resolved with the ATM address(es) of the IP hosts participating in the group. The following should also be noted about the MARS:

- The concept of a cluster is used to define ATM hosts (or routers) that are participating in an ATM level multicast and that share a MARS. A cluster is mapped to a single LIS but it is possible to extend the MARS to support a single cluster over multiple LISs. However, that would require support for multicast routing (e.g., MOSPF, PIM) over ATM, which is an area that requires further study. So for now consider a one-to-one relationship between LIS and cluster.
- Current MARS implementations support UNI 3.1.
- MARS can be extended to support any layer-3 multicast traffic, not just IP.
- MARS can coexist with an ATMARP server or an MCS. However, the MARS does not forward multicast traffic.

The MARS is an architectural extension to the ATMARP server. But instead of maintaining a table of IP to ATM address pairs, it holds an extended table consisting of IP group addresses and then the ATM addresses of the specific cluster members. This is called a *host map*. For example, an entry for members belonging to multicast group 232.200.200.1 might look like this:

```
{232.200.200.1, ATM Address 1, ATM Address 2, …ATM Address N}
```

Figure 11.7 shows a cluster with a MARS and three cluster members or MARS clients. The operation of the MARS is very simple.

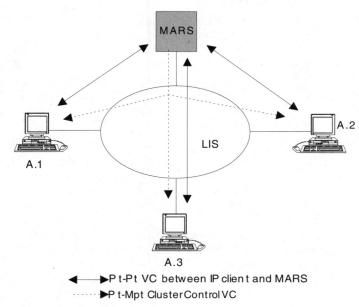

Pt-Pt VC between IP client and MARS

Pt-Mpt ClusterControlVC

Figure 11.7   MARS cluster.

- Clients who wish to participate in a multicast group establish a point-to-point VC with the MARS. Clients register with the MARS by sending a MARS_JOIN message containing the "all nodes" group address (224.0.0.1) as described in RFC1112.

- The MARS will then add the client as a leaf on its ClusterControlVC. The ClusterControlVC is a point-to-multipoint VC that is established between the MARS and all multicast-capable cluster members (hosts or routers). The ClusterControlVC is used by the MARS to distribute group membership updates to all members of the cluster. For example, after host A.2 registers, the MARS will send a MARS_JOIN message out over its ClusterControlVC to all members, indicating that host A.2 has registered and is multicast-capable.

- Clients who wish to join or leave a specific multicast group will send a MARS_JOIN or MARS_LEAVE message to the MARS containing one or more IP group addresses. Again, this information will be propagated to other cluster members over the ClusterControlVC so that sources (roots) can add to or prune their multicast trees.

- Clients send a MARS_REQUEST to the MARS seeking address resolution of a specific IP group address.

- MARS responds with a MARS_MULTI message which contains the host map for the IP group address.

The join address resolution flow is shown in Fig. 11.8. Hosts A.2 and A.3 forward MARS_JOIN messages up to the MARS indicating they wish to join multicast group XYZ. The MARS redirects these messages out over the ClusterControlVC. Host A.1 wishes to send packets to group address XYZ. It issues a MARS_REQUEST message to the MARS which returns a MARS_MULTI message that contains a host map of (XYZ, A.2, A.3). A.1 now has sufficient information to establish a point-to-multipoint VC with the group members A.2 and A.3, and will begin multicasting.

An MCS can also be used to multicast data in a MARS cluster. Figure 11.9 shows the same cluster with an MCS. An MCS will register with the MARS using the MARS_MSERV command. The MARS will then add the MCS as a leaf on a point-to-multipoint VC it maintains called the ServerControlVC. Group membership changes are sent to the MCS(s) over the ServerControlVC. A MARS will contain an additional table for multicast groups that incorporate MCS(s) called the *server map*. It contains an entry for the group address and ATM addresses of one or more MCS(s). If the example above is used for MCS B.1 then the server map for XYZ would be:

```
{XYZ, B.1}
```

The MARS will return the host map to an MCS so that it can build a point-to-multipoint VC to members of the group. The MARS will return the server map to a client so that it can establish a point-to-multipoint VC with the associated MCS(s). In effect, the client is fooled into thinking the MCS(s) is a member (leaf) of the multicast group.

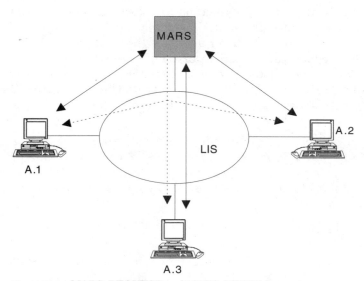

Figure 11.8   MARS_REQUEST and MARS_MULTI flows.

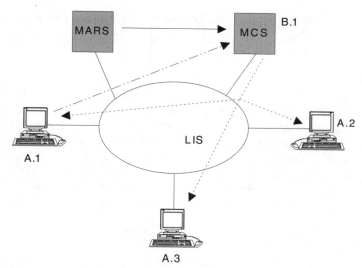

Pt-Mpt server control VC between MARS and MCS
Pt-Mpt VC between multicast sender and MCS
Pt-Mpt VC between MCS and group members

Figure 11.9 MARS multicast server.

It should be noted that it is the option of the system administrator to decide if a VC mesh or MCS should be used to support IP multicast.

11.3.3 IP broadcast

Broadcast is a special case of multicast in which all hosts on a particular network are members. IP broadcast formats are shown in Table 11.4.

The physical network broadcast is important because bootp clients (e.g., diskless workstations) use it to locate their server from which to boot. However, bootp clients typically do not know to which subnet they belong. If MARS is to support physical level broadcast, then it would be a requirement for all stations to join the 255.255.255.255 group. This is called the *broadcast channel*.

MARS is an effective means to support broadcasts for the following reasons:

- Generalized registration process enabling any host to join a broadcast group.

- MARS_MULTI can reduce traffic by returning multiple members in a single command.

TABLE 11.4 IP Broadcast Formats

255.255.255.255	Physical network broadcast
network.subnet.255	Subnet directed broadcast
network.255.255.255	Network directed broadcast

■ MCS can reduce the VCs required by a host to maintain for broadcast support. Only one would be needed.

11.4 Summary

Classical IP and ARP over ATM is the protocol defined for supporting IP over ATM. It supports unicast IP traffic only and is limited to a single LIS. It also includes a standard encapsulation scheme, default MTU size, and UNI signaling flows. The ATMARP server contains a table of IP to ATM address mappings. It is used by hosts to resolve a destination IP address with its corresponding ATM address. IP multicast over ATM is supported using MARS. The MARS is a central registry and distribution entity that contains a table of IP group addresses and associated ATM addresses of the group members.

IP over ATM: Inter-Subnet

The IP model consists of networks interconnected by routers. Packets traveling from one network to another, by definition, must pass through a router. Classical IP over ATM was no exception. ATM connectivity was limited to a single LIS. All inter-LIS traffic still had to pass through a router, even the LISs were attached to a single ATM network. ATM is expected to grow and over time one may find multiple LISs overlaid on a single ATM network. IP is also growing and evolving to support and carry traffic that is no longer just best-effort. Real-time audio and video will be carried over the Internet and intranets, and this kind of traffic can most certainly benefit from the delay guarantees and QoS that ATM offers. Routers will continue to play an important role in forwarding data traffic and providing security and policy controls, but for some applications a direct ATM connection is optimal. In this chapter we will discuss techniques under consideration that enable a source on one LIS to communicate directly over the ATM network to a destination in another LIS without passing through a router. The Next Hop Resolution Protocol (NHRP) is one such technique. NHRP is an inter-LIS address resolution protocol that facilitates direct ATM connectivity between a source and a destination on different subnets without the need for routers in the data path. Another technique under study places the decision to route on the application's traffic and QoS requirements rather than a host's IP address affiliation.

12.1 IP over ATM: Inter-Subnet Considerations

Supporting IP over ATM in a multiple subnet environment warrants consideration of some of the same issues that apply in a single subnet environment. They are addressing, packet encapsulation, address resolution, and broadcast/multicast support. A multiple subnet environment requires that we examine some additional issues. These include:

- *Remote address resolution.*   IP requires that inter-LIS traffic pass through a router. However, if all devices (hosts and routers) are attached to the same ATM network, then it would be possible to establish a direct SVC between any source and destination, even if they are on separate subnets. This would be ideal for traffic requiring some of the special features that ATM offers, such as QoS. Therefore, a technique is required that maps the ATM address to the IP address of a host on a different subnet. Current address resolution protocols such as ARP and ATMARP are confined to a single subnet.

- *Routing protocols.*   IP routing protocols such as RIP and OSPF were discussed in Part 1 of this book. ATM routing uses PNNI, which was discussed in Chap. 10. Again, two models exist: layered and integrated. With layered routing the traditional IP routing protocols run on top of ATM. ATM is another data link protocol on a subnet. ATM runs its own protocol, PNNI, to route SVC requests. Integrated routing combines both IP and ATM routing into a single routing protocol and topology database. Layered routing requires no change to the protocols but assumes no knowledge of the underlying ATM topology. Integrated routing requires both the IP routers and ATM switches to exchange topology information. Thus, with integrated routing, it is possible for an IP route to be computed based on the real IP and ATM topologies.

- *Route hop by hop or establish SVC.*   The current IP model dictates that inter-LIS traffic shall be forwarded hop by hop through routers. But from an IP host perspective it does not matter whether traffic is passed through a series of routers or is directed over an SVC to the destination IP host. The latter requires that the IP host be able to resolve the destination IP address with the matching ATM address. Another issue here is who should make the decision to route or establish SVC. The application or the network?

IP over ATM in a multiple subnet environment is new. We will discuss in more detail these issues and proposed techniques.

12.2   Connectionless versus Connection-Oriented Approaches

IP uses a connectionless mode of operation. This means that a host can begin sending packets to a destination without knowing about the path the packets will take. Packets are forwarded on a best-effort hop-by-hop basis by one or more routers until they reach the destination. If something happens to the packets along the way, no big deal. TCP, a connection-oriented transport protocol running at the end station a layer above IP, will detect the problem and resend the information. It works fine for low-volume data traffic like SMTP and is satisfactory for most everything else as long as there is enough bandwidth and little or no congestion. It is very dynamic and quickly adaptable to change. This is because the routing decision is made on a per-packet basis at each router as it is forwarded through the network.

The connection-oriented approach used by ATM performs the route-decision process up front. Before any information is sent, a path is established from the source to the destination. Resources may even be allocated along that path to support a requested traffic rate and QoS. Once the path is established and the network decides it can support the connection, data will begin to flow. That is the fundamental difference between the two approaches. The connectionless model distributes the route decision-making process to all routers between the source and destination on a per-packet basis. The connection-oriented approach performs the route decision-making process before any data is sent.

Supporting IP over ATM using the connectionless approach would be simple and would require no change whatsoever to the existing IP model. ATM would be viewed as just another data link protocol, albeit a very fast one, that is used to provide connectivity between hosts and routers on the same LIS, as prescribed in RFC1577. Routers attached to the same LIS would establish VCs to each other. Traffic would continue to flow on a hop-by-hop basis from the source LIS to the destination LIS. Even assuming that all ATM hosts and routers were attached to the same ATM network, inter-LIS traffic would continue to flow through routers. This is illustrated in Fig. 12.1.

The advantages to maintaining the existing connectionless model can be summarized as the following: no change to the IP model. However, if the Internet and other IP-based networks intend to carry more and more real-time traffic, then this model may be less than optimal. This is because VCs must be terminated at routers. A router must assemble the cells into a packet on a per-

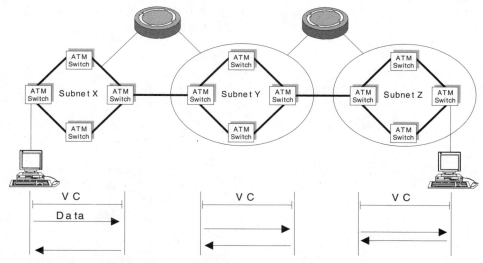

Figure 12.1   Connectionless IP over ATM.

packet basis to perform the route computation. By terminating the VC at the router, one is also terminating the ability to deliver QoS through a router. Real-time applications have strict limitations on network delay and jitter, or they will simply not work. One cannot provide any guarantees on QoS using the connectionless approach.

A connection-oriented approach for supporting IP over ATM would be a dramatic departure from the existing IP model. In effect, each source would establish a direct ATM VC to the destination, bypassing the routers along the way. Of course, staying with the separated addressing model where hosts will support both IP and ATM addresses requires an address resolution protocol. But as illustrated in Fig. 12.2, each host or router would have the ability to set up a cut-through route that would bypass intermediate layer-3 hops along the way.

It is clear that if all or even most traffic was of a nature that could benefit from ATM's traffic management and QoS properties, then this would be the way to go. But it is not. A connection-oriented approach would require signaling overhead and state to be maintained in the network, even for applications lasting a mere couple of packets (e.g., DNS query). This is not an efficient way to make use of network resources.

Thus, it would seem that the best use of network resources would be to provide a combination of both approaches. Applications requiring best-effort service could forward traffic to a default router, which would in turn forward it to the destination using the traditional IP model. This would hold true even if all resources, hosts, and routers were attached to an ATM network. Applications requiring QoS would establish a VC directly to the destination and bypass any routers along the way.

The use of both connectionless and connection-oriented approaches for supporting IP over ATM would require a decision to be made as to whether an

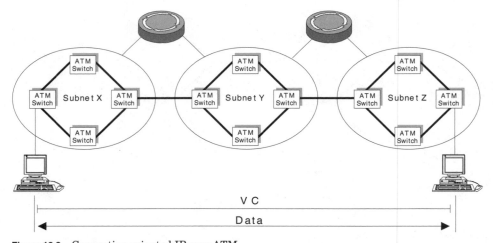

Figure 12.2   Connection-oriented IP over ATM.

application or traffic flow needs a best-effort or some higher level of service with QoS. This could be done beforehand using a signaling protocol like RSVP. Another way would be to have the network inspect the initial traffic flow over a default path and then decide that it requires a higher level of service. The first technique, RSVP, is aligned with the connection-oriented approach. Resources are allocated over a predetermined path based on reservation requests originating from a host. The second technique for deciding to route or cut-through is more or less just an optimization of the traditional connection-less model. That is, packets are forwarded into the network on a best-effort basis and if the network infrastructure identifies a more optimal path based on available resources and the requirements of the traffic flow, then it will take that path. The new path could involve some sort of cut-through routing through the router itself or over the ATM network.

RFC1932 discusses the different approaches for different types of traffic as well as combining both approaches. This is summarized in Table 12.1.

12.3   Next Hop Resolution Protocol

The Next Hop Resolution Protocol (NHRP, pronounced nerp) is an address resolution technique for resolving IP addresses with ATM addresses in a multiple subnet environment. The purpose of NHRP is to provide a host or router with the ATM address of a destination IP address so that one or more layer-3 hops can be bypassed by using a direct connection over the ATM network. NHRP can be considered an extension to the ATMARP process described in RFC1577. Whereas ATMARP is used to map IP and ATM addresses in a single LIS, NHRP is used to map IP and ATM addresses in a multiple LIS environment contained within a single ATM network.

It should be noted that NHRP was originally designed as an extension to classical IP and thus would be limited to IP networks only. But NHRP can sup-

TABLE 12.1   Connectionless and Connection-Oriented Approaches

Application	Connectionless	Connection-oriented	Both
General	Route	Setup VC	Use RSVP or other technique to indicate that VC is required
Short-duration (e.g., DNS, SMTP)	Route	Setup VC	Route
Elastic (TCP) bulk transfer	Route	Setup VC	Route by default but if available use RSVP or other technique to indicate that VC is required
Real time	Route and depend on queue management (WFQ) to bound delay	Setup VC	Route by default unless RSVP states otherwise

port any layer-3 protocol and in fact will be incorporated into the MPOA work being performed in the ATM Forum. NHRP is a result of the work being done in the Routing Over Large Clouds working group of the IETF.*

12.3.1 NHRP terminology

NHRP introduces several terms that are important to understanding its function.

- *Nonbroadcast multiaccess network (NBMA).* An NBMA network is defined as one that (1) does not support an inherent broadcast or multicast capability and (2) enables any host (or router) attached to the NBMA network to communicate directly with another host on the same NBMA network. ATM, Frame Relay, SMDS, and X.25 are all examples of NBMA networks. An NBMA ATM network may contain one or more LISs.

- *Next hop server (NHS).* The NHS provides the NHRP service for NHRP clients in an NBMA network. It contains a cache or table of IP and ATM addresses for devices attached to the ATM network. If the desired destination IP address is not on the ATM network, then the NHS will provide the ATM address of the router nearest to the destination. The NHS should run on a router so as to facilitate forwarding of NHRP requests, replies, and other messages over the default-routed path. The NHS responds to queries from NHRP clients. And the NHS serves a specific set or domain of NHRP clients for whom it is responsible.

- *Next hop clients (NHC).* NHRP clients access the NHS for the purpose of receiving NHRP services.

12.3.2 NHRP configuration

NHRP clients must be attached to an ATM network and must be configured with the ATM address of the NHS that is serving the client. Alternatively, it should have a means of locating its NHS. Techniques under consideration involving other server location requirements such as ATMARP and MARS are a group address and a configuration server. NHRP can run on an ATM-attached host or router. The NHS will likely be located on a station's peer or default router. NHRP clients can be serviced by more than one NHS.

NHRP Servers are configured with their own IP and ATM addresses, a set of IP address prefixes that correspond to the domain of NHRP clients it is serving, and an NBMA (ATM) network identifier. If the NHRP server is located on

---

* *Note:* The actual NHRP specification uses the terms protocol address and NBMA address. To keep it simple and to stay within the context of IP, we will use the terms IP address and ATM address in the discussions to follow. NHRP can work using any layer-3 internetworking protocol (e.g., IPX, Appletalk) over any NBMA network (e.g., Frame Relay, X.25, SMDS, and ATM).

an egress router attached to a non-ATM network, then the NHRP server must exchange routing information between the ATM and non-ATM networks.

12.3.3 NHRP client registration

NHRP clients register with their NHRP server in one of two ways:

- Manual configuration
- NHRP registration packets. The NHRP registration packet contains the following information along with additional values:

```
{NHC's ATMaddress, NHC's IPaddress, NHS's IPaddress}
```

With this information, the NHRP server can begin to build its table of IP and ATM addresses. The use of NHRP registration messages reduces the need for static configuration. The NHRP registration flow is illustrated in Fig. 12.3.

12.3.4 NHRP address resolution

Inter-LIS address resolution in a NHRP environment consists of the following basic steps and will be illustrated based on the sample network topology shown in Fig. 12.4. In that figure we see a single NBMA ATM network that contains two LISs: X and Z (actually three if you count the LIS connecting the two routers, but we have omitted it for simplicity). The LISs are connected by two routers that serve as NHRP servers for subnets X and Z respectively. The routers are running a normal intra-AS routing protocol, OSPF, and are con-

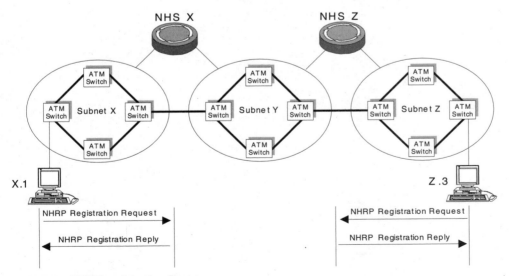

Figure 12.3 NHRP registration flow.

nected by an ATM PVC so they are exchanging routing information. The station attached to subnet X with the IP address of X.1 wishes to communicate with station Z.3.

- Station X.1 builds a packet and addresses it to Z.3. This packet is forwarded over an existing ATM VC to the default router. This causes X.1 to send a NHRP Next Hop Resolution Request message to NHS X with the following information: {AAA, X.1, Z.3}. Station X.1 may also opt to hold onto the packet until a NHRP reply is received or drop it. The first option, the default, is the better choice because that allows data to flow over the default-routed path.

- NHS X checks to see if it serves station Z.3. It also checks to see if it has an entry in its cache for Z.3. Neither is true so the NHRP Next Hop Resolution Request is forwarded to the adjacent NHRP server, NHS Z.

- NHS Z receives the NHRP Next Hop Resolution Request from NHS X. NHS Z determines that it serves the destination IP address contained in the request message. An entry is contained in the cache or table of NHS Z which contains an IP to ATM address mapping for the destination IP address of Z.3. NHS Z resolves the destination IP address, Z.3, with its matching ATM address, BBB. It places this information in a NHRP Next Hop Resolution Reply and returns it to station X.1 over a default-routed path that the request came from. The NHRP Next Hop Resolution Reply could flow

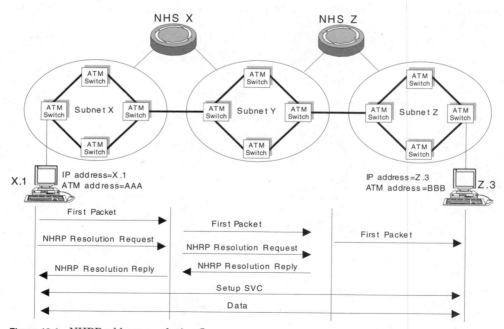

Figure 12.4   NHRP address resolution flow.

directly back to the initiator, station X.1 if (1) a VC exists between station X.1 and NHS Z, (2) an NHRP Reverse NHS record Extension is not included in the request message, and (3) the authentication policy permits direct communication between the initiator, station X.1, and NHS Z. Sending a direct response back to the NHRP initiator may save time but does not enable any of the intermediate NHSs to cache information contained in the NHRP Next Hop Resolution Reply messages.

■ As the NHRP Resolution Reply flows back to station X.1, NHS X may cache the information contained in the packet. This means it could add the entry of {Z.3, BBB} into its cache. This information could be used by NHS X to provide a nonauthoritative NHRP Next Hop Resolution Reply for another station on subnet X that wished to communicate directly with station Z.3. An authoritative reply is a one that is generated by the NHS that serves the NHRP client. If a NHRP client generates an authoritative resolution request, then only the serving NHS can respond authoritatively. If a NHRP client generates a nonauthoritative resolution request, then any NHS that can resolve the request can respond.

■ Station X.1 will receive a NHRP Next Hop Resolution Reply and take two actions, (1) cache the information contained in the reply and (2) establish an ATM SVC directly to station Z.3 and begin data transmission.

The NHRP address resolution flow is shown in Fig. 12.4.

12.3.5 NHRP messages

NHRP packets consist of a fixed part, mandatory part, and an extensions part. Table 12.2 describes the mandatory portions of the NHRP message types and the important elements contained therein. For specific information on packet formats and contents, the actual NHRP specification should be consulted.

The extensions portion of a NHRP message, if present, contains one or more Type/Length/Value fields that are used to carry additional information. This enables NHRP to be adapted as appropriate to different configurations and protocols. Table 12.3 describes the extensions options that can be carried in NHRP messages.

12.3.6 NHRP deployment

There are several important issues to consider as one deploys a network supporting NHRP. Most important to remember and an area that has caused much confusion is the fact that NHRP is not a routing protocol. It does not exchange or advertise reachability information with peer entities like RIP and OSPF do. It does not assist in any way in building a route from a source to a destination. NHRP is a simple inter-LIS address resolution protocol. It needs to run in conjunction with an intra-AS or inter-AS routing protocol. It requires, at least for

TABLE 12.2   NHRP Message Types

Message type	Description
NHRP Next Hop Resolution Request	Query sent from NHRP client to server requesting resolution of destination IP address with ATM address, contains Q-bit (that sent the request, 0=host, 1=router), A-bit (0=nonauthoritative, 1=authoritative), source ATM address, source IP address, destination IP address
NHRP Next Hop Resolution Reply	Response sent by NHRP server in to query, contains Q-bit (copied from request), A-bit (0=nonauthoritative, 1=authoritative), NAK code (see note 1), B-bit (1=stable topology between non-ATM destination IP address and destination ATM address, 0=unstable), source ATM address, source IP address, destination IP address, destination ATM address
NHRP Registration Request	Sent by NHRP client to server to register client's address information, contains source ATM address, source IP address, NHS IP address
NHRP Registration Reply	Response sent by the NHRP server to registration request, contains NAK code (see note 2), source ATM address, source IP address, NHS IP address
NHRP Purge Request	Used to invalidate cached information contained in a NHRP client or server, contains source ATM address, source IP address, destination IP address and target IP address (address to be purged from receiver's database)
NHRP Purge Reply	Sent in response to an NHRP purge request
NHRP Error Indication	Used to convey error information to the sender of the NHRP message, contains the source ATM address, source IP address, destination IP address and the NHRP error code (see note 3)

NOTE 1: NAK error codes for NHRP registration reply

NAK code	Description	Meaning
4.00	Can't serve this address	NHS refuses registration request for administrative reasons
5.00	Registration overflow	NHS cannot serve station due to lack of resources

NOTE 2: NAK code for NHRP Next Hop Resolution Reply

NAK code	Description	Meaning
12.00	No internetworking layer address to NBMA address binding	No IP to ATM address binding

NOTE 3: NHRP error codes

Error code	Description
1.00	Unrecognized extension
2.00	Subnetwork ID mismatch
3.00	NHRP loop detected
6.00	Protocol address unreachable
7.00	Protocol error
8.00	NHRP SDU size exceeded
9.00	Invalid extension
10.00	Invalid Next Hop Resolution Reply received
11.00	Authentication failure

TABLE 12.3   NHRP Extensions

NHRP extension	Description
End of extensions	Terminates extensions list in NHRP packet
Destination prefix length	Used in NHRP Next Hop Resolution Reply to indicate that destination ATM address can reach range of IP addresses that match those specified in destination prefix length.
NBMA subnetwork ID	Unique NBMA ATM network identifier used to ensure that NHRP packet does not leave NBMA network.
Responder address	Identifies both IP and ATM address of responder to NHRP requests.
NHRP forward transit NHS record extension	Contains list of transit NHSs that an NHRP request has passed through.
NHRP reverse transit NHS record extension	Contains list of transit NHHs that an NHRP reply has passed through.
NHRP QoS extension	Contained in NHRP request messages and used to indicate a desired QoS. For resolution requests it is the QoS for the path to the destination.
NHRP authentication	Contains authentication information (e.g., password, keyed MD5) carried in NHRP messages.
NHRP vendor-private additional next Hop entries	Vendor-specific extensions for NHRP used to return multiple Next Hop entries in a single NHRP reply.

an ATM network the SVC routing and signaling function incorporated into UNI Signaling 3.1/4.0 and PNNI Phase I.

The following are items to consider and remember as one contemplates deploying NHRP:

- NHRP clients run on hosts but can also run on any ATM-attached device including routers and edge devices. NHRP client functionality will be deployed in a large number of inexpensive edge devices such as LAN switches with ATM uplinks. This enables edge devices to query a route server, which runs the NHRP server, for an ATM address and then set up a cut-through route directly to the destination workstation or, in the case of a transit ATM network, another edge device. This is illustrated in Fig. 12.5.

- NHRP messages must pass through a contiguous series of NHRP-capable stations. In other words, an NHRP request, for example, must pass through one or more NHRP servers that are adjacent to each other. If this is not the case than the default-routed path will be taken and a cut-through route cannot be established.

- NHRP messages will take the same path as data that is forwarded over the default-routed path.

- NHRP can provide the nearest next-hop or last-hop on the ATM network for devices on the other side of an ATM-attached router. In addition, it will provide aggregated addressing information for non-ATM IP subnets so that subsequent nonauthoritative requests can be quickly responded to. This is

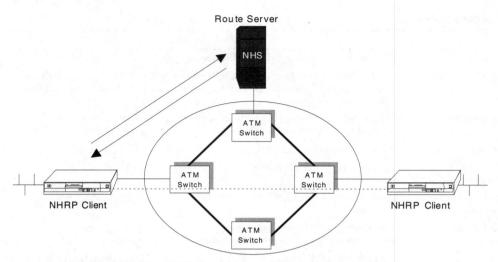

Figure 12.5   NHRP function on ATM edge devices and route servers.

illustrated in Fig. 12.6. An NHRP Next Hop Resolution Request for destination IP address=R.1 is forwarded through the ATM network until it reaches NHS R. NHS R is in fact an egress router which is attached to the ATM network at address=CCC and the non-ATM network called subnet R. The NHRP Next Hop Resolution Reply that is generated by NHS R (remember NHRP packets cannot leave the ATM network) will include the nearest ATM address to host R.1, which is that of NHS R, and it will include a destination prefix length, which is essentially the number of common bits in the IP address prefix of subnet R. This information can be cached by other NHRP servers. This will enable other NHRP clients who are looking for devices on subnet R to quickly receive a nonauthoritative response from an NHS that will direct them to ATM address=CCC.

- NHRP router-to-router configurations are illustrated in Fig. 12.7 which depicts the case where both the NHRP requestor (client) and responder (server) are attached to non-ATM networks and serving as ingress and egress routers, respectively, to the ATM network. Router (I) is attached to net X and is functioning as a ingress router, whereas Router (E) is attached to net Y and is an egress router. Station X.1 begins sending packets to Station Y.3. Router (I) will send out an NHRP Next Hop Resolution Request to which Router (E) will respond. A cut-through route can then be established between router (I) and router (E) for packets sent from Station X.1 to Station Y.3. This is for the most part no problem. However, a situation does exist where a persistent routing loop can be formed. This condition is possible if (1) there is a non-ATM backdoor path between net X and Y as shown and (2) a situation causes the routing protocol to lose attribute information (e.g., trun-

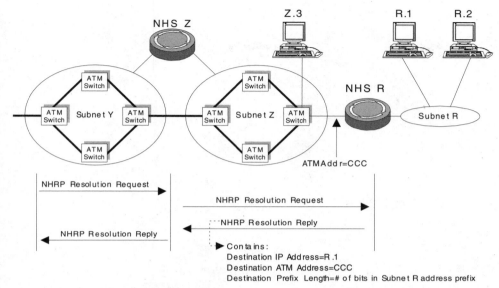

Figure 12.6   NHRP destination address prefix.

cated path vector information in EGPs or lost metric information in IGPs). Possible alternatives under discussion include terminating the NHRP cut-through route at the border of the routing domain and maintain state in the ingress and egress routers to detect change in the routing domain. The routing loop scenario is discussed in more detail in RFC1932.

12.4 IP over ATM
Architectural Extensions

The current IP over ATM model, as characterized in RFC1577, is somewhat restrictive. ATM connectivity (PVC or SVC) is limited to members of the LIS. ATM SVC support is strictly "local" and is based on the IP address of the host. Those that share a common network ID and subnet mask, or in other words, those on the same LIS can benefit from ATM SVC connectivity. No router is required.

Connectivity between members of different subnets requires a router. Even if these particular members are on the same ATM network, it would not be possible to communicate directly using an ATM SVC. This is because they do not share a common network ID and subnet mask. They are "remote" to each other and thus require a router(s) to communicate.

So the current IP over ATM model is as follows:

- Hosts in the same LIS communicate directly using ATM. They are local to each other.

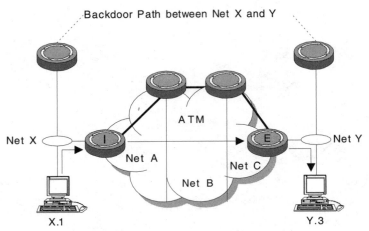

Figure 12.7   NHRP router-to-router topology.

- Hosts in different LISs must communicate through router(s). They are remote to each other.

The decision to route or establish direct SVC connectivity is coupled with the source and destination host's IP address. This is most certainly suboptimal because IP applications constitute a wide range of traffic and QoS characteristics. This spectrum is expected to widen as internets add support for real-time data flows. Short-lived best-effort can continue to be routed hop by hop. Real-time data flows with strict delay requirements can benefit from direct SVC connectivity. But, as it is defined right now an application's traffic and QoS characteristics are not considered when a host decides to route or set up an SVC.

A solution to this problem would be to alter the IP model to perform the local/remote forwarding decision based on the application's requirements and not a source/destination address pair. Any two hosts on an ATM network using ATM SVCs, irrespective of their LIS affiliation, could communicate either through routers or directly. It is up to the application and its respective traffic and QoS requirements as to whether connectivity is local via SVCs or remote through routers. A range of possible options include:

- Best-effort SVC to a local router
- Dedicated SVC to a local router dedicated to a particular service
- Best-effort SVC to a router closest to a particular host
- Dedicated SVC to a host on the same ATM network

This new IP model introduces the notion of a *logical address group* (LAG). A LAG is a set of hosts and routers that share a common IP address prefix. The routers in the LAG would each be a single hop away from the hosts and would also advertise reachability to the LAG's respective address prefix. Because the routers are contained in the LAG and share the common address prefix, these routes would be advertised as directly reachable with a metric of 0. Figure 12.8 shows two LAGs.

The enhanced IP model, as put forth by Rekhter and Kandlur in a preliminary internet draft, offers an efficient mechanism to best utilize the flexibility and performance of ATM SVCs while conserving valuable network resources.

12.5 RSVP/Integrated Services and ATM

The primary objective of the Integrated Services Architecture (ISA) is to support and deliver different service levels to those applications that request them. The integration of these different services will occur at the IP level. ATM has essentially the same goal except the integration occurs at the cell level.

The current set of IP over ATM protocols (RFC1577, NHRP) only support the best-effort model. They do not exploit the powerful QoS capabilities of ATM. The next logical step would be to determine how the ISA model, of which RSVP is a component, and ATM can be integrated.

Work is under way in the IETF to accomplish this. The Integrated Services over Specific Link Layers (ISSLL) is looking at ways of supporting the ISA model over different subnetwork technologies. ATM is a primary focus of work within this group. At the time of this writing several preliminary proposals have been put forth but much work remains.

ISA and ATM have many striking similarities, which should make the interworking of the two quite seamless. They are:

- *Traffic flows.*   Both employ a variant of the leaky bucket to characterize and police traffic flows.

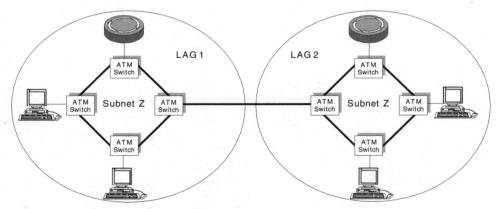

Figure 12.8 Local/remote connectivity for LAGs.

- *Traffic specifications.* ISA uses the r and b parameters of the token bucket while ATM uses the PCR/CDVT and SCR/MBS parameters. In fact the r and b parameters would map quite nicely to the SCR and MBS values.

- *Traffic classes.* The ISA has defined to date guaranteed delay, controlled load, and best-effort. ATM has CBR, VBR, ABR, and UBR. Because it specifies a maximum end-to-end delay, guaranteed delay could be mapped to VBR-rt.

- *Signaling.* Both RSVP and UNI/PNNI signaling are used to transport traffic specifications and QoS parameters into the network. Both employ admission control before accepting a reservation.

But the differences are substantial. This stems from the fact that IP is connectionless and ATM is connection-oriented. IP is a robust and dynamic networking architecture where any changes in topology or resource availability will be addressed by simply rerouting the packets to another path and reestablishing the reservation state. On the other hand, ATM takes the approach that reservations are retained for the duration of the connection. If, however, the topology changes, then ATM must rebuild the connection from scratch.

The issues that may complicate any ISA-ATM interworking are:

- *Multicast.* IP supports bidirectional many-to-many transmissions. ATM supports unidirectional point-to-multipoint. This means that there will be a lot of additional ATM VCs required to emulate the IP multicast model.

- *Heterogeneity.* Receivers in the ISA model can request and receive different levels of QoS. ATM VCs are single QoS. ISA receivers can also renegotiate QoS levels during a connection. ATM currently requires that a new VC with a different QoS be established.

- *Routing.* RSVP and IP routing are separate. ATM signaling and routing (via UNI 3.1/4.0 and PNNI Phase I) are performed concurrently.

12.6 Summary

ATM is expected to grow and over time one may find multiple LISs overlaid on a single ATM network. IP is also growing and evolving to support and carry traffic that is no longer just best-effort. Real-time audio and video will be carried over the Internet and intranets, and this kind of traffic can most certainly benefit from the delay guarantees and QoS that ATM offers. Routers will continue to play an important role in forwarding data traffic and providing security and policy controls, but for some applications a direct ATM connection is optimal. In this chapter we discussed techniques under consideration that enable a source on one LIS to communicate directly over the ATM network to a destination in another LIS without passing through a router. The Next Hop

Resolution Protocol (NHRP) is one such technique. NHRP is an inter-LIS address resolution protocol that facilitates direct ATM connectivity between a source and a destination on different subnets without the need for routers in the data path. Another technique under study places the decision to route on the application's traffic and QoS requirements rather than a host's IP address affiliation.

13

LAN Emulation and MPOA

The ATM Forum's mission is to develop implementation agreements among its participating members, which will foster the growth of ATM. LAN Emulation (LANE) and Multiprotocol over ATM (MPOA) are two such efforts which will enable traditional LANs and internetworks to run on top of and coexist with ATM switched-based networks. LAN Emulation enables a group of ATM-attached workstations to emulate the functions and protocols of a traditional token-ring or ethernet LAN. An emulated LAN (ELAN) can interwork with traditional legacy LANs through a bridge function. MPOA will enable multiple protocols to be routed and bridged over an ATM network. MPOA networks can internetwork with traditional router-based networks.

13.1 LANE Overview

LAN Emulation can be best characterized as a service developed by the ATM Forum that will enable existing LAN applications to run over an ATM network. To do so this service must emulate the characteristics and behaviors of traditional ethernets and token-rings. It must support a connectionless service. Current LAN stations send data without first establishing a connection. It must support broadcast and multicast traffic such as the kind allowed over shared media LANs like ethernet and token-ring. It must enable the interconnection of traditional LANs (real ethernets and token-rings) with the emulated LAN (those workstations directly attached to an ATM network). It must maintain the MAC address identity associated with each individual device attached to a LAN. And finally, and perhaps most important, it must protect the vast install base of existing LAN applications and enable them to work unchanged over an ATM network.

Thus, LAN Emulation V1.0 was created and indeed does address the following key requirements:

- Connectionless service is emulated over ATM.

- Broadcast and multicast traffic is supported over an emulated LAN even though ATM does not have an inherent broadcast mechanism.

- Legacy LANs can bridge onto an emulated LAN using standard techniques such as transparent and source-route bridging.

- MAC addresses are still used to indentify emulated LAN workstations. Similar to the ATMARP server approach, a server exists (LES) which maintains a table of MAC-to-ATM addresses.

- LAN applications can run unchanged over an emulated LAN. In fact, LAN applications have no knowledge that they are running over an ATM network.

The services provided by the LAN Emulation specification can be best summarized in Fig. 13.1. In that figure we see an ATM network with two workstations connected, as well as a bridge to a legacy ethernet. These are the LANE clients. The emulation services are MAC-to-ATM address resolution, broadcast, and configuration. These are the servers. The two workstations and bridge connect to and utilize the LAN Emulation services so that in essence they "think" they are running on a traditional ethernet. The underlying ATM fabric is used so that the two workstations, if desired, can establish a direct ATM VC and realize some of the benefits of high bandwidth and performance that ATM can offer. In addition, the install base of LAN applications is left intact and unchanged. The legacy ethernet workstations can bridge to the emulated LAN using standard transparent bridging.

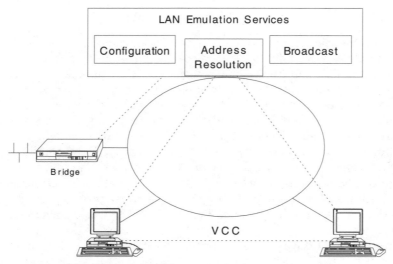

Figure 13.1   LAN Emulation architecture

In summary LAN Emulation provides the following functions:

- Defines the protocols and operation for a collection of workstations functioning as a single emulated LAN (ELAN). The ELAN can be IEEE 802.3/Ethernet or IEEE 802.5 Token-Ring.

- Specifies a set of services for each instance of an ELAN. The services provide configuration, address resolution, and broadcast function. Membership in an ELAN is not based on physical location but rather on the association with a specific set of services. This makes LAN Emulation ideal for constructing and managing what are known as *virtual LANs* (VLANs).

- Multiple LANE clients can use the single set of services. A LANE client can be a workstation with a MAC address identity or a bridge which provides a proxy MAC appearance.

- Control messages and data frames flow on different VCCs.

13.2   LANE Architecture

The architecture of LAN Emulation is defined from two perspectives. First of all there is a traditional layered architecture that defines how and where the LAN Emulation entity is positioned and operates within a LAN workstation. In other words, for a given workstation running LAN Emulation there is a set of functional layers with ATM at the bottom, the LAN application at the top, and a LAN Emulation entity between the two. Second, there is a series of protocols that exist between LAN Emulation clients and servers. More specifically, this is a user-to-network interface which specifices how LANE clients and servers interact to achieve the emulated LAN service over an ATM network.

13.2.1   LAN Emulation functional layers

The functional layers of a device running LAN Emulation are shown in Fig. 13.2. The PHY and ATM layers are common to any end user or switch implementing ATM. LAN Emulation makes use of standard AAL services to support signaling and data transfer. The functional layers interact through a set of specified interfaces that include:

- Interface between the LAN Emulation layer and the higher layers used to transmit and receive data frames. Because the intent of LAN Emulation is to hide the presence of ATM below, the LAN Emulation layer presents a MAC-level interface and addressing scheme to the higher layers. Again, the higher layers, as far as they are concerned, are running on either a token-ring or ethernet.

- Interface between the LAN Emulation layer and AAL used to transmit and receive AAL5 frames. Interface service access points are identified by a SAP-

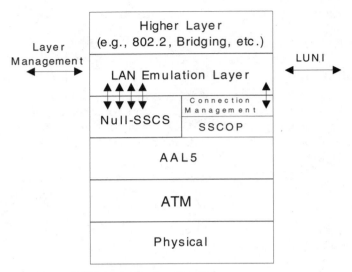

Figure 13.2   LAN Emulation functional layers.

ID which map on a one-to-one basis with specific VCCs. A LAN Emulation entity (client or server) will maintain several SAPs which map to the different connection that a LANE entity will support.

■ Interface between the LAN Emulation layer and a connection management entity. This enables a LANE entity to set up or release ATM VCCs. PVCs and SVCs are supported.

■ Interface between the LANE entity and layer management that includes facilities for initialization, control, and status.

13.2.2 LUNI

LANE clients and server interact over the LAN Emulation *user-to-network interface* (LUNI). Figure 13.3 shows a logical depiction of the LUNI between two LANE clients and the LANE servers. The functions performed over the LUNI are:

■ *Initialization.*   Obtain the ATM address(es) of the LANE services available and join or leave a particular emulated LAN specified by these ATM addresses.

■ *Registration.*   Inform the LANE services of client's MAC addresses or source-route descriptors.

■ *Address resolution.*   Obtain the ATM address representing the LANE client with a particular unicast or broadcast MAC address or segmant/bridge pair (for source-routing bridges).

■ *Data transfer.*

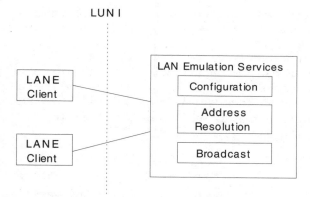

Figure 13.3 LUNI.

13.3 LANE Components

The components of an emulated LAN consist of both a LEC that typically resides on workstation, file servers, bridges and routers, and the LANE services (LECS, LES, and BUS). They are defined as the following:

- *LAN Emulation client (LEC).* A LEC can be a workstation, bridge, or router. The LEC performs address resolution, data forwarding, and other control functions. The LEC presents a MAC-level interface to the higher layers and implements LUNI when communicating with other components on the ELAN.

- *LAN Emulation configuration server (LECS).* The LECS is used to initialize a LEC with information specific to the ELAN that the LEC will be joining. The LECS will provide a LEC with the ATM address of the LES. The LECS can provide this information to the LEC, based on the client's ATM address, MAC address, or some other preconfigured policy. The LECS enables a LEC to autoconfigure itself and provides some level of control as to who can join an ELAN.

- *Broadcast and unknown server (BUS).* The BUS handles data addressed to the MAC broadcast address (x'FFFFFFFFFFFF'), all multicast traffic, and unicast frames sent by a LEC before the ATM address of the destination has been resolved. All LECs maintain a connection to the BUS and are leave on a point-to-multipoint VC with the BUS as a root. This enables LECs to send data frames without first setting up a connection, thus maintaining the presence of a connectionless data-transfer service to the higher-layers service present in each LEC.

- *LAN Emulation server (LES).* The LES functions as a registry and address resolution server for LECs attached to the ELAN. The LES provides a facility for LECs to register their MAC and ATM addresses. A LEC may also query a LES for resolution of a MAC to ATM address. The LES will either respond directly to the LEC or forward the query to other LECs that may be able to respond.

The server entities (LECS, LES, and BUS) can reside in a single physical device or can run in separate devices over an emulated LAN. An emulated LAN requires a single instance of a LES/BUS pair and supports only one type of emulated LAN: token-ring *or* ethernet. In other words, a single LES/BUS cannot support some clients that are emulating token-ring and others that are emulating ethernet.

13.4   LANE Connections

Data transfer on an ELAN consists of the exchange of control messages between LANE entities and encapsulated data frames that flow between LECs. Control VCCs carry control messages between a LEC and either the LECS or the LES. Data VCCs connect the LECs to each other and to the BUS. The following control VCCs are defined and used in the LANE specification:

- *Configuration Direct VCC.*   This is a bidirectional point-to-point VCC that is established between the LEC and the LECS as part of the LECS Connect phase. It is used by the LEC to obtain configuration information such as the ATM address of the LES.
- *Control Direct VCC.*   This is a bidirectional point-to-point VCC that is established between the LEC and the LES for the purpose of sending control information.
- *Control Distribute VCC.*   This is an optional unidirectional point-to-point or point-to-multipoint VCC that is established from the LES to one or more LECs.

Figure 13.4 depicts the control VCCs between the LEC and the LECS and LES.

Data VCCs are established between a pair of LECs to the BUS. They carry encapsulated ethernet or token-ring frames depending on the type of emulated LAN. The Data VCCs consist of the following:

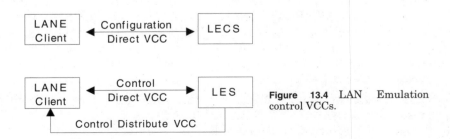

Figure 13.4 LAN Emulation control VCCs.

- *Data Direct VCC.* This is a bidirectional point-to-point VCC that is established between two LECs. When a source LEC wishes to communicate with a destination LEC but does not know its ATM address, it issues an LE_ARP request and sends it over the Control Direct VCC to the LES. Once the LE_ARP response is received over the Control Distribute VCC, the source LEC can establish a Data Direct VCC to the destination LEC.

- *Multicast Send VCC.* This is a bidirectional point-to-point VCC that is established between the LEC and the BUS. This VCC is used for sending multicast data frames to the BUS, as well as initial unicast data frames whose ATM address is not known to the source LEC. A LEC may receive data frames over this VCC.

- *Multicast Forward VCC.* This is either a unidirectional point-to-point or point-to-multipoint VCC that is established from the BUS to one or more LECs. This VCC is used for forwarding multicast data frames to ELAN members.

Figure 13.5 shows the LAN Emulation Data VCCs.

13.5   LANE Functions

The basic functions performed by LAN Emulation consist of the following:

- *Initialization.* LEC obtains the ATM address of the LES and establishes connections with the LES and BUS.

- *Registration.* LEC registers its MAC address(es) with the LES.

- *Address resolution.* Enables a source LEC to obtain the ATM address of the destination LEC for the purpose of establishing a Data Direct VCC.

- *Data transfer.* Determine which VCC to send data on and then encapsulate in AAL5 frames.

13.5.1   Initialization

The initialization of a LANE client consists of the following steps:

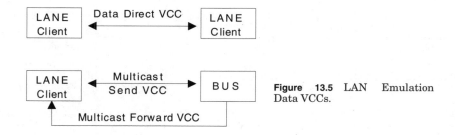

Figure 13.5 LAN Emulation Data VCCs.

- LECS connect phase
- Configuration phase
- Join phase
- BUS connect phase

In the LECS connect phase, the LEC establishes a Configuration Direct VCC with the LECS. Three methods are defined for locating the LECS:

- LEC obtains the LECS ATM address using SNMP ILMI commands from the adjacent switch.
- Use the well-known ATM address of the LECS assigned by the ATM Forum.
- Use the well-known PVC (VPI=0, VCI=17) to connect to the LECS.

If none of the three are successful, then the LEC may choose to connect directly to the LES. The Configuration Direct VCC does not exist, obviously, and the next or configuration phase would be skipped.

In the configuration phase, the LEC obtains the ATM address of the LES and, optionally, several other configuration parameters. Table 13.1 shows the control frames that flow between the LEC and LECS over the Configuration Direct VCC and some of the important operational variables that are carried. Notice that the response will carry the C2 LAN Type variable which specifies whether the LEC will be token-ring or ethernet as well as the C9 variable, the ATM address of the LES.

In the JOIN phase, the LEC establishes a Control Direct VCC to the LES and attempts to join as a member of the ELAN. Table 13.2 shows the control frames that are sent from the LEC to the LES over the Control Direct VCC and from the LES to the LEC over the Control Distribute VCC. The join request control frame may optionally carry the C6 variable which is the unique MAC address associated with the LEC. This enables the LEC to register this address and its associated ATM address, the C1 variable with the LES. The join response contains, among other values, the C14 variable, the LECID which is a unique value that is assigned by the LES for every LEC that joins the ELAN.

In the final phase of LANE initialization, the LEC connects to the BUS. The LEC locates the BUS by sending an LE_ARP_REQUEST to the LES, specifying resolution of the MAC broadcast address. The LES returns the ATM

TABLE 13.1   LAN Emulation Configuration Phase Control Frames

Control frame	Direction	Information
LE_CONFIGURE_REQUEST	LEC—>LECS	■ C1 LEC ATM address
LE_CONFIGURE_RESPONSE	LEC<—LECS	■ C2 LAN Type
		■ C3 max frame size
		■ C5 ELAN name
		■ C9 target ATM address (LES)

TABLE 13.2   LAN Emulation JOIN Phase Control Frames

Control frame	Direction	Information
LE_JOIN_REQUEST	LEC—>LES over Control Direct VCC	■ C1 LEC ATM address ■ C2 LAN Type ■ C3 max frame size ■ C4 proxy LEC ■ C5 ELAN name ■ C6 local unicast MAC address (optional)
LE_JOIN_RESPONSE	LEC<—LES over Control Distribute VCC	■ C2 LAN Type ■ C3 max frame size ■ C5 ELAN name ■ C14 LECID

address of the BUS. The LEC uses this to establish a Multicast Send VCC to the BUS. The BUS will then automatically add the LEC to an existing point-to-multipoint Multicast Forward VCC or establish a new one. Once the BUS connect phase is complete, the LEC is initialized and data transfer can begin.

Figure 13.6 shows all the Control and Data VCC that are established during the initialization phase.

13.5.2 Registration

The address registration function of LAN Emulation enables a LEC to register additional LAN and ATM destination pairs that were not registered during the JOIN phase. Table 13.3 shows the four control frames that are sent between the LEC and LES to register and unregister this information with the LES.

13.5.3 Address resolution

The address resolution function of LAN Emulation is used by the source LEC to associate a destination MAC address with the matching ATM address. The

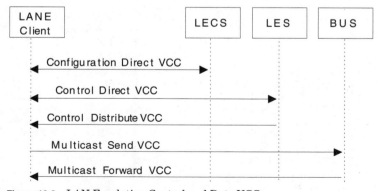

Figure 13.6   LAN Emulation Control and Data VCCs.

purpose is to provide to the source LEC the ATM address of the destination LEC. The destination LEC could be a workstation or a bridge (transparent or source-routing) which is providing a proxy LEC function for the legacy MAC devices behind it.

When the source LEC has a frame to transmit to a destination MAC address and it does not already have a Data Direct VCC open nor does it have an entry in its own MAC-to-ATM address cache (C16 variable), it sends an LE_ARP_REQUEST over the Control Direct VCC to the LES.

How the LES behaves depends on whether the MAC destination address is registered with the LES. The LES can respond to the address resolution request in the following manner:

- If the LE_ARP_REQUEST contains the broadcast MAC address (all ones) as the destination MAC address, then the LES will respond with the ATM address of the BUS in the LE_ARP_RESONSE. This is performed during the BUS connect phase of the LEC initialization process.

- If the destination MAC address is known to the LES (registered), then the LES will return the destination ATM address to the source LEC in an LE_ARP_RESPONSE. This control frame is sent over the Control Direct VCC or Control Distribute VCC. Forwarding it over the latter will enable other LECs to update their LE_ARP caches (C16) but will incur some network and LEC processing overhead.

- If the destination MAC address is unknown to the LES, then the LES will forward the LE_ARP_REQUEST to other LECs over the Control Direct VCC or Control Distribute VCC. This will typically be the case if the destination MAC address belongs to a workstation attached to a legacy LAN on the other side of a bridge.

TABLE 13.3 LAN Emulation Address Registration Control Frames

Control frame	Direction	Information
LE_REGISTER_REQUEST	LEC—>LES over Control Direct VCC	■ C1 LEC ATM address ■ C6 local unicast MAC address ■ C8 route descriptor (if SRB) ■ C14 LECID
LE_REGISTER_RESPONSE	LEC<—LES over Control Direct VCC or Control Distribute VCC	■ Status ■ C14 LECID
LE_UNREGISTER_REQUEST	LEC—>LES over Control Direct VCC	■ C1 LEC ATM address ■ C6 local unicast MAC address ■ C8 route descriptor (if SRB) ■ C14 LECID
LE_UNREGISTER_RESPONSE	LEC<—LEC over Control Direct VCC or Control Distribute VCC	■ Status ■ C14 LECID

An example of registered address resolution is shown in Fig. 13.7. LANE Client #1 wants to send a frame to another LEC (not shown) that has registered its MAC address with the LES. It will then send an LE_ARP_REQUEST over the Control Direct VCC to the LES. The LES will respond with an LE_ARP_RESPONSE, which contains the ATM address of the destination LEC. The source LEC install the new MAC-to-ATM address mapping in its own LE_ARP cache (C16) and then sets up a Data Direct VCC to the destination LEC.

Address resolution for unregistered MAC addresses involves a little bit more. Remember, only LECs that are directly attached to the ATM network are allowed to register their own MAC addresses. Devices such as ATM LAN bridges are allowed to register only their own MAC addresses, or if they are token-ring source-route bridges, then their route descriptors. For example, an ethernet-to-ATM transparent bridge will not register with the LES any of the MAC addresses of real ethernet-attached workstations that it has learned about. Instead, it will respond to LE_ARP_REQUESTS that have been forwarded to it from the server with its own ATM address, the MAC address of the actual ethernet-attached workstation, and a flag indicating that the MAC address is "remote" from the LEC that responded.

An example of this is shown in Fig. 13.8. LANE Client #1 wishes to transmit a frame to a destination MAC address that is unregistered. It is in fact an ethernet workstation that is attached to LANE Client #2. LANE Client #2 is actually an ethernet-to-ATM bridge. So after LANE Client #1 sends the first frame to the BUS which will in turn forward it out its Multicast Forward VCC to all LECs on the ELAN, it sends an LE_ARP_REQUEST to the LES. Because it is unregistered the LES forwards the request on its Control Distribute VCC to all LECs on the ELAN. LANE Client #2 receives the request, checks its own MAC

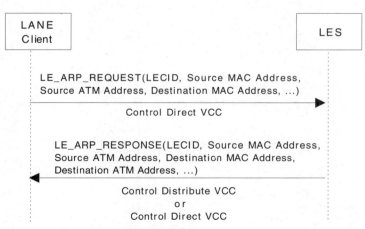

Figure 13.7 Registered address resolution.

address cache (it is a transparent learning bridge) and determines that it contains a match for the destination MAC-address value in the request. LANE Client #2 then issues an LE_ARP_RESPONSE that contains the destination MAC address (C27), its own ATM address, and sets a flag to indicate that the address is remote. The response is forwarded back to LANE Client #1 who caches the information and now can set up a Data Direct VCC.

There are four types of address resolution control frames and they are shown in Table 13.4 along with some of the important values that are contained within. LE_ARP requests and responses have been explained. The LE_NARP _REQUEST is used when a LEC (typically a proxy LEC) wishes to invalidate an existing MAC-to-ATM address mapping. The LE_TOPOLOGY_REQUEST will be sent out by either a LEC or the LES to inform other members of the ELAN that a change in network topology is under way.

13.5.4   Data transfer

Data frames can flow between a source LEC and a destination LEC in one of two ways:

- Data Direct VCC
- Multicast Send VCC to the BUS and then back out over the Multicast Forward VCC.

If a source LEC has already established a Data Direct VCC to a destination LEC, then all unicast frames will flow over that connection. If the source LEC

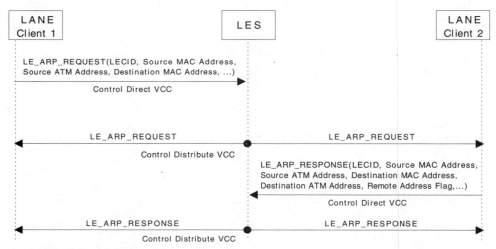

Figure 13.8   Unregistered address resolution.

TABLE 13.4 LAN Emulation Address Resolution Control Frames

Control frame	Direction	Information
LE_ARP_REQUEST	LEC—>LES over Control Direct VCC	▪ Source MAC address ▪ Source ATM address ▪ Destination MAC address ▪ C14 LECID
LE_ARP_RESPONSE	LEC<—LES over Control Direct VCC or Control Distribute VCC	▪ Source MAC address ▪ Source ATM address ▪ Destination MAC address ▪ Destination ATM Address ▪ Remote flag ▪ C14 LECID
LE_NARP_REQUEST	LEC—>LES over Control Direct VCC	▪ MAC address that is no longer valid ▪ Source ATM address ▪ Destination ATM address that was previously representing the invalid MAC address ▪ C14 LECID
LE_TOPOLOGY_REQUEST	LEC<—>LES over Control Direct VCC or forwarded by LES over Control Distribute VCC	▪ Topology change flag ▪ C14 LECID

does not have a Data Direct VCC established, then it may forward the frames up to the BUS via the Multicast Send VCC. The BUS in turn will forward the frames back out its Multicast Forward VCC to the destination LEC or may use the Multicast Send VCC. It is up to the BUS implementation to decide which one to use, but both cannot be used at the same time. In this mode LAN Emulation does indeed provide a connectionless service because the source LEC can begin transmitting without having to first set up a Data Direct VCC.

All multicast and broadcast frames are forwarded to the BUS over the Multicast Send VCC. Again the BUS can use either the Multicast Send VCC or Multicast Forward VCC to propagate the multicast or broadcast frames to the members of the ELAN. In this operation it is possible for a sending LEC to receive a copy of its own broadcast frame. However, the sending LEC inspects the LECID that is contained in each frame. Those frames that contain a LECID that matches that of the sending LEC are filtered out.

It may be possible for two paths to exist between a source and destination LEC pair: one through the BUS and one through a Data Direct VCC. This could introduce a situation where frames are delivered out of order. To address this situation, a mechanism called the LAN Emulation Flush Protocol was developed.

If a source LEC detects that it is receiving frames over both a Data Direct VCC and a Multicast Forward VCC, it will send an LE_FLUSH_REQUEST over one of the paths to ensure that all frames on the path have reached their destination. The source LEC will not send any frames over the path it sent the flush request until it receives a flush response with a matching transaction ID. The LEC receiving the flush request will return a response. The flush messages are shown in Table 13.5.

13.5.5 LAN Emulation signaling

Signaling over the LUNI interface is based on UNI 3.0/3.1. The signaling flows for establishing ATM SVCs were discussed in Chapter 8. The signaling for establishing a Data Direct VCC is shown in Figure 13.9. Excluding the READY _IND and READY_QUERY messages which are specific to Data Direct VCC establishment, the flows for setup and teardown are similar to those for point-to-point and point-to-multipoint SVCs. In this example the source LEC that wishes to initiate a Data Direct VCC, LANE Client #1 will generate a SETUP message. The information elements contained in this message include AAL parameters (AAL5), traffic descriptors (forward/backward PCR), broadband bearer capability (BCOB-X), QoS class (0 for best-effort), and a broadband lower-layer information (BLLI) which indicates the type of LANE connection that is being established (e.g., Data Direct VCC, Control Direct VCC). Once LANE Client #1, receives a CONNECT message it is ready to start sending data. However, LANE Client #1 must first send a READY_IND message as soon as it is ready to receive frames on the newly established VCC. At that point, it will consider call establishment to be complete. If for some reason the READY_IND message is lost, the destination LEC, LANE Client #2 will wait a period of time and then send a READY_QUERY message to LANE Client #1.

13.6 LAN Emulation Summary

LAN Emulation was created by the ATM Forum and is the standard for emulating either token-ring or ethernet LANs on top of an ATM network. It is based on a client/server model with the server functions providing configuration, address resolution, and broadcast/multicast support, and the client being a component that runs on a workstation or bridge that interfaces the standard higher-layer LAN applications and protocols to the lower-layer ATM function. The server functions are the LECS, LES, and BUS, and the client component is the LEC.

TABLE 13.5 LAN Emulation Flush Control Frames

Control frame	Direction	Information
LE_FLUSH_REQUEST	LEC—>Data Direct VCC or Multicast Send VCC	■ Transaction ID ■ Destination MAC address ■ Destination ATM address
LE_FLUSH_RESPONSE	LEC—>LES over Control Direct VCC for forwarding to LEC	■ Transaction ID ■ Destination MAC address ■ Destination ATM address

The functions and operation of LAN Emulation can best be summarized by the following:

- LANE enables a token-ring *or* ethernet LAN to be emulated on an ATM network.
- LAN Emulation servers are the LECS, LES, and BUS. The LECS provided configuration and ELAN membership information to the client; the LES maintains a cache of MAC-to-ATM addresses and is an address resolution server, and the BUS is used to forward broadcast, multicast, and unknown data frames to members of the ELAN.
- The LAN Emulation Client (LEC) is a software layer that interfaces the higher-layer LAN interfaces the higher-layer application and protocols to the physical ATM network. In effect, it hides the ATM network from the LAN application
- LAN Emulation can be used to construct VLANs as a backbone between sites and to connect real token-rings or ethernets into an ATM network.
- LAN Emulation only supports a single ELAN. In other words, a single instance of the LES/BUS pair is dedicated to a specific ELAN. It certainly is possible to have multiple ELAN overlaid on a single ATM network but to traverse ELAN boundaries, one does require the use of a bridge or router.

13.7   MPOA Overview

Many networks today run a multitude of different protocols (e.g., IP, IPX, Appletalk) and will continue to do so for the foreseeable future. The fact that

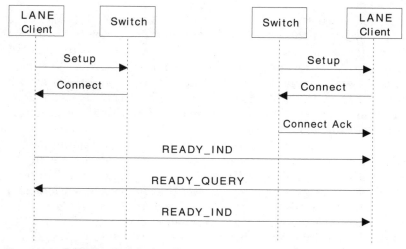

Figure 13.9   LAN Emulation signaling.

these layer-3 internetworking protocols exist would correctly imply the existence of multiple networks. That is, routers would be required to connect and forward packets from one IP subnet to another, and indeed that is the case. The same would hold true for IPX, Appletalk, and other routable protocols. Solutions exists for internetworking IP (RFC1577, NHRP, MARS) over an ATM network and those were covered in previous chapters. LAN Emulation supports multiple protocols but only over a single ELAN. A single ELAN is logically a flat network so there is, by definition, no need to route. However, if a network consists of multiple ELAN that need to be connected, and the ELANs represent different layer-3 subnets, than a router is needed.

So the ATM Forum examined this problem and decided to develop the Multiprotocol over ATM specification. Like LAN Emulation, MPOA is a service, and the purpose of this service is to support layer-3 internetworking for hosts attached to ELANs (running a LEC), hosts attached to ATM networks, and hosts attached to legacy LANs. Of course this could all be accomplished using traditional routers. But the real premise behind MPOA is to provide and deliver the function of a router and take advantage of the underlying ATM network as much as possible.

Under a single standards umbrella, the ATM Forum, MPOA is attempting to consolidate a number of different internetworking over ATM solutions. For example, the IETF has developed intra- and inter-subnet address resolution protocols (ATMARP and NHRP), thus enabling clients to establish direct SVCs from a source to a destination. MARS supports IP multicast. The ATM Forum has come up with a solution, LAN Emulation, for emulating token-ring or ethernet LAN behavior on an ATM network. However, this is restricted to a single subnet. MPOA can and will incorporate these solutions and other work ongoing in the IETF and ATM Forum as it builds toward providing a comprehensive internetworking solution.

Another important concept to understand and to illustrate what MPOA is attempting to accomplish is the *virtual router*. A virtual router has two key functions, path computation and packet forwarding, which are distributed across an ATM network. For example, Fig. 13.10*a* shows a diagram of a single router or what is known as a *unified router*. The CPU, bus, and ports are all contained in one box. The CPU in the router typically performs such functions as path computation, routing-table maintenance, and reachability propagation. It runs whichever routing protocol is needed (e.g. OSPF, NLSP). The ports on the router consist of adapters that perform inbound and outbound packet forwarding and may even cache some routing-table entries. Packets going in one port may travel over a high-speed bus to the outbound port. There is nothing wrong with this design except for the fact that faster applications and link speeds may outpace the router's ability to keep up. Or to keep up, the router may have to be outfitted with more expensive adapters, a faster CPU, and bus, and multiply that by the number of routers in the data path and it is easy to see that this could become too costly. Figure 13.10*b* shows the same routing functions distributed over an ATM network. There is a centralized route server that performs path computation, routing-table maintenance, and reachability propagation. This is the CPU of the virtual router. The ATM network is the bus. The virtual router ports are contained in inexpensive data forwarding devices that are attached to the ATM network. A virtual router port could be contained in a ATM-attached workstation. Wherever it's located, the idea behind the virtual router is to establish a direct path or connection from one port to another over the ATM network. The advantages of a virtual router can be summarized in the following points:

- Distributes the routing function between route servers that run the routing protocol and inexpensive, high-performance data forwarding devices.

- Separates routing from switching functions.

- Enables direct VCCs between data forwarding devices.

- Removes router CPU from data path.

- Scales in cost and performance much better than tradition unified router.

- Leverages performance and QoS capabilities of ATM network.

- Enables direct connections between ELANs rather than passing through traditional router.

- Enables subnet members to be distributed across entire ATM network rather than physically colocated to unified router port.

- Interwork with unified routers.

13.8   MPOA Components

Similar to classical IP and LAN Emulation, MPOA is based on a client/server model. MPOA clients establish VCCs with the MPOA server components to forward data packets or request information so that the client can establish a more direct path. The basic components of MPOA are:*

- *Subnet.*   A collection of devices that share a common layer-3 address prefix. The MPOA baseline refers to this as an Internetwork Address Subgroup (IASG). This is not an MPOA client or server but is an important concept to understand.

---

* *Note:* At the time of this writing, the MPOA baseline text was still in an early state of development and was likely to undergo some change. The authors feel that the terminology used in the baseline text was difficult to pronounce much less conceptualize. We have therefore taken the liberty to describe in more friendly terms the components and operation of MPOA.

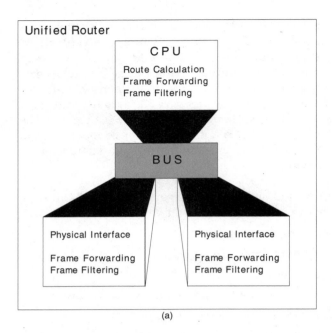

(a)

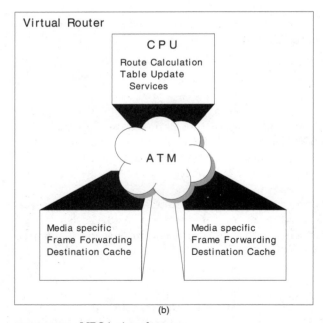

(b)

Figure 13.10   MPOA virtual router.

- *Edge device.*   This is a physical device that forwards packets from a legacy LAN to an ATM LAN, at any protocol. An edge device may use a destination's network address or MAC address to forward a packet. An edge device can also query an MPOA server for information before forwarding a packet. An edge device is an MPOA client. Also called an Edge Device Functional Group.

- *ATM host.*   Another MPOA client implementation that may query an MPOA server as well as forward packets at the network or MAC level. Also called an ATM Host Functional Group.

- *Route server.*   The route server runs routing protocols, responds to queries from MPOA clients, and participates in layer-3 to ATM address resolution. Also called a Route Server Functional Group.

- *Intra-Subnet Coordination Functional Group.*   This MPOA server entity supports the distribution of a single subnet range across multiple legacy ports on edge devices or ATM hosts. This is called the IASG Coordination Function Group (ICFG). The ICFG is coresident with the route server and one exists for each IASG that the route server is attached to. For example, if the route server was supporting IP and IPX there would be two ICFGs, one for IP and one for IPX.

- *Other MPOA server components.*   Intra- and inter-subnet default forwarders (Default Forwarder and Remote Forwarder Function Groups, respectively) and a MARS.

Figure 13.11 summarizes the basic components of the MPOA. In that figure, two subnets are logically connected to a single route server. The MPOA server components are shown to be separate but could in fact be part of the same route server device. In addition, MPOA clients can use LANE to communicate on an intra-IASG basis.

13.9   MPOA Flows

The basic information flows of the MPOA service consist of:

- *Configuration.*   Clients establish VCCs with servers to retrieve and register configuration information.

- *Data transfer.*   Ideally this is a direct VCC between two MPOA clients, but data packets can also be forwarded through a default-forwarding function.

- *Client/server.*   Used by clients to inform or query servers for information.

- *Server/server.*   Used by servers to distribute and update other MPOA servers.

There are two types of client/server MPOA flows. The first, called the RSFG Control (RSCtl), is used by an MPOA client or ICFG to obtain information from

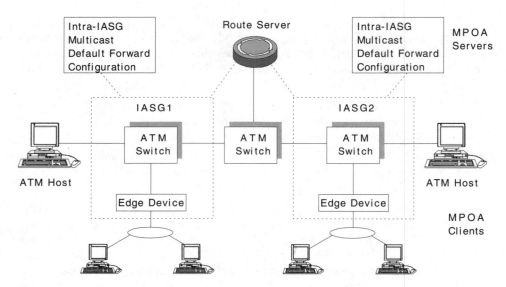

Figure 13.11   MPOA components.

the MPOA route server when attempting to resolve a destination layer-3 address to an ATM address. The second, called the ICFG Control (ICCtl), is used by MPOA clients to obtain information from the ICFG so that it can resolve an intra-IASG destination address.

There are two distinct types of MPOA server/server flows. One is between route servers and is called the RSPeer flow. The RSPeer flow is used by a route server to forward destination resolution queries for IASG destinations not served by the source route server. In addition, route servers may exchange path and topology information over this flow. The second type is between ICFG and is called the ICPeer flow. This is used by ICFGs to distribute topology information among all of the ICFGs that are supported within a single IASG. The MPOA client/server, server/server, and a data transfer flow between two MPOA clients are illustrated in Fig. 13.12. An MPOA client can be an edge device or an ATM host.

MPOA will use LLC/SNAP encapsulation as defined in RFC1483 for all VCCs over a given flow.

13.10   MPOA Operation

The MPOA service performs the following operations:

- *Configuration.*   This ensures that all MPOA components (clients and servers) contain the appropriate set of administrative information.

- *Registration and discovery.*   Registration is performed by MPOA clients and servers to inform each other of their existence and identity. Discovery is the process by which edge devices may inform the ICFG of any legacy-attached devices.

- *Destination resolution.*   The process by which the MPOA service resolves a destination layer-3 address to an ATM address, thus enabling an MPOA client to establish a cut-through SVC.

- *Data transfer.*   Forwarding layer-3 packets from one MPOA client to another.

- *Intra-IASG coordination.*   This function enables IASGs to be distributed across multiple physical interfaces.

- *Routing protocol support.*   This enables an MPOA virtual router to interact with routers on legacy networks.

- *Spanning-tree support.*   This enables an MPOA service to interact with conventionally extended (those using bridging) LANs.

- *Replication support.*   This enables key components to be replicated to increase capacity and availability.

13.11 LANE versus MPOA

There are a number of basic similarities as well as significant differences between LANE and MPOA. Both are intended to provide support for existing

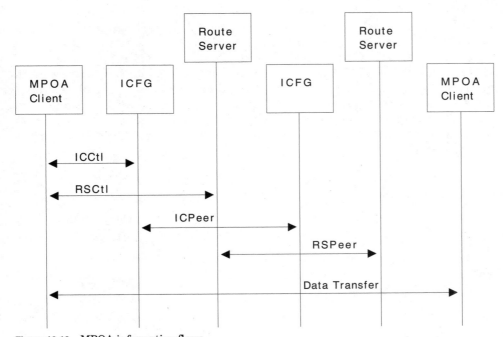

Figure 13.12   MPOA information flows.

LANs running over an ATM network. Both desire to enable users to leverage the performance and scalability of ATM by establishing point-to-point VCCs between a source and destination. Both are based on a client/server model in which inexpensive client function can be distributed across the ATM network while the intelligence of routing, multicasting, default packet forwarding, and so on is consolidated in a set of servers. And finally, both have been embraced and sanctioned by the ATM Forum and all of the participants who have contributed to the implementation agreements.

But of course there are very basic and significant differences. LANE is really a single subnet solution. MPOA supports multiple subnets. LANE may not scale as well as MPOA for the same reason that bridged networks cannot scale as well as routed networks—broadcast propagation, logical-addressing limitations, policy, organizational, and otherwise. LANE solves one problem—emulating a legacy LAN. MPOA is attempting to consolidate into one implementation agreement a number of different solutions that address many problems—LANE, NHRP, MARS, and so on. LANE, though, is a mature and stable specification and there are a large number of vendors who are shipping products. MPOA is still under development and it may be some time before it is completed and MPOA products begin to ship.

Nevertheless, it is envisioned that when the MPOA specification is completed it will provide a superior level of service over that of LANE.

13.12   Summary

LAN Emulation (LANE) and Multiprotocol over ATM (MPOA) are two efforts of the ATM Forum that will enable traditional LANs and internetworks to run on top of and coexist with ATM switched-based networks. LAN Emulation enables a group of ATM-attached workstations to emulate the functions and protocols of a traditional token-ring or ethernet LAN. An emulated LAN (ELAN) can internetwork with traditional legacy LANs through a bridge function. MPOA will enable multiple protocols to be routed and bridged over an an ATM network. MPOA networks can internetwork with traditional router-based networks.

Glossary

AAL ATM adaptation layer. A collection of standardized protocols that provide services to higher layers by adapting user traffic to a cell format. The AAL is divided into the convergence sublayer (CS) and the segmentation and reassembly (SAR) sublayer.

AAL1 AAL type 1. A protocol standard used for the transport of constant bit rate (CBR) traffic (i.e., audio and video) and for emulating TDM-based circuits (i.e., DS1, E1).

AAL2 AAL type 2. A protocol standard for supporting time-dependent variable bit rate (VBR-RT) of connection-oriented traffic (i.e., packetized video and audio).

AAL3/4 AAL type 3 and 4. A protocol standard for supporting both connectionless and connection-oriented variable bit rate (VBR) traffic. Used also to support SMDS.

AAL5 AAL type 5. A protocol standard for supporting the transport of lightweight variable bit rate (VBR) traffic and signaling messages. Also used to support frame relay services.

ABR available bit rate. One of the two best-effort service types (the other one is UBR), where the network makes no absolute guarantee of cell delivery. However, it does guarantee a minimum bit rate for user transmission. An effort is also made to keep cell loss as low as possible.

access control byte The byte following the start delimiter of a token or frame that is used to control access to the token-ring network.

access priority The maximum priority that a token can have for the adapter to use it for transmission.

access rate The bit-per-second (bps) rate at which a user can transmit over the network's lines.

access unit A unit that allows multiple attaching devices access to a token-ring network at a central point. Sometimes these devices may also be referred to as a concentrator.

ACK Acknowledgment. A message that acknowledges the reception of a transmitted packet. ACKs can be separate packets or piggybacked on reverse-traffic packets.

acknowledgment In data communications, the transmission of characters from the receiving device indicating that data sent has been received correctly.

ACR Allowed (or Available) cell rate. The available bandwidth, in cells per second, for a given QoS class, which is dynamically controlled by the network.

active (1) Operational. (2) Pertaining to a file, page, or program that is in main storage or memory, as opposed to a file, page, or program that must be retrieved from auxiliary storage. (3) Pertaining to a node or device that is connected or is available for connection to another node or device.

active monitor A function in a single adapter on a token-ring network that initiates the transmission of tokens and provides token error recovery facilities. Any active adapter on the ring has the ability to provide the active monitor function if the current active monitor fails.

active program Any program that is loaded into memory and ready to be executed.

active session The session in which a user is currently interacting with the computer.

adapter address Twelve hexadecimal digits that identify a LAN adapter.

Adapter Card A hardware card that provides the interface between the computer (DTE) and the physical network circuit. (See also **NIC.**)

adaptive routing A method of routing packets of data or data messages in which the system's intelligence selects the best path. This path might change with traffic patterns or link failures.

adaptive session-level pacing A form of session-level pacing in which session components exchange pacing windows that may vary in size during the course of a session. This allows transmission within a network to adapt dynamically to variations in availability and demand of buffers on a session-by-session basis. Session-level pacing occurs within independent stages along the session path according to local congestion at the intermediate nodes.

address (1) A character or group of characters that identify data source or destination or a network node. (2) The destination of a message sent through a communications system. In computer network terms, it is a set of numbers that uniquely identifies a workstation on a LAN.

adjacent In a network, pertaining to devices, nodes, or domains that are directly connected by a data link or that share common control.

adjacent link station A link station directly connected to a given node by a link connection over which network traffic can be carried.

adjusted ring length (ARL) In a multiple-wiring-closet ring, the sum of all wiring closet-to-wiring closet cables in the main ring path less the length of the shortest of those cables.

Advanced Peer-to-Peer Networking (APPN) An extension to SNA featuring (a) greater distributed network control that avoids critical hierarchical dependencies, thereby isolating the effects of single points of failure; (b) dynamic exchange of network topology information to foster ease of connections and reconfiguration, adaptive route selection, and simplified network definition; (c) automated resource registration and directory lookup. APPN extends the LU 6.2 peer orientation for end-user services to network control; APPN also uses LU 6.2 protocols on its own control-point sessions that provide the network control.

advanced program-to-program communication (APPC) (1) The general facility characterizing the LU 6.2 architecture and its various implementations in products. (2) Sometimes used to refer to the LU 6.2 architecture and its product implementation as a whole, or an LU 6.2 product feature in particular, such as an APPC application program interface.

AIR Additive Increase Rate. The cell rate a source can transmit after increasing its rate by the RIF.

AIS Alarm indication signal. One of the OAM function types used for fault management. (See also **CC, RDI.**)

alert A message sent to a management services focal point in a network to identify a problem or an impending problem.

algorithm A prescribed finite set of well-defined rules or processes for the solution of a problem in a finite number of steps. In normal English, it is the mathematical formula for an operation, such as computing the check digits on packets of data that travel via packet-switched networks.

all-routes broadcast frame A frame that has bits in the routine information field set to indicate the frame is to be sent to all LAN segments in the network. The destination address is not examined and plays no role in bridge routing.

all-stations broadcast frame A frame whose destination-address bits are set to all ones. All stations on any LAN segment on which the frame appears will copy it. It is independent of all-routes broadcasting.

ANSI American National Standards Institute. An U.S. technology standards organization.

API See **application programming interface.**

application A program or set of programs that perform a task.

application program interface (API) The formally defined programming language interface that allows a programmer to write to the interface.

application transaction program A program written for or by a user to process the user's application; in an SNA network, an end user of a type 6.2 logical unit.

applications layer The seventh and highest layer of Systems Network Architecture (SNA) and Open Systems Interconnection (OSI). It supplies functions to applications or nodes allowing them to communicate with other applications or nodes.

APPN end node A type 2.1 end node that provides full SNA end-user services and supports sessions between its local control point (CP) and the CP in an adjacent network node to dynamically register its resources with the adjacent CP (its network node server), to send and receive directory search requests, and to obtain management services; it can also attach to a subarea network as a peripheral node.

APPN intermediate routing The capability of an APPN network node to accept traffic from one adjacent node and pass it on to another, with awareness of session affinities in controlling traffic flow and outage notifications.

APPN intermediate routing network The portion of an APPN network consisting of the network nodes and their connections.

APPN network A type 2.1 network having at least one APPN node.

APPN network node A type 2.1 (T2.1) node that, besides offering full SNA end-user services, provides intermediate routing services within a T2.1 network, and network services to its local LUs and attached T2.1 end nodes in its domain; it can also attach to a subarea network as a peripheral node.

APPN node An APPN network node or an APPN end node.

ARP   Address Resolution Protocol. A TCP/IP protocol used for resolving local network addresses by mapping a physical address (i.e., a MAC address) to an IP address.

asynchronous   Asynchronous transmission. An approach for acquiring synchronization on a per-byte basis. Start and stop bits are used as delimiters.

Asynchronous transfer   An efficient approach for transmitting information where time slots are used on a demand basis (ATDM, ATM) rather than on a periodical one (TDM, STM).

asynchronous transmission   A method of data transmission which allows characters to be sent at irregular intervals by preceding each character with a start bit, and following it with a stop bit. No clocking signal is provided. This is in contrast to synchronous transmission.

ATDM   Asynchronous time-division multiplexing. An asynchronous and intelligent TDM where time slots are allocated to the users on demand (dynamically).

ATM   Asynchronous Transfer Mode. A broadband switching and multiplexing, connection-oriented, high-performance, and cost-effective integrated technology for supporting B-ISDN services (i.e., multimedia). Since no clock control is necessary it is called asynchronous. (See also **STM**.) Information is transmitted at very high rates (up to hundreds of Mbps) in fixed-size format packets called cells. Traffic streams are distinguished and supported according to different QoS classes.

ATM CSU/DSU   ATM Channel/Data Service Unit. A device that converts information bits (i.e., transmitted over the telephony network) or frame-based information into (or from) a stream of ATM cells. (See **CSU, DSU, DXI**.)

ATM Forum   Originally founded by a group of vendors and telecommunication companies, this formal standards body is comprised of various committees responsible for making recommendations and producing implementation specifications.

ATM layer   The second layer of the ATM protocol stack model that constructs and processes the ATM cells. Its functions also include usage parameter control (UPC) and support of QoS classes.

ATM-SAP   ATM-service access point. The physical interface at the boundary between the AAL and the ATM layer. (See also **SAP, PHY-SAP**.)

AToMMIB   ATM MIB. IETF-defined management information base (MIB) for managing VP/VC links and ATM PVC-supported services and interfaces.

attenuation   A decrease in magnitude of current, voltage, or electrical or optical power of a signal in transmission between points. It may expressed in decibels or nepers.

average cell rate   The mean number of cells that the source can inject into a network over a given virtual connection (VC).

average cell transfer delay   The arithmetic average of a number of cell transfer delays (CTD). (See also **mean cell transfer delay**.)

B-ICI   Broadband-intercarrier interface. An interface that supports service connections (such as CRS, CES, SMDS, FR) across public ATM networks and/or carriers.

B-ISDN   Broadband Integrated Services Digital Network. An ITU-T-introduced protocol platform to support the integrated, high-speed transmission of data, audio, and video in a seamless fashion. ATM emerged as a suitable transport standard.

backbone   A LAN, a WAN, or a combination of both dedicated to providing connectivity between subnetworks in an enterprisewide network. Subnetworks are connected to the backbone via bridges and/or routers and the backbone serves as a communications highway for LAN-to-LAN traffic.

backbone LAN segment   In a multisegment LAN configuration, a centrally located LAN segment to which other LAN segments are connected by means of bridges or routers.

backup path   In an IBM Token-Ring Network, an alternative path for signal flow through access units and their main ring-path cabling.

backup server   A program or device that copies files so at least two up-to-date copies always exist.

balun   Balanced/unbalanced. An impedance matching transformer. Baluns are small passive devices that convert the impedance of coaxial cable so that its signal can run on twisted-pair wiring. They are used often so that IBM 3270-type terminals, which traditionally require coaxial cable connection to their host computer, can run on twisted pair.

bandwidth   The range of electrical frequencies a device can handle.

BASize   Buffer allocation size. A 1-byte field in the CPCS-PDU header to indicate to the receiving end the buffer space that needs to be reserved for reassembling the CPCS-PDU.

beacon   A token-ring frame sent by an adapter indicating that it has detected a serious ring problem, such as a broken cable or a multistation access unit. An adapter sending these frames is said to be beaconing.

BEC   Backward error correction. An error-correction scheme where the sender retransmits any data to be found in error, based on the feedback from the receiver.

best effort   A QoS class in which no specific traffic parameters and no absolute guarantees are provided. Best effort includes UBR and ABR. (See also **service types.**)

bisynchronous transmission   Also called BISYNC. A data character-oriented communications protocol developed by IBM for synchronous transmission of binary-coded data between two devices.

bit   Abbreviation for binary digit. The smallest unit of information (data) and the basic unit in data communications. A bit can have a value of 0 or 1.

bit rate   The number of bits of data transmitted over a communications line each second.

BNC   A bayonet-locking connector for slim coaxial cables.

BOM   Beginning of message. A PDU that constitutes the beginning of a message.

bps (bits per second)   A measurement of data transmission speeds.

BRI   Basic rate interface. An ISDN service specification that provides two 64-kbps data B-channels and one 16-kbps control D-channel, all sharing the same physical medium.

bridge   (1) An interface connecting two similar local area networks. (2) A device that connects two local area networks. It performs its functions at the data link control (DLC) layer.

bridge ID   The bridge label combined with the adapter address of the adapter connecting the bridge to the LAN segment with the lowest LAN segment number.

bridge label   A two-byte hexadecimal number that the user can assign to each bridge.

bridge number   The bridge identifier that the user specifies in the bridge program configuration file. The bridge number distinguishes between parallel bridges.

broadcast   The simultaneous transmission of data to more than one destination.

broadcast message   A message from one station sent to all other users. On a token-ring LAN, the destination address is unspecified, thus all devices receive the message.

brouter   In local area networking, a device that combines the dynamic routing capabilities of an internetwork router with the ability of a bridge to interconnect local area networks.

BSC   Binary Synchronous Communication. A set of IBM operating procedures for synchronous transmission used in teleprocessing networks.

BT   Burst tolerance. Proportional to the MBS, burst tolerance is used as a measure (leaky bucket parameter) for conformance checking of the SCR.

buffer   In data transmission, a buffer is a temporary storage location for information being sent or received. Usually located between two different devices that have different abilities or speeds for handling the data.

burstiness   A source traffic characteristic that is defined as the ratio of the peak cell rate (PCR) to the average cell rate. It is a measure of the intercell spacing. (See also **MBS**).

bus   A network configuration in which nodes are interconnected through a bidirectional transmission medium.

BUS   Broadcast and unknown server. A server that forwards multicast, broadcast and unknown-destination address traffic to the attached LECs.

BW   Bandwidth. Transmission capacity of a communications medium.

byte   A binary character operated upon as a unit and usually shorter than a computer word. It is eight consecutive bits representing a character.

cable loss   The amount of radio frequency signal attenuation caused by a cable.

cable riser   Cable running vertically in a multistory building to serve the upper floors.

CAC   Connection admission control. An ATM function which determines whether a virtual circuit (VC) connection request should be accepted or rejected.

campus   A networking environment in which users—voice, video, and data—are spread out over a broad geographic area, as in a university, hospital, medical center, etc. There may be several LANs on a campus. They will be connected with bridges and/or routers communicating over telephone or fiber-optic cable.

carrier   A wave or pulse train that may be varied by a signal bearing information to be transmitted over a communication system.

CAT-3   Category 3 unshielded twisted. A type of UTP commonly used with ATM interfaces for cell transmission at low speeds, 25–50 Mbps and at distances up to 100 meters.

CAT-5   Category 5 unshielded twisted pair. A type of UTP commonly used with ATM interfaces for higher-speed cell transmission (more than 50 Mbps).

CBR   Constant (or continuous) bit rate. One of the five ATM classes of service which supports the transmission of a continuous bit stream of information where traffic, such as voice and video, needs to meet certain QoS requirements. (See also **QoS classes.**)

CC   Continuity cell. A cell used periodically to check whether a connection is idle or has failed (i.e., at the cross-connect nodes), in order to guarantee a continuation in the flow of the information cells. Continuity checking is one of the OAM function types for fault management. (See also **AIS, RDI.**)

CCITT   Consultative Committee on International Telegraphy and Telephony. A standards and specifications body whose published recommendations cover a wide spectrum of areas which include definition of terms, basic principles and characteristics, protocol design, description of models, and other specifications. Currently known as ITU-T.

CCR   Current cell rate. A field in the RM cell header that indicates the current complying cell rate a user can transmit over a virtual connection (VC).

CDV   Cell delay variation. A QoS parameter that measures the difference between a single cell's transfer delay (CTD) and the expected transfer delay. It gives a measure of how closely cells are spaced in a virtual circuit (VC). CDV can be introduced by ATM multiplexers (MUXs) or switches.

CDVT   Cell-delay variation tolerance. Used in CBR traffic it specifies the acceptable tolerance of the CDV (jitter).

cell   Basic ATM transmission unit. It is a 53-byte packet, comprised of a 5-byte header and a 48-byte payload. User traffic is segmented into cells at the source and reassembled at the destination.

cell header   The 5-byte ATM cell header contains control information regarding the destination path and flow control. More specifically, it contains the following fields: GFC, VPI, VCI, PT, CLP, and HEC.

cell layer   Same as ATM layer.

CER   Cell error rate. A QoS parameter that measures the fraction of transmitted cells that are erroneous (they have errors when they arrive at the destination).

CES   Circuit emulation service. An ATM-provided class of service, where TDM-type, constant-bit-rate (CBR) circuits are emulated by the AAL1.

CI   Congestion indication. A bit in the RM cell to indicate congestion (it is set by the destination if the last cell received was marked).

CIF   Cell Information Field. The payload (48 bytes) of an ATM cell.

CIR   Committed information rate. A term used in frame relay which defines the information rate the network is committed to provide the user with, under any network conditions.

circuit emulation   A virtual-circuit (VC) service offered to end users where the characteristics of an actual, digital bit-stream (i.e., video traffic) line are emulated (i.e., a 2- or 45-Mbps signal).

class 4   Specifies the parameters for connectionless data transfer. AAL3/4 or AAL5 can be used to support this class.

class of service (COS)   A designation of the transport network characteristics, such as route security, transmission priority, and bandwidth, needed for a particular session. The class of service is derived from a mode name specified by the initiator of a session.

classical IP   IETF-defined protocols for developing IP over ATM networks (i.e., IP support for the QoS classes, ARP over SVC, and PVC networks) so that common applications (i.e., FTP, Telnet, SMTP, SNMP) can be supported in an ATM environment. The main issues in the transport of IP over ATM are the packet encapsulation and the address resolution.

CLP   Cell loss priority. A 1-bit field in the ATM cell header that corresponds to the loss priority of a cell. Lower priority (CLP=1) cells can be discarded under congestion situations.

CLR   Cell loss ratio. A QoS parameter that gives the ratio of the lost cells to the total number of transmitted cells.

CMIP   Common Management Information Protocol. An ITU-T -defined management interface standard that can support administration, maintenance, and operation information functions. (See also **OAM&P.**)

CMIP   Common Management Information Protocol. A protocol formally adapted by the International Standards Organization used for exchanging network management information over OSI. Typically, this information is exchanged between two management stations. It can be used to exchange information between an application and a management station. Though designed for OSI networks, it is transport independent. Theoretically, it can run across a variety of transports, including IBM's SNA.

CMOT (CMIP over TCP/IP)   The use of CMIP over a TCP/IP-based transport.

CMR   Cell misinsertion rate. A performance measure that is defined as the number of misinserted cells (those that arrive from the wrong source) per (virtual) connection second.

CO   Central Office. Premises of a carrier service provider where customer lines (i.e., telephone lines) are multiplexed and switched to other COs.

coaxial cable   A cable composed of an insulated central-conducting wire wrapped in another cylindrical conducting wire. The whole thing is usually wrapped in another insulating layer and an outer protective layer. A coaxial cable has great capacity to carry great quantities of information. It is typically used to carry high-speed data and in cable TV.

COM   Continuation of message. A PDU that is part of a message.

communication   The transmission and reception of data.

communication adapter   A circuit card with associated software that enables a processor, controller, or other device to be connected to a network.

communication network management (CNM)   The process of designing, installing, operating, and managing distribution of information and control among user of communication systems.

communications line   The physical link (such as wire or a telephone circuit) that connects one or more workstations to a communications control unit or that connects one control unit to another.

communications manager   A component of OS/2 Extended Edition that lets a work-station connect to a host computer and use the host resources as well as the resources of other personal computers to which the workstation is attached, either directly or through a host.

communications port   (1) An access point for data entry or exit to or from a communi-cation device such as a terminal. (2) On a personal computer or workstation, a synchro-nous or asynchronous serial port to which a modem can be attached.

composite end node   To a type 2.1 node, a group of nodes that appears to be a single end node.

concurrent   Pertaining to the occurrence of two or more activities within a given inter-val of time.

CONFIG.SYS   A file that contains configuration options for an OS/2 or DOS program installed on a workstation or personal computer. It defines the devices, system parame-ters, and resource options of a workstation or personal computer.

congestion control   A resource and traffic management mechanism to avoid and/or prevent excessive situations (buffer overflow, insufficient bandwidth) that can cause the network to collapse. There exist various congestion control methods. (See also **flow control.**)

connection-oriented   See connection-oriented network.

connection-oriented network   Communications service where an initial connection between the endpoints (source and destination) has to be set up. Examples are ATM and frame relay. (See also **virtual circuit VC.**)

connectionless network   Communications service where packets are transferred from source to destination without the need of a preestablished connection. Examples are IP and SMDS. (See also **datagram.**)

connectionless service   A networking node in which individual data packets in a local area network traveling from one point to another are directed from one intermediate node to the next until they reach their ultimate destination. The receipt of a transmis-sion is typically acknowledged from the ultimate destination to the point of origin.

control point (CP)   A component of a node that manages resources of that node and optionally provides services to other nodes in the network.

control vector   One of a general class of RU substructures that has variable length, is carried within some enclosing structure, and has a 1-byte key used as an identifier.

controller   A unit that controls input/output operations for one or more devices.

conversation   A logical connection between two transaction programs using an IBM LU 6.2 session.

corporate network   May also be called an internetwork or a wide area network or enterprise network. A network of networks that connects most or all of a corporation's local area networks. Connections between networks and LANs are made with bridges and routers.

COS   Class of service. (See **QoS classes.**)

CPCS   Common part convergence sublayer. Part of the AAL convergence sublayer (CS). It has to always be present in the AAL implementation. Its task is to pass primitives to the other AAL sublayers (SAR, SSCS). It supports the functions of the standardized common part AALs: AAL1, AAL3/4, and AAL5.

CPE   Customer premises equipment. Computer and communications equipment (hardware and software) used by a carrier's customer and located at the customer's site. (See also **DTE.**)

CPI   Common part indicator. A 1-byte field in the header of the CPCS-PDU in AAL3/4 that indicates the number of bits the BASize field consists of.

CRC   Cyclic redundancy check. A bit-errors detection technique that employs a mathematical algorithm, where, based on the transmitted bits, it calculates a value attached to the information bits in the same packet. The receiver using the same algorithm recalculates that value and compares it to the one received. If the two values do not agree the transmitted packet is then considered to be in error.

CRC   Cyclic redundancy check. A process used to check the integrity of a block of data.

CRM   Cell rate margin. A measure of the residual useful bandwidth for a given QoS class, after taking into account the SCR.

CRS   Cell relay service. A bearer service offered to the end users by an ATM network that delivers (transports and routes) ATM cells.

CS   Convergence sublayer. The upper half of the AAL. It is divided into two sublayers, the common part (CPCS) and the service specific (SSCS). It is service dependent and its functions include manipulation of cell-delay variation (CDV), source clock frequency recovery, and forward error correction (FEC). Though each AAL has its own functions, in general the CS describes the services and functions needed for conversion between ATM and non-ATM protocols. (See also **SAR.**)

CS-PDU   Convergence Sublayer Protocol Data Unit. The PDU used at the CS for passing information between the higher layers and the SAR, where they are converted into cells.

CSF   Cell switch fabric. (See **switch fabric.**)

CSR   Cell missequenced ratio. A performance measure that is defined as the number of missequenced cells (those that arrive in the wrong order) per (virtual) connection second.

CSU   Channel service unit. Equipment at the user end that provides an interface between the user and the communications network. CSU can be combined with DSU in the same device. (See **DCE.**)

CTD   Cell transfer delay. A QoS parameter that measures the average time for a cell to be transferred from its source to its destination over a virtual connection (VC). It is the sum of any coding, decoding, segmentation, reassembly, processing, and queuing delays.

data circuit-terminating equipment (DCE)   The equipment installed at the user's premises that provides all the functions required to establish, maintain, and terminate a connection for data transmission, and the signal conversion and coding between the data terminal equipment device and the line.

data communication   The transmission and reception of data.

data link   A physical link, like a wire, that connects one or more devices or communication controllers.

data link control (DLC)   (1) The physical means of connecting one location to another for the purpose of transmitting and receiving data. (2) In SNA, the second layer of the seven layer architecture. (3) In OSI, the second layer of the seven-layer architecture.

datagram   A packet transport mode where packets are routed independently and may follow different paths, thus there is no guarantee of sequence delivery. (See also **VC**.)

datastream   (1) All data transmitted through a data channel in a single read or write operation. (2) A continuous stream of data elements being transmitted, or intended for transmission, in character or binary-digit form, using a defined format.

DCE   Data circuit-terminating equipment or data communications equipment. Device at the user end, typically a modem or other communications device, which acts as an access point to the transmission medium.

dependent logical unit (DLU)   An LU controlled by an SNA host system.

destination   In a network, any point or location, for example, a node, a station, or a terminal, to which data is to be sent.

destination address   That part of a message which indicates for whom the message is intended. Synonymous with the address on an envelope. IBM Token-Ring Network addresses are 48 bits in length.

device   (1) An input/output unit such as a terminal, display, or printer. (2) In computers it may be used for direct access storage (e.g., hard disk).

differential Manchester encoding   A transmission encoding scheme in which each bit is encoded as a two-segment signal with a signal transition (polarity change) at either the bit time or half-bit time. Transition at a bit time represents a 0. No transition at a bit time indicates a 1.

diskless workstation   A workstation without a hard disk or diskette drive.

distributed processing   A network of computers such that the processing of information is initiated in local computers, and the resultant data is sent to a central computer for further processing with the data from other local systems. A LAN is an example of distributed processing.

domain   In IBM's SNA, a host-based systems services control point (SSCP), the physical units (PUs), logical units (LUs), links, link stations, and all the affiliated resources that the host (SSCP) controls.

downloading   The act of receiving data from one computer into another.

downstream physical unit (DSPU)   A controller or a workstation downstream from a gateway that is attached to a host.

DQDB   Distributed queue dual bus. The IEEE 802.6 standard is a MAN protocol based on 53-byte packets that can support connectionless and connection-oriented, isochronous integrated services. It is implemented as two unidirectional buses configured in a physical ring topology.

DS-0   Digital signal 0. Physical interface for digital transmission at the rate of 64 kbps.

DS-1   Digital signal 1. Physical interface for digital transmission at the rate of 1.544 Mbps. Also, known as a T-1 standard, it can simultaneously support 24 DS-0 circuits.

DS-2   Digital signal 2. Physical interface for digital transmission at the rate of 6.312 Mbps.

DS-3   Digital signal 3. Physical interface for digital transmission at the rate of 44.736 Mbps.

DSU   Data service unit. Equipment at the user end that acts as a telephony-based interface between low-rate (i.e., 56 kbps) services and higher rate circuits.

DTE   Date terminal equipment. The host computer (PC or workstation) to provide the end user with access to a communications network. The DTE is connected to a DCE which performs the signaling operation. (See also **CPE**).

DXI   Data exchange interface. A frame-based ATM interface between a DTE (such as a router or a local switch) and a DCE. DXI interfaces to the ATM UNI and has been chosen by the ATM Forum as an affordable solution for providing ATM capabilities over WAN.

E-1   European Digital Signal 1. European standard for digital physical interface at 2.048 Mbps.

E-3   European Digital Signal 3. European standard for digital physical interface at 34.368 Mbps. It can simultaneously support 16 E-1 circuits.

E-4   European Digital Signal 4. European standard for digital physical interface at 139.264 Mbps.

E.164   An ITU-T–defined 8-byte address format. In ATM, it is typically used in public networks and is provided by the telecommunication carriers, while 20-byte NSAP format addresses are used within private networks.

early token release   This is a method of token passing which allows the token to be released prior to completion of transmission by the station. It is used on 16-Mbps token-ring networks.

EFCI   Explicit Forward Congestion Indication. A 1-bit field in the PTI that contains information whether congestion at an intermediate node has been experienced. The EFCI bit is set when, for example, a buffer threshold has been exceeded.

ELAN   Emulated LAN. (See **LAN Emulation.**)

end user   The ultimate source or destination of application data flowing through a network. An end user can be an application program or a human operator.

end-node domain   An end-node control point, its attached links, and its local LUs.

ENR   Enterprise Network Roundtable. An ATM Forum associated group of ATM users who provide feedback on ATM-related issues and also present the users with completed interoperable capabilities and functionality.

ER   Explicit rate. A field in the RM cell header specifying the cell rate a user should use for transmission over a virtual connection (VC), as it is dictated by the RM. (See also **CCR**).

error rate   In data transmission, the ratio of the number of incorrect elements transmitted to the total number of elements transmitted.

ETSI   European Telecommunications Standards Institute. The corresponding body of ANSI in Europe, involved in providing and adapting standards for the European telecommunications.

FDDI   Fiber Distributed Data Interface. An ANSI-defined standard for implementing a high-speed (100 Mbps) LAN over fiber.

FDM   Frequency-division multiplexing. A technique that allows for the channel bandwidth of a circuit to be subdivided into many little channels (one per traffic stream).

FEC   Forward error correction. An error correction technique where there are no retransmissions, and therefore, the receiver is responsible for correcting any errors in the packets.

file   A set of related records treated as a unit.

file server   A device which serves as a central location for commonly used files by everyone on a LAN.

flow control   A method used in networking for congestion avoidance and traffic regulation. There are three techniques: window-based control, where a sliding window is used to determine how many cells can be transmitted during a predefined period; rate-based control, where the rate at which the source can transmit is monitored and controlled; and credit-based control, where a source can transmit a cell if there is a credit available. CAC is also part of the flow control.

Forum   Same as ATM Forum.

FR   Same as frame relay.

frame   A group of bits sent serially (one after another). It is a logical transmission unit.

frame check sequence   In a token-ring LAN, a 32-bit field which follows the data field in every token-ring frame.

frame relay   A packet-switching technology to provide a very reliable packet delivery over virtual circuits (VCs). Some of the concepts used in frame relay have been incorporated in ATM networks.

FRM   Fast resource management. A form of network management for allocating resources (buffers, bandwidth) dynamically.

front end processor   Off-loads line control, message handling, code conversion, error control, and routing of data from the host computer. IBM's 3725 and 3745 are examples of front end processors. Also known as a communication controller.

FTP   File Transfer Program. A protocol used for transferring files between different machines across a network.

functional address   In IBM network adapters, this is a special kind of group address in which the address is bit significant, each "on" bit representing a function performed by the station (e.g., active monitor, ring-error monitor, LAN error monitor, or configuration report server).

gateway   A functional unit that connects two different computer network architectures.

gateway function   (1) A capability of a subarea node to provide protocol support to connect two or more subarea networks. (2) The component that provides this capability.

Gbps   Gigabits per second. Transmission speed or rate of a hundred million bits per second.

GCRA   Generic cell rate algorithm. A reference model proposed by the ATM Forum for defining cell-rate conformance in terms of certain traffic parameters. It is usually referred as the leaky bucket algorithm. (See also **traffic shaping.**)

GFC Generic Flow Control. A 4-bit field in the ATM cell header in order to support multiplexing functions. Its default value is '0000', when the GFC protocol is not enforced. The GFC mechanism is intended to support simple flow control in ATM connections.

group address In a LAN, a locally administered address assigned to two or more adapters to allow the adapters to copy the same frame.

group SAP A single address assigned to a group of service access points (SAPs).

half-session A session-layer component consisting of the combination of data flow control and transmission control components comprising one end of a session.

hard error An error condition on a network that requires the source of the error to be removed or that the network be reconfigured before the network can resume reliable operation.

header The portion of a message that contains control information for the message. Usually find at the beginning of a frame.

HEC Header Error Check or Header Error Control. A 1-byte field in the cell header used for the header error correction and detection. Due to the information contained in the header, HEC is quite significant.

hertz (Hz) A unit of frequency equal to one cycle per second.

hexadecimal A numbering base where 4 bits are used to represent each digit. The digits can have one of 16 values, 0, 1, 2, . . . , 9, A, B, C, D, E, F.

hierarchical network A multisegment network configuration providing only one path through intermediate segments between source segments and destination segments.

HOL Head-of-line. The head position of a buffer (i.e., inside a switch). A blocking phenomenon is associated with the HOL, which refers to the fact that cells in the queue have to wait for the HOL cell to depart first.

hop In token-ring networking, the connection between ring segments. The connection is usually made using bridges.

hop count The number of ring segments spanned to establish a session between two workstations. In IBM Token-Ring Networks the maximum is seven.

host node (1) A node at which a host computer is situated. (2) In SNA, a subarea node that contains an SSCP.

host system (1) A data processing system that is used to prepare programs and the operating environments for use on another computer or controller. (2) The data processing system to which a network is connected and with which the system can communicate.

HSSI High-speed serial interface. An interface between CSU/DSU and DXI.

ICR Initial cell rate. The rate at which a source is allowed to start up following an idle period. It is established at connection setup and is between the MCR and the PCR.

IEEE Institute of Electrical and Electronic Engineers. A standards and specification organization with extensive activities in the areas of computers and electronics.

IEEE 802 IEEE committee on local area networks.

IEEE 802.1 IEEE standard for overall architecture of LANs and internetworking.

IEEE 802.2 IEEE data link control layer standard used with IEEE 802.3, 802.4, 802.5.

IEEE 802.3 IEEE carrier-sense multiple access with collision detection (CSMA/CD). A physical layer standard specifying a LAN with a CSMA/CD access method on a bus topology. Ethernet and Starlan both follow subsets of the 802.3 standard. Typically, they transmit at 10 Mbps.

IEEE 802.4 IEEE physical layer standard specifying a LAN with a token-passing access method on a bus topology. Used with Manufacturing Automation Protocol (MAP) LANs. Typical transmission speed is 10 Mbps.

IEEE 802.5 IEEE physical layer standard specifying a LAN with a token-passing access method on a ring topology. Used by IBM's Token-Ring Network. Typical transmission rates are 4 Mbps and 16 Mbps.

IETF Internet Engineering Task Force. A body, which was initially responsible for developing specifications required for the interoperable implementation of IP. One of the issues IETF has been focusing on is the implementation of classical IP over ATM.

IISP Interim Interswitch Signaling Protocol. A protocol that uses UNI-based signaling for switch-to-switch communication. (See also **NNI.**)

ILMI Interim local management interface. An ATM Forum -defined network management system (NMS) based on SNMP that can provide configuration, performance and fault-management information concerning virtual circuits (VCs) connections available at its UNI (public and private). It operates over AAL3/4 and AAL5 and will be eventually replaced once it becomes standardized by ITU-T.

impedance The combined effect of resistance, inductance, and capacitance on a signal at a particular frequency.

independent logical unit (ILU) In SNA, a logical unit that does not require assistance from an SSCP to establish an LU-LU session.

Institute of Electrical and Electronic Engineers (IEEE) A publishing and standards-making body responsible for many standards used in LANs.

International Standards Organization (ISO) An international standards-making body for creating internationally accepted standards. One such standard is Open Systems Interconnection (OSI).

IP Internet Protocol. A networking protocol for providing a connectionless (datagram) service to the higher-transport protocol. It is responsible for discovering and maintaining topology information and for routing packets across homogeneous or heterogeneous networks. Combined with TCP, it is commonly known as the TCP/IP platform.

IPX A protocol similar to IP that was developed by Novell.

ISDN Integrated Services Digital Network. An early, CCITT-adopted protocol reference model intended for providing a ubiquitous, end-to-end, interactive, digital service for data, audio, and video.

isochronous Refers to the fact that a time slot can be divided into equal-size minislots allocated to different channels for synchronous transmission of information (used in DQDB).

ITU-T   International Telecommunications Union-Telecommunications Standards Sector. A formal international standards, specifications, and recommendations body, formerly known as CCITT–ITU-T is part of the International Telecommunications Union (ITU) founded in 1948 and sponsored by the United Nations to promote telephone and telegraphy issues.

IXC   Inter-exchange carrier. A public switching network carrier that provides connectivity across and between LATAs.

jitter   The cell delay variation (CDV).

jitter   Undesirable variation in the arrival time of a transmitted digital signal.

JPEG   Joint Photographic Experts Group. A standard developed for encoding, transmitting, and decoding still images.

Kbps   Kilobits per second. Transmission speed or rate of one thousand bits per second.

LAG   Logical address group. Similar to a LIS except that the decision to establish a direct SVC is made on a traffic and QoS requirement rather than the destination IP address.

LAN   Local area network. A network that interconnects PCs, terminals, workstations, servers, printers, and other peripherals at a high speed over short distances (usually within the same floor or building). Various LAN standards have been developed, with Ethernet as the most widely used.

LAN adapter   A circuit board installed in workstations that connects the workstation with the LAN media.

LAN Emulation   A technique that specifies the interfaces and protocols needed for providing LAN-supported functionality and connectivity in an ATM environment, so that legacy protocols can be interoperable with the ATM protocols, interfaces, and devices.

LAN Emulation Service   An ATM Forum appointed technical workgroup to address LAN Emulation.

LANE   Same as LAN Emulation.

LATA   Local access and transport area. Geographically defined telecommunication areas, within which a local carrier can provide communications services. (See also **LEC, IXC.**)

layer   In networking architectures, a collection of network processing functions that together comprise a set of rules and standards for successful data communication.

LE   Same as LAN Emulation.

LE-ARP   LAN Emulation ARP. The ARP used in LAN Emulation for binding a requested ATM address to the MAC address.

leaky bucket   A flow-control algorithm, where cells are monitored to check whether they comply with the connection parameters. Nonconforming cells are either tagged (as violators) or dropped from the network. The analogy is taken from a bucket (memory buffer) with a hole in its bottom that allows the fluid (cells) to flow out at a certain rate. (See also **GCRA, traffic contract, UPC.**)

leased line   A dedicated communications link usually owned by a telecommunications provider that charges for the use of the line.

LEC LAN Emulation client. Typically located in an ATM end system (i.e., ATM host, LAN switch), its task is to maintain address resolution tables and forward data traffic. It is uniquely associated with an ATM address.

LECS LAN Emulation configuration server. A server whose main function is to provide configuration information to a LEC (such as the ELAN it belongs to or its LES).

LENNI LAN Emulation network node interface. Same as LNNI.

LES LAN Emulation server. A server which provides support for the LAN emulation address resolution protocol (LE-ARP). The LECs register their own ATM and MAC addresses with the LES. A LES is uniquely identified by an ATM address.

LI Length indicator. A 6-bit field in the AAL3/4 SAR-PDU trailer that indicates the number of bytes in the SAR-PDU that contain CPCS information.

LIS Logical IP subnet. Group of ATM-attached devices that share a common address prefix. LIS members can communicate using direct virtual connections.

LLC Logical link control. The upper-half of the data link layer in LANs that performs error control, broadcasting, multiplexing, and flow control functions. (See also **MAC.**)

LMI Local management interface. An ITU-T -defined interface to provide an ATM end-system user with network management information. (See also **ILMI**).

LNNI LAN Emulation network node interface. Specifies the NNI operation between the LANE servers (LES, LECS, BUS).

lobe A term used to describe the connection from a workstation to a token-ring concentrator such as a multistation access unit.

local area network (LAN) A network of two or more computing units connected to share resources over moderate-sized geographic area, such as an office, a building, or campus.

Local Exchange Carrier An intra-LATA communication services provider.

locally administered address (LAA) An adapter address that the user can assign to override the universally administered address (UAA).

logical connection In a network, devices that can communicate or work with one another because they share the same protocol.

logical link The conceptual joining of two nodes for direct communications. Several logical links may be able to utilize the same physical hardware.

logical link control (LLC) A protocol developed by the IEEE 802 committee, common to all of its LAN standards, for data link-level transmission control; the upper sublayer of the IEEE layer 2 (OSI) protocol that complements the media access control protocol; IEEE standard 802.2.

Logical Link Control Protocol (LLC Protocol) In a local area network, the protocol that governs the exchange of frames between data stations independently of how the transmission medium is shared.

logical unit (LU) An access port for users to gain access to the services of a network.

LU-LU session In SNA, a session between two logical units in an SNA network. It provides communication between two end users, or between an end user and an LU services component.

LUNI LAN Emulation user network interface. Specifies the UNI between a LEC and the network providing the LAN Emulation.

MAC Medium access control. A set of protocols that are (the lower) part of the data link layer and consist the basis of the IEEE-LAN specifications. Generally, MAC determines the way devices can transmit in a broadcast network. (See also **LLC.**)

MAC frame Frames used to carry information to maintain the ring protocol and to exchange management information.

MAC protocol The LAN protocol sublayer of data link control (DLC) protocol that includes functions for adapter address recognition, copying of message units from the physical network, and message unit format recognition, error detection, and routing within the processor.

MAN Metropolitan area network. A term to describe a network that provides regional connectivity within a metropolitan area (such as a city). MANs are classified to be between LANs and WANs.

MARS Multicast Address Resolution Server. Used to support IP Multicast over ATM. Contains table of IP multicast addresses and associated ATM addresses.

Mbps Megabits per second. Transmission speed or rate of one million bits per second.

MBS Maximum burst size. A traffic parameter that specifies the maximum number of cells that can be transmitted at the peak rate (PCR).

MCDV Maximum cell delay variation. As the name suggests, it is the maximum CDV over a given QoS class.

MCLR Maximum cell loss ratio. As the name suggests, it is the maximum CTD over a given QoS class, defined for CBR and VBR traffic and for cells with CLP=0.

MCR Minimum cell rate. A parameter that gives the minimum rate that cells can be transmitted by a source over a virtual connection (VC).

MCTD Maximum cell transfer delay. As the name suggests, it is the maximum CTD over a given QoS class.

mean cell transfer delay The average of the processing, queuing, and propagation delays.

medium access control (MAC) A media-specific access control protocol within IEEE 802 specifications. The physical address of a station is often called the MAC address.

mesh network A multisegment network configuration providing more than one path through intermediate LAN segments between source and destination LAN segments.

MIB Management information base. A data structure that defines objects for referencing variables such as integers and strings. In general, it contains information regarding network's management and performance, i.e., traffic parameters. (See also **ILMI, AToMMIB.**)

MID Multiplex identification. A 10-bit field in the AAL3/4 SAR-PDU header for identifying the different CPCS-PDUs multiplexed over the same VCC.

MIN Multistage interconnection network. A switch fabric built from switching elements organized in series and/or in parallel, for providing physical connections between the inputs and the outputs of a switch.

mips Million instructions per second. A measure of computer speed.

modem (modulated/demodulator) A device that converts digital data from a computer to an analog signal that can be transmitted on a telecommunication line and converts the received analog signal to digital data for the computer.

MPEG Motion Picture Experts Group. A video technology standard that specifies the digital encoding, transmission, and decoding protocols, capable of presenting VCR quality motion video.

MPOA Multiprotocol over ATM. A set of standards to support, other than IP, (distributed) routing protocols. Developed on top of LANE and NHRP it will support switches, route servers, and hosts, all attached to an ATM network.

MR Mean rate. Same as average cell rate.

Multimedia A way of presenting to the user a combination of different forms of information such as text, data, images, video, audio, and graphics (i.e., videoconference).

multiple-domain network In SNA, a network with more than one SSCP. In APPN, a network with more than one network node.

Multiprotocol Encapsulation Multiprotocol Encapsulation over ATM provides for higher protocols, such as IP, to perform bridging and routing functions over an ATM network.

MUX Multiplexer. A networking local device where multiple streams of information are combined so they can share a common physical medium.

N-ISDN Narrowband integrated services digital network. Predecessor to the B-ISDN, N-ISDN, encompasses the original standards for the ISDN.

native applications Applications that have been developed for non-ATM environment communications platforms (i.e., LAN applications).

NAU In SNA, network addressable unit. In APPN, network accessible unit.

NDIS Network driver interface specification. Generic name for a device driver for a NIC, which is independent of any hardware or software implementation.

NetBIOS network basic input/output system. Provides an interface to allow programs to operate the token-ring adapter in a personal computer or workstation.

network A group of nodes and the links interconnecting them.

network addressable unit (NAU) It is the origin or destination of data transmitted by the path control layer. Synonymous with network accessible unit.

network management The conceptual control element of a station that interfaces with all of the architectural layers of that station and is responsible for the resetting and setting of control parameters, obtaining reports of error conditions, and determining if the station should be connected to or disconnected from the network.

network management vector transport (NMVT) One of the SNA formats used for the transmission for communications and systems management data.

NHRP Next Hop Resolution Protocol. A protocol proposed to be used for ATM address resolution based on classical IP. In particular, if an address request cannot be served by a node it is forwarded to the next server node on the path to the destination until finally the ATM-IP address mapping can be accomplished.

NIC   Network interface card or controller. The hardware communications interface (circuit board) required for the DTE (workstation, PC) to access the network (same as adapter card).

NMS   Network management system. Set of OAM&P functions for setting the required hardware and software parameters used in managing a network.

NNI   Network node interface (or network-to-network interface). ITU-T-specified standard interface between nodes within the same network. The ATM Forum distinguishes between two standards: one for private networks called P-NNI and one for public networks known as public NNI.

node   A device connected into a network.

node type   The classification of a network device based on the protocols it supports and the network addressable unit it can contain.

noise   A disturbance that affects a signal and that can distort the information carried by the signal.

nonbroadcast frame   A frame containing a specific destination address and that may contain routing information specifying which bridges are to forward it. A bridge will forward a nonbroadcast frame only if that bridge is included in the frame's routing information.

NPC   Network parameter control. Traffic management mechanism (performed at the NNI) exercised by a network for traffic received by another network.

NSAP   Network services access point. In the OSI environment, it is the SAP between the network and the transport layers, which identifies a DTE by a unique address.

OAM   Operations and maintenance. Set of administrative and supervisory actions regarding network performance monitoring, failure detection, and system protection. Special-type cells are used to carry OAM-related information.

OAM&P   Operations, administration, maintenance and provisioning. A set of network management functions and services that interact to provide the necessary network management tools and control.

OC-n   Optical carrier-n. ITU-T–specified physical interface for transmission over optical fiber at n times 51.84 Mbps (i.e., OC-3 is at 155.52 Mbps, OC-12 at 622.08 Mbps, OC-48 at 2.488 Mbps).

Octet   8 bits or one byte.

Open Systems Interconnection (OSI)   The only internationally accepted framework for communication between two systems made by different vendors. It is a seven-layer architecture developed by ISO.

operating system   A software program which manages the basic operation of a computer system.

OSI   Open systems interconnection. The OSI Reference Model introduced by the International Organization for Standardization (ISO) consists of seven layers, each specifying the protocols and functions required for two nodes to communicate using the underlying network infrastructure (physical medium, switches, routers, bridges, multiplexers, intermediate nodes).

OSIRM   Open Systems Interconnection Reference Model. (See **OSI.**)

P-NNI   Private network node interface. The NNI used in private networks.

P-UNI   Private user network interface The UNI used between a user and a private network.

pacing   In data communications a technique by which receiving the receiving-device controls the rate of transmission of a sending device to prevent overrun.

parallel bridge   One of the two or more bridges that connect the same two LAN segments in a network.

payload   Part of the ATM cell, it contains the actual information to be carried. It occupies 48 bytes. (See also **PTI.**)

PBX   Private branch exchange. A circuit switch that relays telephones, terminals or other equipment, and provides access to the public telephone system.

PC   Priority control. A congestion control function that uses the CLP bit to perform priority queuing and scheduling actions.

PCR   peak cell rate. A traffic parameter that characterizes the source and gives the maximum rate at which cells can be transmitted. It is calculated as the reciprocal of the minimum intercell interval (time between two cells) over a given virtual connection (VC). Field in the RM cell header indicating the maximum acceptable ER.

PDH   Plesiochronous digital hierarchy. A hierarchy that refers to the DS-0, DS-1, DS-2, and DS-3 interfaces for digital transmission. Originally developed to efficiently carry digitized voice over twisted pair.

PDU   Protocol data unit. Term originally used in the OSI model, also known as message, to describe the primitive passed across different layers and contains header, data, and trailer information.

permanent virtual circuit   A virtual connection established by the network management between an origin and a destination that can be left up permanently (used in X.25 and FR protocols).

PHY   Physical layer. The bottom layer of the ATM protocol reference model, it is subdivided into two sublayers, the transmission convergence (TC) and the physical medium (PM). It provides the ATM cells transmission over the physical interfaces that interconnect the ATM devices.

PHY-SAP   Physical layer service access point. The physical interface at the boundary between the PHY and the ATM layers. (See also **SAP, ATM-SAP.**)

physical unit (PU)   The component that manages and monitors the resources of a node.

PL   Physical layer. (See **PHY.**)

PLCP   Physical Layer Convergence Protocol. A protocol that specifies a TC mapping of ATM cells to DS-3 frames.

PM   Physical medium. One of the two PHY sublayers that provides the bit timing and performs the actual transmission of the bits over the physical medium.

PMD   Physical medium dependent. Same as PM.

port A physical connection to the link hardware. May also be referred to as an adapter.

PRI Primary rate interface. An ISDN specification that provides twenty-three 64-kbps B channels and one 64-kbps D channel intended for use over a single DS1 or an E-1 line.

print server A computer or program providing LAN users with access to a centralized printer.

private network A communications network comprised of dedicated circuits between DTEs and other devices (multiplexers, switches, routers) where bandwidth is dedicated and network management is much simpler. (See also **PVN, public network.**)

protocol The set of rules governing the operation of functional units of a communication system that must be followed if communication is to be achieved.

PT Payload type. (See **PTI.**)

PTI Payload Type Identifier. A 3-bit cell-header field for encoding information regarding the AAL and EFCI.

public network A communications network where users have shared access to the network resources. Network services are usually provided by common carriers (i.e., telephone companies). (See also **private network.**)

PVC Permanent (or provisioned) virtual connection. A virtual connection (VPC/VCC) provisioned for indefinite use in an ATM network, established by the network management system (NMS). (See also **SVC.**)

Q.2110 ITU-T recommendation for specifying the UNI SSCOP.

Q.2130 ITU-T recommendation for specifying the UNI SSCF.

Q.2931 ITU-T recommendation derived from both Q.931 and Q.933 to provide SVC specifications and standards.

Q.931 ITU-T recommendation for specifying the UNI signaling protocol in N-ISDN.

Q.933 ITU-T recommendation for specifying the UNI signaling protocol in frame relay.

Q.93B Currently called Q.2931.

QoS Quality of service. A term which refers to the set of ATM performance parameters that characterize the traffic over a given virtual connection (VC). These parameters include the CLR, CER, CMR, CDV, CTD, and the average cell transfer delay.

QoS classes Quality of service classes. Five service classes are defined by the ATM Forum in terms of the QoS parameters. Class 0—refers to best-effort service. Class 1—specifies the parameters for circuit emulation, CBR (uncompressed) video and for VPN. AAL1 supports this kind of connection-oriented service. Class 2—specifies the parameters for VBR audio and video. AAL2 supports this delay-dependent, connection-oriented class. Class 3—specifies the parameters for connection-oriented data transfer. AAL3/4 and mostly AAL5 support this delay-independent class of service.

RBOC Regional Bell Operating Company. Local service telephone companies that resulted from the breakup of AT&T.

RDF Rate decrease factor. A factor by which a source should decrease its transmission rate if there is congestion. (See also **RIF.**)

RDI Remote defect indication. One of the OAM function types used for fault management. (See also **AIS, CC.**)

repeater   A device inserted at intervals along a circuit to boost and amplify a signal being transmitted.

RFC   Request for comment. Draft documents that contain proposed standards and specifications. RFCs can then be approved or just archived as historical recommendations.

RIF   Rate increase factor. A factor by which a source can increase its transmission rate if the RM cell indicates no congestion. This can result in an additive cell rate (ACR). (See also **RDF.**)

ring error monitor (REM)   A function that compiles error statistics reported by adapters on a network, analyzes the statistics to determine probable error cause, sends reports to network manager programs, and updates network status conditions. It assists in fault isolation and correction.

ring in (RI)   The receive or input receptacle on an access unit or repeater.

ring out (RO)   The transmit or output receptacle on an access unit or repeater.

RM   Resource management. The management of critical network resources, such as bandwidth and buffers, at the node level. A value of 6 is reserved in the PTI to indicate an RM cell.

route   An ordered sequence between origin and destination stations that represents a path in a network between the stations.

router   An intelligent device that connects two LAN segments which use similar or different architectures at the network layer.

routing   A network management function responsible for forwarding the packets from the source to their destination. Numerous algorithms exist that satisfy various network topologies and requirements.

RSVP   ReSerVation Protocol. A protocol developed for supporting different QoS classes in IP applications (such as videoconference, multimedia).

RTT   Round-trip time. Round-trip time between a source and a device, such as a switch, and it is usually measured in number of cells (which depends on the buffering capabilities of the device). It is used as a window in flow control.

SAAL   Signaling AAL service-specific parts of the AAL protocol responsible for signaling. Its specifications, being developed by ITU-T, were adopted from N-ISDN.

SAP   Service access point. Physical interface between the layers in the OSI model through which lower layers provide services to the higher layers passing over the protocol data units (PDUs).

Subnetwork attachment point   The unique address maintained by a subnetwork for each of the DTEs attached to it.

SAR   Segmentation and reassembly. The lower half of the AAL. It inserts the data from the information frames into the cell. It adds any necessary header or trailer bits to the data and passes the 48-octet to the ATM layer. Each AAL type has its own SAR format. At the destination, the cell payload is extracted and converted to the appropriate PDU. (See also **CS.**)

SAR-PDU   Segmentation and Reassembly Protocol data unit. The 48-octet PDU that the SAR sublayer exchanges with the ATM layer. It comprises of the SAR-PDU payload and any control information that the SAR sublayer might add.

SCR   Sustainable cell rate. A traffic parameter that characterizes a bursty source and specifies the maximum average rate at which cells can be sent over a given virtual connection (VC). It can be defined as the ratio of the MBS to the minimum burst interarrival time.

SDH   Synchronous digital hierarchy. A hierarchy that designates signal interfaces for very high-speed digital transmission over optical fiber links. (See also **SONET.**)

SEAL   Simple efficient adaptation layer. The original name and recommendation for AAL5.

segment   In IBM Token-Ring Network, (1) A portion of a LAN that consists of cables, components, or lobes up to a bridge. (2) An entire ring without bridges.

segment number   The identifier that uniquely distinguishes a LAN segment in a multisegment LAN.

server   A computer providing a service to LAN users. Services may be a shared file.

service access point (SAP)   The point of access to services provided by the layers of a LAN architecture.

service types   There are four service types: CBR, VBR, UBR, and ABR. CBR and VBR are guaranteed services while UBR and ABR are described as best-effort services.

session   A connection between two stations that allows them to communicate.

SIG   SMDS Interest Group. An industry forum active in producing specifications in the area of SMDS. It has also joined some of the ATM Forum activities.

single-route broadcast   The forwarding of specially designated broadcast frames only by bridges which have single-route broadcast enabled. If the network is configured correctly, a single-route broadcast frame will have exactly one copy delivered to every LAN segment in the network.

SIR   Sustained information rate. A flow control mechanism used in SMDS.

SMDS   Switched multimegabit digital service. A connectionless, MAN service, based on 53-byte packets, that target the interconnection of different LANs into a switched public network.

SMTP   Simple Mail Transfer Protocol. The protocol standard developed to support electronic mail (E-mail) services.

SN   Sequence number. Part of the header of the SAR-PDU (2 bits in AAL1, 4 bits in AAL3/4), it is used as a sequence counter for detecting lost, out-of-sequence or misinserted SAR-PDUs.

SNA   Systems network architecture. A host-based network architecture introduced by IBM, where logical channels are created between endpoints.

SNMP   Simple Network Management Protocol. An IETF-defined standard for handling management information. It is normally found as an application on top of the User Datagram Protocol (UDP).

SNP   Sequence number protection. A 4-bit field in the header of the AAL1 SAR-PDU that contains the CRC and the Parity Bit Fields.

soft error   An intermittent error on a network that causes data to be transmitted more than once to be received.

SONET Synchronous Optical Network. An ANSI-defined standard for high-speed and high-quality digital optical transmission. It has been recognized as the North American standard for SDH.

source routing A method used by a bridge for moving data between LAN segments. The routing information is embedded in the token.

source routing transparent (SRT) bridge A combination bridge utilizing IBM's source-routing mechanism along with transparent-routing mechanism.

SPANS Simple Protocol for ATM Network Signaling. A protocol supported by FORE Systems switches that provides SVC tunneling capability over a PVC network.

SPVC Switched or semipermanent virtual connection. A PVC-type connection where SVCs are used for call setup and (automatic) rerouting. It is also called smart PVC.

SS7 Signaling System Number 7. A common channel signaling standard developed by CCITT. It was designed to provide the internal control and network intelligence needed in ISDNs.

SSCF Service-specific coordination function. Part of the SSCS portion of the SAAL. Among other functions it provides a clear interface for relaying user data and providing independence from the underlying sublayers. (See also **SSCOP.**)

SSCOP Service-Specific Connection-Oriented Protocol. Part of the SSCS portion of the SAAL. SSCOP is an end-to-end protocol that provides error detection and correction by retransmission and status reporting between the sender and the receiver, while guaranteeing delivery integrity. (See also **SSCF.**)

SSCS Service-specific convergence sublayer. One of the two components of the convergence sublayer (CS) of the AAL that is particular to the traffic service class to be converted. It is developed to support certain user applications such as LAN Emulation, transport of high-quality video, and database management.

SSM Single-segment message. A message that constitutes a single PDU.

ST Segment Type. A 2-bit field in the SAR-PDU header that indicates whether the SAR-PDU is a BOM, COM, EOM, or SSM.

station An input or output device that uses telecommunications facilities.

STDM Statistical time-division multiplexing. Same as ATDM.

STM Synchronous transfer mode. A packet-switching approach where time is divided in time slots assigned to single channels during which users can transmit periodically. Basically, time slots denote allocated (fixed) parts of the total available bandwidth. (See also **TDM.**)

STM-1 Synchronous transport module-1. An ITU-T–defined SDH physical interface for digital transmission in ATM at the rate of 155.52 Mbps.

STM-*n* Synchronous transport module-*n*. An ITU-T–defined SDH physical interface for digital transmission in ATM at n times the basic STM-1 rate. There is a direct equivalence between the STM-n and the SONET STS-3*n* transmission rates.

STP Shielded twisted pair. Two insulated copper wires twisted together and wrapped by a protective jacket shield. (See also **UTP**).

STS-1   Synchronous Transport Signal-1. SONET signal standard for optical transmission at 51.84 Mbps. (See also **OC-1.**)

STS-*n*   Synchronous Transport Signal-*n*. SONET signal format for transmission at *n* times the basic STS-1 signal (i.e., STS-3 is at 155.52 Mbps).

subarea   A portion of an SNA network consisting of the subarea node and any attached resources to that node.

subarea address   A value defined to identify the subarea node and is placed in the subarea address field of the network address.

subarea network   The interconnection of subareas.

subarea node   A node that uses subarea addressing for routing.

SVC   Switched virtual connection. A connection that is set up and taken down dynamically through signaling. (See also **PVC**).

switch fabric   The central functional block of the ATM switch which is responsible for buffering and routing the incoming cells to the appropriate output ports.

switch, ATM   An ATM device responsible for switching the cells. There exist various switch architectures which can be classified according to different aspects (i.e., buffering, switch matrix, interconnection design, division multiplexing).

switched line   A telecommunications line in which the connection is established by dialing.

switched virtual circuit   A connection where control signaling is used to establish and tear it down dynamically. Examples are the telephone system, ISDN, X.25.

symbolic name   A name that may be used instead of an adapter or bridge address to identify an adapter location.

Synchronous Data Link Control (SDLC)   A bit-oriented synchronous communications protocol developed by IBM.

synchronous time-division multiplexing   A TDM scheme where the interleaved time slots are preassigned to the users.

system services control point (SSCP)   A function within IBM's VTAM that controls and manages an SNA network and its resources.

Systems Network Architecture (SNA)   IBM's seven-layer networking architecture.

T1   A TDM digital channel carrier that operates at a rate of 1.544 Mbps. Known also as a repeater system, it is often referred to as DS-1.

T1   A digital transmission link with a capacity of 1.544 Mbps.

T3   A TDM digital channel carrier that operates at 44.736 Mbps. It can multiplex 28 T1 signals and it is often used to refer to as DS-3.

TAXI   Transparent asynchronous transmitter/receiver interface. An interface that provides connectivity over multimode fiber links at a speed of 100 Mbps.

TC   Transmission convergence. One of the two PHY sublayers that is responsible for adapting the ATM cells into a stream of bits to be carried over the physical medium. (See also **PM.**)

TCP   Transmission Control Protocol. A standardized transport protocol developed for interconnecting IP-based networks. Operating on top of IP (combined known as TCP/IP), it is responsible for multiplexing sessions, error recovery, end-to-end reliable delivery, and flow control.

TCP/IP   A protocol platform, known also as the Internet protocol suite, that combines both TCP and IP. Widely used applications, such as Telnet, FTP, and SMTP interface to TCP/IP.

TCS   Transmission convergence sublayer. Same as TC.

TDJ   Transfer delay jitter. (See **CDV.**)

TDM   Time-division multiplexing. A technique for splitting the total bandwidth (link capacity) into several channels to allow bit streams to be combined (multiplexed). The bandwidth allocation is done by dividing the time axis into fixed-length slots and a particular channel can then transmit only during a specific time slot.

telephone twisted pair (TTP)   One or more twisted pairs of copper wire in the unshielded voice-grade cable commonly used to connect a telephone to its wall jack. It is also known as unshielded twisted pair (UTP).

Telnet   An asynchronous, virtual terminal protocol that allows for remote access to the network.

TM   Traffic management. Means for providing connection admission (CAC), congestion and flow control (i.e., UPC, traffic shaping).

token   A sequence of bits passed from one device to another on the token-ring network that signifies permission to transmit over the network. It consists of a starting delimiter, an Access Control Field, and an end delimiter.

token passing   In a token-ring network, the process by which a node captures a token, inserts a message, addresses the token and adds control information, and then transmits the frame and generates another token after the original token has made a complete circuit.

token ring   A network with a ring topology that passes tokens form one attaching device to another.

token-ring interface coupler (TIC)   The hardware interface for connecting front-end processors and controllers to a token-ring network.

token-ring network   A network that uses a ring topology in which tokens are passed in a sequence from one node to another.

topology   The physical or logical arrangement of nodes in a computer network.

traffic contract   An agreement between the user and the network management agent regarding the expected QoS provided by the network and the user's compliance with the predetermined traffic parameters (i.e., PCR, MBS, burstiness, average cell rate).

traffic descriptors   A set of parameters that characterizes the source traffic. These are the PCR, MBS, CDV, and SCR.

traffic shaping   A method for regulating noncomplying traffic (i.e., violates the traffic parameters, such as PCR, CDV, MBS as specified by the traffic contract). (See also **GCRA.**)

Transmission Control Protocol/Internet Protocol (TC/IP)   A set of protocols that allows cooperating computers to share resources across a heterogeneous network.

transmission group (TG)   A single link or a group of links between adjacent nodes logically grouped together. In SNA, these nodes are adjacent subarea nodes. In APPN, it is a single link.

transparent routing   A method used by a bridge for moving data between two networks through learning the station addresses on each network.

twisted pair   A transmission medium that consists of two insulated conductors twisted together to reduce noise.

type 2.0 (T2.0) node   A node that attaches to a subarea network as a peripheral node and provides full end-user services but no intermediate routing services.

type 2.1 (T2.1) node   An SNA node that can be configured as an endpoint or intermediate routing node in a T2.1 network, or as a peripheral node attached to a subarea network. It may act as an end node, network node, or intermediate node in an APPN network.

type 4 node   An SNA subarea node that provides routing and data link control functions for a type 5 node. Type 5 nodes control type 4 nodes.

type 5 node   An SNA subarea node that contains an SSCP and controls type 4 and type 2 SNA node types.

UBR   Unspecified bit rate. One of the best-effort service types (the other one is ABR). Realistically, no traffic parameters are specified by the source, so, no actual quality commitment is made by the network management.

UDP   User Datagram Protocol. A connectionless transport protocol without any guarantee of packet sequence or delivery. It functions directly on top of IP.

UME   UNI Management Entity. Software at the UNIs for providing the ILMI functions.

UNI   User network interface. The interface—defined as a set of protocols and traffic characteristics (i.e., cell structure)—between the CPE (user) and the ATM network (ATM switch). The ATM Forum specifications refer to two standards being developed, one between a user and a public ATM network, called public UNI, and one between a user and a private ATM network, called P-UNI.

UNI 2.0   ATM Forum UNI specification for the physical (PHY) and the ATM layers, the ILMI, OAM (traffic control), PVC support.

UNI 3.0   An upgrade of UNI 2.0 with traffic control for PCR and the operation over current transmission systems as some of the additional features.

UNI 3.1   A corrected version of UNI 3.0, this specification also includes SSCOP standards.

UNI 4.0   This UNI specification refers to signaling issues in ABR, VP, and QoS negotiations.

universally administered address (UAA)   The address permanently encoded in an adapter at the time of manufacture. All universally administered addresses are unique.

unnumbered acknowledgment (UA)   A data link control command used in establishing a link and in answering receipt of logical link control frames.

unshielded twisted pair (UTP)   (See **telephone twisted pair.**)

UPC   Usage parameter control. A form of traffic control that checks and enforces user's conformance with the traffic contract and the QoS parameters. Commonly known as traffic policing, it is performed at the UNI level.

UTOPIA   Universal test & operation physical interface. An interface to provide connectivity at the PHY level among ATM entities.

UTP   Unshielded twisted pair. A twisted pair (copper) wire without any protective sheathing, used for short distances wiring (i.e., building). There are two categories specified by the ATM Forum for cell transmission: 3 (CAT-3) and 5 (CAT-5).

VBR-nrt   Variable bit rate-nonreal time. One of the service types for transmitting traffic where timing information is not critical and which is characterized by the average and peak cell rates. It is well suited for long data packets transfers.

VBR-rt   Variable bit rate-real time. One of the service types for transmitting traffic that depends on timing information and control and which is characterized by the average and peak cell rates. It is suitable for carrying traffic such as packetized (compressed) video and audio.

VC   Virtual channel. A term to describe unidirectional flow of ATM cells between connecting (switching or end-user) points that share a common identifier number (VCI).

VCC   Virtual channel connection. Defined as a concatenation of virtual channel links.

VCI   Virtual channel identifier. A 16-bit value in the ATM cell header that provides a unique identifier for the virtual channel (VC) that carries that particular cell.

VF   Variance factor. It is the CRM normalized by the variance of the total cell rate over a given circuit.

virtual channel   (See **VC.**)

virtual circuit   A connection set up across the network between a source and a destination where a fixed route is chosen for the entire session and bandwidth is dynamically allocated. (See also **datagram.**)

virtual connection   A connection established between end users (source and destination), where packets are forwarded along the same path and bandwidth is not permanently allocated until it is used.

Virtual Telecommunications Access Method (VTAM)   A set of programs that control communication between nodes and application programs in SNA.

VLAN   Virtual LAN. A networking environment where users on physically independent LANs are interconnected in such a way that it appears as if they are on the same LAN workgroup. (See also **LANE.**)

VOD   Video on demand. A technology that enables the customer to remotely select and play a video, transmitted over communications links.

VP   Virtual path. A term to describe a set of virtual channels (VCs) grouped together, between crosspoints (i.e., switches).

VPC   Virtual path connection. Defined as a concatenation of VP links.

VPCI/VCI   Virtual path connection identifier/virtual channel identifier. A combination of two numbers, one for identifying the VP and one for VCI.

VPI   Virtual path identifier. An 8-bit value in the cell header that identifies the VP and, accordingly, the virtual channel the cell belongs to.

VPN   Virtual private network. Network resources provided to users, on demand, by public carriers such that the users view this partition of the network as a private network. The advantage of the VPNs over the dedicated private networks is that the former allow a dynamic allocation of network resources.

WAN   Wide area network. A network that covers long-haul areas and usually utilizes public telephone circuits.

WATM   Wireless ATM. An emerging technology for interfacing wireless and ATM networks.

wide area network (WAN)   LAN segments, bridged or routed, using communication lines increasing the geographic size of the LAN.

workstation   A terminal or computer attached to a network.

X.25   One of the first CCITT standardized, public (data), packet-switching network protocols. Originally designed to operate over unreliable communications links, it supported both virtual circuit (VC) and datagram services.

Bibliography

Alles, Anthony, ATM Internetworking, Cisco Systems, 1995.

Armitage, G. and T. J. Smith, IP Broadcast over ATM Networks, Internet Draft, 1995.

Armitage, G., Support for Multicast over UNI 3.0/3.1 based ATM Networks, Internet Draft, 1996.

Atkinson, R., Default IP MTU for use over ATM AAL5, RFC1626, 1994.

ATM Forum, ATM User-Network Interface (UNI) Specification Version 3.1, Prentice Hall, 1995.

ATM Forum, LAN Emulation Over ATM Version 1.0, 1995.

ATM Forum/94-0471R15, PNNI Draft Specification, 1996.

ATM Forum/95-0013R10, Traffic Management Specification V4.0, 1996.

ATM Forum/95-0326R2, Draft Proposal for Specification for FEC-SSCS for AAL Type 5, 1995.

ATM Forum/95-0824R7, Baseline Text for MPOA, ATM Forum, 1996.

ATM Forum/95-1438R8, UNI Signalling 4.0, 1995.

Black, Uyless, *ATM: Foundation for Broadband Networks,* Prentice Hall, 1995.

Bonomi, F. and K. W. Fendick, The Rate-Based Flow Control Framework for the Available Bit Rate ATM Service, IEEE Network, March/April 1995.

Breyer, Robert and Sean Riley, *Switched and Fast Ethernet: How It Works and How to Use It,* Ziff-Davis Press, 1995.

Callon, R. and J. Halpern, "Technical Tutorial on ATM and Internetworking," Next Generation Networks '95 Conference, 1995.

Canserver, D. H., NHRP Protocol Applicability Statement, Internet Draft, 1996.

Dutton, Harry J. R. and Peter Lenhard, *Asynchronous Transfer Model Technical Overview,* 2d ed., IBM, Prentice Hall, 1995.

Floyd, S. and A. Romanov, *The Dynamics of TCP Traffic over ATM Networks,* Sigcomm '94 Proceedings, 1994.

Gaddis, Mike, et al., *Quantum Flow Control Specification Revision 2.0,* 1995.

Guha, Aloke, "Addressing the Traffic Management Issue in ATM," Next Generation Networks '95 Presentation Notes, 1995.

Heinanen, Juha, Multiprotocol Encapsulation over ATM Adaptation Layer 5, RFC1483.

Huitema, Christian, *Routing in the Internet,* Prentice Hall, 1995.

IBM International Technical Support Centers, "TCP/IP Tutorial and Technical Overview," GG24-3376, 1989.

"The Basics of IP Network design," SG24-2580, 1995.

IBM International Technical Support Organization, "High-Speed Networking Technology: An Introductory Survey," 1995.

"New and Improved! IBM Multisegment LAN Design Guidelines," 1994.

ITU Recommendation I.113, "Vocabulary of Terms for Broadband Aspects of ISDN," 1991.

ITU Recommendation I.121, "Broadband Aspects of ISDN," 1991.

ITU Recommendation I.150, "B-ISDN Asynchronous Transfer Mode Functional Characteristics," 1993.

ITU Recommendation I.311, "B-ISDN General Network Aspects," 1993.

ITU Recommendation I.321, "B-ISDN Protocol Reference Model and Its Application," 1991.

ITU Recommendation I.327, "B-ISDN Functional Architecture," 1993.

ITU Recommendation I.361, "B-ISDN ATM Layer Specification," 1993.

ITU Recommendation I.362, "B-ISDN ATM Adaptation Layer (AAL) Functional Description," 1993.

ITU Recommendation I.371 Draft, Traffic Control and Congestion Control in B-ISDN, 1995.

ITU Recommendation I.413, "B-ISDN User-Network Interface," 1993.

ITU Recommendation Q.2931, "B-ISDN DSS2 User-Network Interface (UNI) Layer-3 Specification for Basic Call/Connection Control," 1993.

Iwata, A. et al., ATM Connection and Traffic Management Schemes for Multimedia Internetworking, Communications of the ACM, Feb. 1995.

Katz, D., et al., NBMA Next Hop Resolution Protocol, Internet Draft, 1996.

Laubach, M. and J. Halpern, Classical IP and ARP over ATM, Internet Draft, 1996.

Laubach, Mark, Classical IP and ARP over ATM, RFC1577, 1993.

Le Boudec, Jean-Yves, "The Asynchronous Transfer Mode: A Tutorial," IBM Research Division, 1991.

Lyon, T., Simple and Efficient Adaptation Layer (SEAL), ANSI T1S1.5/91-292, 1991.

Mankin, A. and M. Maher, ATM Signalling Support for IP over ATM-UNI 4.0 Update, Internet Draft, 1996.

McDysan, D. E. and D. L. Spohn, *ATM Theory and Application,* McGraw-Hill, 1995.

Metz, Christopher, A Survey of Routing Protocols and Models in ATM Networks, IBM, 1995.

——, A Survey of Routing Protocols over ATM, ATM Year '96 Presentation, 1996.

Flow Control for Best-Effort Data Traffic in ATM Networks, IBM, 1994.

Miller, Mark A., *Analyzing Broadband Networks,* M&T Books, 1994.

Newman, Peter, Traffic Management for ATM Local Area Networks, IEEE Communications, Aug. 1994.

Nicolas, Laurant, ATM Support in TNN and NBBS, IBM Development, 1995.

Onvural, Raif, Asynchronous Transfer Mode Performance Issues, Artech House, 1994.

Partridge, Craig, Gigabit Networking, Addison-Wesley, 1993.

Perez, M., et al., ATM Signaling Support for IP over ATM, RFC1755, 1995.

Perlman, Radia, Interconnections: Bridges and Routers, Addison-Wesley, 1992.

Peterson, David M., *TCP/IP Networking: A guide to the IBM Environment,* McGraw-Hill, 1995.

Ranade, Jay and George C. Sackett, *Introduction to SNA Networking,* 2d ed., McGraw-Hill, 1995.

Rekhter, Y., NHRP for Destinations off the NBMA Subnetwork, Internet Draft, 1996.

Rekter, Y. and D. Kandlur, "Local/Remote" Forwarding Decision in Switched Data Link Subnetworks, Internet Draft, 1995.

Sackett, George C., *IBM's Token-Ring Networking Handbook,* McGraw-Hill, 1992.

Talpade and Ammar, Multicast Server Architectures for MARS-based ATM Multicasting, Internet Draft, 1996.

Villamizar, Curtis, et al., IP over ATM: A Framework Document, Internet Draft, 1996.

Index

About the Authors

George C. Sackett is Managing Director of NetworX Corporation and one of today's knowledgeable networking experts dealing with corporate systems. He has 15 years of technical and managerial experience with corporate networks, specializing in merging legacy systems and network systems (SNA) to multiprotocol client/server systems and networks. Christopher Y. Metz is a senior network specialist for IBM's U.S. Marketing and Services Division. His main focus is on implementation of TCP/IP, SNMP, and other networks into large corporate systems.